Thinki   n

Thinking cepts in pr research. which to rigorous, produces

Derrida – Spivak – Foucault Butler – Deleuze - Barad – n

phical con- qualitative es through complish a d the data ncluding:

Thinking analysis s narratives ches prec research refusing a the move.

Special fe new theoret concept and theorist; and detailed chapters that plug the same data set into a specific concept. This vital tool will help researchers understand and fully utilize their powers of data analysis, and will prove invaluable to both students and experienced researchers across all the social sciences.

itative data transparent stic approa- ory" pushes ferently. By meaning on

hat might be a particular

Alecia Y. Jackson is Associate Professor at the Department of Leadership and Educational Studies, Reich College of Education, Appalachian State University, USA. She is co-editor with Lisa A. Mazzei of *Voice in Qualitative Inquiry* (Routledge).

Lisa A. Mazzei is Associate Professor, Doctoral Program in Leadership Studies, Gonzaga University, USA. She is also Visiting Research Fellow at the Education and Social Research Institute, Manchester Metropolitan University, UK. She is co-editor with Alecia Y. Jackson of *Voice in Qualitative Inquiry* (Routledge), and author of *Inhabited Silence in Qualitative Research*.

Thinking with Theory in Qualitative Research

Viewing data across multiple perspectives

Alecia Y. Jackson and Lisa A. Mazzei

Routledge
Taylor & Francis Group

LONDON AND NEW YORK

First published 2012
by Routledge
2 Park Square, Milton Park, Abingdon, Oxon OX14 4RN

Simultaneously published in the USA and Canada
by Routledge
711 Third Avenue, New York, NY 10017

Routledge is an imprint of the Taylor & Francis Group, an informa business

British Library Cataloguing in Publication Data
A catalogue record for this book is available from the British Library

Library of Congress Cataloging in Publication Data
Jackson, Alecia Youngblood, 1968-
Thinking with theory in qualitative research : viewing data across multiple perspectives / Alecia Youngblood Jackson, Lisa A Mazzei. -- 1st ed.
p. cm.
1. Qualitative research--Methodology. 2. Interviewing--Technique. 3. Women college teachers--United States--Research. 4. First generation college students--United States--Research. 5. Poststructuralism. I. Mazzei, Lisa A. II. Title.
H62.J295 2012
001.4'2--dc23
2011026121

ISBN: 978-0-415-78099-5 (hbk)
ISBN: 978-0-415-78100-8 (pbk)
ISBN: 978-0-203-14803-7 (ebk)

Typeset in Galliard
by Taylor & Francis Books

Contents

Acknowledgments

Lone scholars we are not. We would like to express our sincere thanks to colleagues near and far who helped us as we conceptualized and wrote this book. We are especially grateful to those who were generous enough to read chapters in draft form: Sara Childers, Alexa Dare, Stephanie Daza, Ken Gale, Susanne Gannon, Fran Huckaby, Maggie MacLure, Kate McCoy, Nancy McEachran, Chaz Preston, Phillip Prince, Hillevi Lenz Taguchi, and Cate Watson. We are also grateful to Jennifer Greene for comments on an earlier version of Chapter 1 that was presented at the 2011 Annual Meeting of the American Educational Research Association.

This book would not have been possible without the immediate enthusiasm of our editor at Routledge, Philip Mudd, and the generosity of time and candor from our participants. We owe a special debt to Cassandra and Sera. We are also indebted to various agencies at Appalachian State University for funding for our project: the University Research Council, the Office of Academic Affairs, the Reich College of Education Dean's Office, and the Department of Leadership and Educational Studies. We would also like to thank Gonzaga University for funding to support our week of intensive work together in Boone, NC. We express gratitude to Beth Armstrong and Christopher Horsethief for their editorial assistance, and to students in Lisa's Advanced Qualitative course who served as 'readers' for two of the chapters. And lastly we are in deep appreciation to our mentors who introduced us to the joys of theory, and colleagues who showed an interest in this project from the very beginning.

Lisa thanks Alecia for thinking with her, laughing with her, and challenging her. Lisa cannot think of anyone (besides Phillip) whom she would rather be joined with at the hip for a year! She is especially grateful to Phillip for sharing her love of philosophy and for sharing life.

Alecia is indebted to Lisa for her positive energy, creative mind, and willingness to stay "in the threshold" with her, no matter what. Alecia owes Kristian, Silas, and Jude a big thank you for their unconditional willingness to give her the time and space to think with theory.

Introduction

In this time of researching situations that we no longer understand – what Deleuze describes as "situations which we no longer know how to react to, in spaces which we no longer know how to describe"[1] – we hope that what we are calling *Thinking with Theory in Qualitative Research: Viewing Data Across Multiple Perspectives* is a move to begin creating a language and way of thinking methodologically *and* philosophically together that is up to the task. In this book, we endeavor to explain how we think with theory in our current project, which centers on a rather conventional qualitative interview study (detailed here in the Introduction) of women professors in the academy who are first-generation college graduates. Drawing on six poststructural philosophers (Derrida, Spivak, Foucault, Butler, Deleuze, and Barad), we "plug in" the common data set and the theorists' philosophical concepts. We read the same data across multiple theorists by plugging the theory and the data into one another, in keeping with Deleuze's[2] conceptual play of the zigzag: "The zigzag is the lightning bolt spark of creation and the 'crosscutting path from one conceptual flow to another', a path set off by the spark of creation, unpredictable, undisciplined, anti-disciplinary, and non-static."[3] The result of "thinking with theory" across the data illustrates how knowledge is opened up and proliferated rather than foreclosed and simplified.

Methodology: working within/against interpretivism

Our purpose in this book is to challenge qualitative researchers to use theory to think *with* their data (or use data to think *with* theory) in order to accomplish a reading of data that is both *within and against interpretivism*. We argue that qualitative data interpretation and analysis does not happen via mechanistic coding, reducing data to themes, and writing up transparent narratives that do little to critique the complexities of social life; such simplistic approaches preclude dense and multi-layered treatment of data. Furthermore, we challenge simplistic treatments of data and data analysis in qualitative research that, for example,

---

[1] Gilles Deleuze, *Cinema II*, trans. Hugh Tomlinson and Robert Galeta (Minneapolis: University of Minnesota Press, 1989), xi.

[2] Gilles Deleuze and Claire Parnet, *Dialogues II*, trans. Hugh Tomlinson and Barbara Habberjam (1987; repr. New York: Columbia University Press, 2002).

[3] Lisa Mazzei and Kate McCoy, "Thinking with Deleuze in Qualitative Research." *International Journal of Qualitative Studies in Education* 23, no. 5 (2010): 505. Note that Mazzei and McCoy are citing Stivale within the quote.

beckon voices to "speak for themselves," or that reduce complicated and conflicting voices and data to thematic "chunks" that can be interpreted free of context and circumstance.[4]

We came to this project the way many methodologists come to different approaches to their data: the processes we were using (coding) were insufficient and we could no longer ignore what we had put up with before.[5] In the context of qualitative research, specifically qualitative research that concerns itself with an analysis of speech and conversations, good methodologists are taught to organize what they have "seen, heard, and read"[6] in order to make sense of and represent what they have learned. Well trained methodologists are carefully taught to be attentive to their field notes and transcription data in order to sort and sift and identify the codes and categories that emerge from the data. Perhaps, we realized, we were no longer good methodologists. Perhaps we were becoming post-methodologists in the way that Patti Lather[7] and Elizabeth St Pierre[8] have described.

While the research project that informs the chapters is an orthodox interview study in many ways, all of the poststructural theorists whom we use demand that we attempt to decenter some of the traps in humanistic qualitative inquiry: for example, data, voice, narrative, and meaning-making.[9] In other words, our methodological aims are against interpretive imperatives that limit so-called "analysis" and inhibit the inclusion of previously unthought "data."[10] It is such a rethinking of an interpretive methodology that gets us out of the representational trap of trying to figure out what the participants in our study "mean," and helps us to avoid being seduced by the desire to create a coherent and interesting narrative that is bound by themes and patterns.

Interview methods in interpretive qualitative inquiry oblige researchers to "center" the subject. We as researchers ask participants to be selective in 1) their telling, 2) their interpretation of experience, 3) the representation of themselves, and 4) the assumptions they make about who that self is (during the telling). What emanates from such centering is a supposedly coherent narrative that represents truth. However, our methodology-against-interpretivism disrupts the centering compulsion of traditional qualitative research; our project is about cutting into the center, opening it up to see what newness might be incited.

To acknowledge and accept the centeredness of interviewing practices is to work both within and against a project that is failed from the start. Yet, starting with the interview as a failed practice does not mean that we give up on the interview as method. Rather, we make very specific assumptions about data, voice, and truth (these assumptions are taken up first in

---

[4] See *Voice in Qualitative Inquiry*, edited by Alecia Y. Jackson and Lisa A. Mazzei (London: Routledge, 2009).

[5] In the book *Dialogues II* by Gilles Deleuze and Claire Parnet, it is written that "it is rather when everything is going well, or everything goes better on the other line, that the crack happens on this new line – secret, imperceptible, marking a threshold of lowered resistance, or the rise of a threshold of exigency: you can no longer stand what you put up with before, even yesterday" (p. 126).

[6] Corrine Glesne, *Becoming Qualitative Researchers*, 2nd edn (New York: Longman, 1999), 130.

[7] Patti Lather, *Getting Lost: Feminist Efforts Toward a Double(d) Science* (Albany: SUNY Press, 2007).

[8] Elizabeth A. St Pierre, "Afterword: Decentering Voice in Qualitative Inquiry." In *Voice in Qualitative Inquiry*, edited by Alecia Y. Jackson and Lisa A. Mazzei (London: Routledge, 2009): 221–36.

[9] Readers who are new to poststructural theory may want to proceed directly to 'Interlude IV, Why Butler?' to read about language in humanism, structuralism, and poststructuralism.

[10] See for example Elizabeth A. St Pierre, "Methodology in the Fold and the Irruption of Transgressive Data." *International Journal of Qualitative Studies in Education* 10, no. 2 (1997) and Lisa A. Mazzei, *Inhabited Silence in Qualitative Research* (New York: Peter Lang, 2007).

Chapter 1 and then discussed throughout the chapters). A recognition of the limits of our received practices does not mean that we reject such practices; instead, we work the limits (and limitations) of such practices. For example, we accept in our research, and in the conversations with the women in this study, that the data are partial, incomplete, and always in a process of a re-telling and re-membering. The methodological implications of this view are that we, as researchers, question what we ask of data as told by participants, question what we hear and how we hear (our own privilege and authority in listening and telling), and deconstruct why one story is told and not another.[11] As Cixous and Calle-Gruber wrote, "all narratives tell one story in place of another story."[12] If one narrative – the one that we use to frame the book – has been told in place of another, then not only "data" but also "analysis" become *something else*. This *something else* is our refusal to tell the stories of the women; that is, a refusal to create thematic patterns to represent the essence of the participants in our study. Readers of this book will not find generalized stories that represent the experiences of all first-generation women faculty in academia. Readers of this book *will* find repeated data excerpts that are viewed across multiple, conceptual perspectives, a viewing that opens up and diffracts, rather than crystalizes, representation. However, the repeated data excerpts were not intentionally extracted by us as a result of their fitting neatly into the theoretical concept; rather, there was a *constitution and emergence* of the data and concept that occurred simultaneously as we were thinking with/in the larger theoretical framework. A description of this analytic maneuver is taken up more specifically in Chapter 1. In this Introduction, we offer a background of the study, including the method and participants.

Method and participants

The idea for this project emerged over a lovely dinner with Philip Mudd, our editor at Routledge, during the 2009 International Congress of Qualitative Inquiry. We had been discussing the failures of coding within a poststructural research method, and we talked about the ways in which each of us had been using theory in our previous and current work with qualitative data. Neither of us coded data anymore, but we could not describe systematically what happened when we "thought with theory." We became excited about the prospect of creating a process-oriented book that might continue to shift the qualitative research field into a post-framework. Philip urged us on.

We each had lots of data that we had collected for previous projects, yet for this book, we wanted to collect new data together. We asked ourselves, "Who do we want to talk to?" As women in the academy, we immediately realized that we wanted to talk with other academic women. We needed to narrow the "sampling pool," so we tossed around several identity categories before we settled on first-generation academic women. We were interested in this particular category because first-generation is rather invisible, and we suspected that women who claimed the category would have unique and complex perspectives on their lives. One of us is a first-generation academic, and the other is a daughter of a first-generation college graduate (her father graduated from college on the GI Bill, but her mother did not attend college). Though definitions of first-generation vary, the interpretation adopted by

---

[11] Linda Alcoff, "The Problem of Speaking for Others," *Cultural Critique* 20 (1991), 5–33.

[12] Hélène Cixous and Mireille Calle-Gruber, *Hélène Cixous Rootprints: Memory and Life Writing*, trans. Eric Prenowitz (London: Routledge, 1997), 178.

the U.S. Department of Education TRIO programs states that graduates are considered first-generation if neither parent *graduated from* a four-year college or university, so we used the same conditions for participants in our study. We finessed our research purpose statement and questions to get us started.

> In this qualitative research study, we interviewed ten first-generation women faculty and administrators in order to understand their educational, socio-cultural, and professional experiences. The research questions that guided this study were:
>
> 1. What is the importance given to life events and/or individuals in the participants' decisions to pursue first undergraduate, then graduate study?
> 2. How have participants negotiated entry, survival, and advancement in the academy?
> 3. What have they learned as a result of forging new territory without familial/social role models?
> 4. How do they understand/articulate multiple identities?

Even though we were not going to use this book to advance knowledge about the essence or phenomenon of first-generation women academics, we poked around in the literature to see what had been said and to gain some insight into constructing our interview guide. To our surprise, we could find no previous research on first-generation academic women. The first-generation research seemed to stop with undergraduate college students (male and female), with a smattering of studies that looked at graduate school students. We did find two first-generation faculty narrative projects at Ohio University and California State University-Fresno,[13] but the only research that related to our project was in two articles by Sandra Jones: her research draws from data that she collected with female professors from the working class.[14]

Our next step was to prepare Institutional Review Board (IRB) materials for both of our governing institutions. After we garnered IRB approvals, we continued to tweak the semi-structured interview guide that we would use while we recruited participants. We intended to include both women faculty and administrators who had obtained a terminal degree, and we did not exclude any women on the basis of demographic characteristics. In fact, we achieved diversity in the sample by including women of various ages, races, ethnicities, and regional backgrounds. We recruited using purposeful sampling via academic listservs; the email included the purpose of the study and the requirements for participation. We secured ten participants within a couple of weeks of our initial email request by gaining their consent and sending them the interview guide. The semi-structured interview guide consisted of the following questions.

1. Take me back to your first day of college and reconstruct the events of the day. (Include decisions, people, circumstances, etc.)
2. What was influential in your decision to pursue advanced graduate study?
3. What tensions have you experienced between the culture of your upbringing and the culture of the academy?

[13] See "The Importance of First Generation Faculty & Staff," www.ohio.edu/univcollege/firstgeneration/index.cfm and "First Generation Story Project," http://firstgeneration.csufresno.edu/stories/default.htm.
[14] Sandra J. Jones, "A Place Where I Belong: Working-Class Women's Pursuit of Higher Education." *Race, Gender & Class* 11, no. 3 (2004): 74–87 and Sandra J. Jones, "Complex Subjectivities: Class, Ethnicity, and Race in Women's Narratives of Upward Mobility." *Journal of Social Issues* 59, no. 4 (2003): 803–20.

4. What were some of the most difficult experiences you had when you first entered the academy? (as well as in the years following).
5. What were some of the most pleasurable experiences you had when you first entered the academy? (as well as in the years following).
6. Is the academic life what you expected? If not, how has it differed? Did you know what to expect?
7. What are the most rewarding aspects of your academic life? Most frustrating? How do these correspond (or not) with your personal life?
8. What relationships in your life have changed as a result of becoming an academic? What is the nature of these changed relationships?
9. What other changes in your life have you experienced as a result of your achievements?
10. What does it mean to be a "good professor" in your department? How well have you "fit in" to this definition?
11. Has your understanding of what is valued or understood as constituting a good professor changed over time? If so, can you point to any key events or factors affecting this shift?
12. Are there any parts of yourself you put away or keep hidden in your personal relationships? In your work relationships? Say more about this.
13. What do you want other academics to know about your experiences as a woman in the academy? As a first-generation student?
14. Is there anything I should have asked but didn't?

Each interview lasted anywhere from one to three hours and was conducted face-to-face (with the exception of one that was done via telephone). We asked the participants to choose the location and time/day of the interview, and we had their permission to audio-record the interview and send it to an outside vendor for transcription. After we received the transcriptions, we offered them to the participants for review.

Although we interviewed ten women, we settled on using data from only two of the women's interviews for the purposes of this book. We detail this process and decision in Chapter 1, so for now we want to leave readers with a bit of background information on the two women participants who appear in this book: Cassandra and Sera. (All people and place names that appear in the data are pseudonyms.) We struggled with how much of Sera's and Cassandra's background to offer readers; as we have explained, this book is not about telling their stories or creating portraits of their lives, so inserting a backstory here in the Introduction "feels" like we are attempting to start with some beginnings. However, most of the data that we use in the book are focused on their academic lives, and through the interviews we learned that their journeys to higher education offer (selectively) important contexts and insights. After much doubt and debate, we decided to include limited backstories for both Sera and Cassandra. We thought it only fair to readers who might desire some inkling of background, and we realized that we ourselves held these backstories in our minds as we "thought with theory." However, we caution that these backstories do not provide fullness to the data, but serve more as an entrée into some sort of chronological capture of their lives from their childhood to their entry, as undergraduate women, into higher education. As Tamsin Lorraine writes,

Chronological time suggests that each moment in our existence is securely established and that our deeds and accomplishments are somehow enshrined in a past that remains stable – even as it recedes from us. As each moment slides from the present into the past, we can reassure ourselves that we are adding recognisable blocks to a building of our future we collectively share. A time out of joint suggests that there is no way to calibrate the pasts of our lived experience into a unified chronology. Chronological time is constructed out of the habitual reactions of bodies, the memories and expectations of conscious reflection, and collective forms of interpreting the past insisting in our present. We erase incongruities and smooth our paradox in order to create the delusion of time as a seamless whole.[15]

In other words, the backstories are as limited as all the data excerpts that appear in Chapters 2–7. The backstories are present here not as a stable or seamless whole, but as "time out of joint" – something that *appears* unified but is simply constructed (by us) for a specific purpose: not to calibrate coherence, but to show how their past is "insistent" in the tellings of their present. That is, included in the backstories are pieces of their lives that Cassandra and Sera deemed important to their present positionings in the academy.

Cassandra's backstory

Cassandra was born in the 1940s, the oldest child in an African-American family living in the Deep South. "I come from a very small rural town," she stated. "The population then, and probably now, is less than a thousand." Her father had a fifth-grade education while her mother had completed the eighth grade. "We lived by farming," Cassandra reported. Her family had about three acres of their own land, on which they grew food for their personal use. "We pretty much lived off of what we had accumulated ... We had always had big vegetable gardens and things like that, so we were able to pretty much grow what we ate ... We lived very, very meagerly."

Her family worked for other people with larger farms, doing "anything that we could do to make some money ... Whether it was picking vegetables, or whether it was working in tobacco or cotton, whatever kind of work that was available, we did it." She noted, "From the time of the planting of the crops in the spring until the harvesting of the crops in the fall, my family was regularly employed. And then, of course, in the wintertime there was no income ... That was our life."

A turning point for her future was realized in those fields. She explained, "I remember that one very, very hot day one of my sisters and I were working in a tobacco field and it was grueling and I said to her, 'I'm not gonna do this for the rest of my life.' ... I decided that I didn't know exactly what I was gonna do, but I wasn't gonna work on the farms for the rest of my life." She went on to say that, however, "very, very few people actually got a college education out of my hometown ... In the black folk, about the only people who really went to college were the valedictorian and the salutatorian."

Cassandra worked hard in school. "One of the things [I] learned as I was coming up even in grade school and high school was [I] have to be twice as good to be considered as good." Cassandra's high school guidance counselor recognized her academic ability. "At that time, you would be placed in either a vocational track or an academic track in high school, depending on what your performances had been in your classes ... I was always really good

---

[15] Tamsin Lorraine, "Living a Time Out of Joint." In *Between Deleuze & Derrida*, edited by Paul Patton and John Protevi (London: Continuum, 2003), 44.

in school and so my guidance counselor ... put me in an academic track." She was ultimately honored as valedictorian of her class.

"It wasn't until sometime in my senior year of high school that I actually began to think about what college I was gonna go to," Cassandra said. She originally thought she would attend the small, liberal arts college from which her pastor had graduated, but a conversation at school changed her mind. "[I] was talking with the principal one day, who was also a graduate of that institution, and he asked me where I was going. I told him, and he asked me, 'Why do you want to go there?' And I was really surprised because I thought as a person who graduated from there, he would be happy." As she reflected upon that conversation, she recalled, "What he suggested was that I could do a lot better." She applied to another school at the last minute: a small, historically black state university about two hours from her home town.

"Almost everybody that I knew who was college educated were teachers." This was Cassandra's original plan as well. "My life goal after I decided to go to college was just to get my bachelor's and to become a teacher and to teach in a public school not too far from my hometown, in one of the little towns around or something." After her arrival at the university, however, she decided to consider science-related programs. "I went to school thinking that I was going to be a scientist because I was really, really good in those courses in high school ... But then I got my grades in chemistry [and they] were not that great. And so at the end of the freshman year when [I] had to decide a major, I went into the college catalog and decided that I was going to find a major that was as far away from science as I could possibly get."

Cassandra described her parents as "very supportive" and "very proud" of her decision to go to college. While some of her cousins had gone to college and become teachers, Cassandra was the only member of her immediate family to complete her bachelor's degree; it was conferred upon her in 1966. "I have one sister who ... graduated from community college, and there's another one who went, but I'm not sure that she graduated."

Sera's backstory

Sera is an only child whose mother became single when Sera's dad "hit the party road" when Sera was two and her mom "hit the hell of minimum wage and single parenting." Throughout her childhood, she bounced around from adult to adult: "There wasn't very much consistency in my life. I lived with my grandma some, my dad some, and my mom some." She described her upbringing as "poverty and struggle." She grew up in a white working-class milieu, "sitting next to the juke box in bars while [her] parents were drinking and in different places because they weren't together."

During her early teens, Sera's mother determined to settle down. "She wanted me to be in one place for high school ... She was like, 'We're going to high school. We're going to be there all four years.'" Sera had two schools from which to choose; she selected a "pretty large public high school ... in [an] inner city." There she got involved in many activities.

Planning for college was not a significant component of Sera's high school experience, despite scoring forty-fifth out of the 400 students in her class on a college entrance exam. "I never had it in my mind that I would go to college ... I just really didn't think much about it." She ended up filling out college applications as "a matter of course" at school. She explained, "Somehow I was in a situation where I was filling out application forms. And somehow, I was in a situation where I was filling out financial aid forms."

Two major state universities denied Sera admission because she lacked requisite coursework on her high school transcript. She stated, "But then I got an acceptance letter to [a large state school], and I was like okay, now it's a possibility. Like I didn't even think – and then I thought okay, well, what would that be like? That sounds kind of cool. You know, I don't know what I'm going to do next year. I could do this."

Finances for school came together as well, in part because of her grandparents. "They lived in San Francisco for a long time and owned a hotel, but they retired to California to Lake Tahoe, where you could gamble. And my grandfather would go up to the casinos for his fun thing to do, and he would come home, and he would give the winnings to my grandmother. And she, for years, would just save this money … She always thought that it would be for my college." Sera summarized, "So I had $10,000, I was in a state school, I had financial aid, I had acceptance, but none of it was by my sort of design or goals or yearning or whatever. And then I headed off."

While her mother supported her decision to go to college, she was not physically present when the time came for Sera to transition to campus. She had taken a job cooking on a tugboat partway through Sera's senior year, and was only home to visit about once a month. Sera related what her mother said to her: "Well, here's the keys to the car. Drive yourself over, pack your stuff, lock the house. I'll see you back in probably September or October." She continued, "So I drove across the state all by myself with my little crates in my mom's pickup truck."

Sera had never visited the university campus prior to her departure; she had selected her housing based on what she learned from a brochure. She explained, "I chose a dorm because it said it had a dark room and a radio station. You know, it was pretty exciting to think about what that was going to be like." Anticipation turned to shock when she arrived at the university. "I got to campus and I was completely overwhelmed. I'd never been to any place like this." She got lost and ended up among hordes of students partying on Greek Row. "I didn't know where I was going. And I didn't have anybody to ask. And I ended up just parking and sobbing, sobbing, sobbing, getting that together, and then finding my dorm, and checking in."

On her second day at the university, Sera made a friend who helped influence her academic future. "I met this girl, [Mandy], and she was just a big party all the time." Her friendship with Mandy spurred her in her studies. "[Mandy] had had an upbringing of an expectation that she would go to college. So she knew more about what that was – she was more comfortable, I guess, with the fact that she was going to go to classes and do really well, which made me very competitive. So we took our classes together, we lived together, and I think a lot of how I did well was because of her."

University pseudonyms and descriptions

Catholic University is a private Catholic university. Total enrollment is nearly 8,000, 5,000 of whom are undergraduate students. Established in the late 1800s, the university belongs to a long tradition of humanist, Catholic education and employs approximately 370 full-time faculty members. Catholic University is Sera's current employer.

Prairie College is a private, residential liberal arts college with a denominational affiliation. Total enrollment is approximately 3,000, nearly all of whom are undergraduates (2,700). Founded in 1890, the college's mission is to prepare graduates to honor God and Christ in their service to humanity. The university has approximately 150 full-time faculty. Prairie

College is where Sera began her academic career as an assistant professor, before teaching at Catholic University.

Regional State University enrolls approximately 17,000 students, the majority of whom come from within the state. Undergraduate enrollment accounts for approximately 15,000 of total enrollment. Located in a rural setting, the university employs approximately 870 full-time faculty and is classified as a master's comprehensive. Cassandra has worked as an academic at Regional State University since 1992.

Southern State University was founded in 1896 as a land-grant college. Today it is designated as a land-grant, senior comprehensive institution of approximately 5,000 students. At the time of its founding, Southern State University was the state's sole public college for black youth. Since the mid-1960s it has been open to white students and faculty, but it has largely retained its mission and focus as a historically black institution. Cassandra attended Southern State University as an undergraduate and began her academic career as an assistant professor there.

Chapter 1

Plugging one text into another

There is no difference between what a book talks about and how it is made. Therefore a book also has no object. As an assemblage, a book has only itself, in connection with other assemblages and in relation to other bodies without organs. We will never ask what a book means, as signified or signifier; we will not look for anything to understand in it ... A book exists only through the outside and on the outside. A book itself is a little machine ... [1]

Plugging in

However readers choose to enter this assemblage, they will encounter a concept that we picked up from Deleuze and Guattari to capture our thinking with theory in qualitative research. That little phrase is "plugging in." We first encountered plugging in on page 4 of Deleuze and Guattari's *A Thousand Plateaus*: "When one writes, the only question is which other machine the literary machine can be plugged into, *must* be plugged into in order to work."[2] In our thinking with theory, we were confronted with multiple texts – or literary machines: interview data, tomes of theory, conventional qualitative research methods books that we were working against, things we had previously written, traces of data, reviewer comments, and so on *ad infinitum*. That is, we had a sense of the ceaseless variations possible in having co-authored texts that relied on a plugging in of ideas, fragments, theory, selves, sensations. And so we moved to engage plugging in as a *process* rather than a *concept*, something we could put to work, for as Rosi Braidotti urges in this time of change, "the challenge lies in thinking about processes, rather than concepts."[3]

Conceptualizing the process of plugging in is the easy part. Putting it to work requires much more acumen. Plugging in to produce something new is a constant, continuous process of making and unmaking. An assemblage isn't a thing – it is the *process* of making and unmaking the thing. It is the process of arranging, organizing, fitting together. So to see it at work, we have to ask not only how things are connected, but also what territory is claimed in that connection. What we aim to do here in Chapter 1 is attempt to recapture our process of plugging in multiple machines in this assemblage, and ask what new territories are claimed within the field of qualitative research methods.

[1] Gilles Deleuze and Félix Guattari, *A Thousand Plateaus: Capitalism & Schizophrenia*, trans. Brian Massumi (Minneapolis, MN: University of Minnesota Press, 1987), 4.

[2] *Ibid.*

[3] Rosi Braidotti, *Metamorphoses: Toward a Materialist Theory of Becoming* (Malden, MA: Polity, 2002), 1.

We likened our previous experience authoring pieces together as emphasizing a "genera-tion of sensations," as Elizabeth Grosz wrote about in a discussion of artistic production.[4] Certainly what we envisioned for this project was not grounded in traditional coding and thematic, conventional analysis of data, with emphasis on the production of an end or commodity. Rather, we positioned our project as a production of knowledge that might emerge as a creation out of chaos.[5] Coding and data reduction then would be seen as commodification and the process of plugging in as a production of the new, *the assemblage in formation*. Imagine this production of knowledge – emerging as assemblage, creation from chaos – not as a final arrival, but as the result of plugging in: an assemblage of "continuous, self-vibrating intensities" that required discarding the

> tripartite division between a field of reality (the world) and a field of representation (the book) and a field of subjectivity (the author). Rather, an assemblage establishes con-nections between certain multiplicities drawn from each of these orders, so that a book has no sequel nor the world as its object nor one or several authors as its subject.[6]

Here in Chapter 1, we take up each of these "fields" that make up this assemblage that readers have before them, an assemblage that will inevitably be plugged in to readers' own machines: their own theories, data, methods, becomings, and so on. For us and our project, we connect a "field of reality" (data, theory, method), a "field of representation" (producing different knowledge, resisting stable meaning), and a "field of subjectivity" (becoming-researcher). In this next section of "Plugging in" we present the field of reality, or how certain connectivities *emerged in between* data and theory. In the second part of Chapter 1, we move into another figuration called "The threshold"; in that section, we explore our field of representation – or how various assemblages (or analytical questions) sprouted via our plugging in. Finally, in the figuration "Folding and flattening," we explore a field of sub-jectivity, in which we follow various lines of flight in regard to researcher selves – and how the assemblage made and unmade us as "authors." That is, we acknowledge that we alone are not the authors of this assemblage; the research participants and the theorists inserted themselves in the process. As well, folding and flattening pushed us as "authors" (qualitative researchers) away from conventional interpretation into realms of post-humanist "data analysis."

In the field of reality, what did we plug in? As mentioned in the Introduction, we interviewed ten women who were the first generation in their families to graduate from college, and who then went on to earn doctorates and become academics. Our initial aim was to view the data across theoretical constructs (phenomenology, critical theory, poststructuralism). We did not

---

[4] In drawing on Deleuze and Guattari's discussion of affect in the book *What is Philosophy?* Elizabeth Grosz in her book *Chaos, Territory, Art* writes the following: "Sensations, affects, and intensities, while not readily identifiable, are clearly closely connected with forces, and particularly bodily forces, and their qualitative transformations. What differentiates them from experience, or from any phenomenological framework, is the fact that they link the lived or phenomenological body with cosmological forces, forces of the outside that the body itself can never experience directly." (p. 3) Our writing and plugging in together has been much like this. We create from the sensations of our thinking with and against each other, the data, the theory, and ourselves.

[5] Elizabeth Grosz, *Chaos, Territory, Art: Deleuze and the Framing of the Earth* (New York: Columbia University Press, 2008).

[6] Deleuze and Guattari, *A Thousand Plateaus*, op. cit., 23.

set out to focus on theoretical frameworks in the abstract; rather, we wanted to engage the implication of those concepts for qualitative methodology, analysis, and representation. However, becoming more enmeshed in the process of making the thing, we found that there was too much data to be read across the theoretical frameworks. We sought to resist an easy story, and yet to illustrate from *all* of the data was to revert to the macro and to sweeping generalizations. We were haunted by the question: How were we to show the method of "plugging in" if readers couldn't experience the same thing opened up and distorted repeatedly? In order to illustrate what we were attempting, we had to focus intently on specific data "chunks" that could be repeated and re-viewed across the various theorists and concepts.

And so we narrowed down and focused on two transcripts for purposes of discussion: Cassandra's and Sera's. Before we explain the choice of data (and we are not quite convinced that the data did not *choose us*), we want to offer some words on data, voice, and experience, and how we positioned the data excerpts as we plugged them into theory. We are well aware that, as researchers, we asked Cassandra and Sera to share their truths and experiences, but in our analysis we were keeping an eye toward their experiences not as this "thing" that has happened "to" them, but something that has been filtered, processed, and already interpreted. There is nothing pure about what they told us, yet we needed their "stories" to knead the dynamics among philosophy, theory, and social life to see what gets made, not understood. That is, Cassandra and Sera had already "made meaning" of their experiences in that they chose to tell them in a particular way – in their selection, what they emphasized, and what they chose not to reveal. We assume that data is partial, incomplete, and always being re-told and re-membered. This is not something we have arrived at on our own, nor is it something that has come to us through the process of writing this book. It has been a long time coming, beginning with our doctoral studies, in our efforts to resist the containment of interpretivism, and in our reading and doing of research under the influence of poststructural theories. In fact, we have published widely using poststructural theories of language, subjectivity, power, and desire to trouble the concept of voice in conventional and critical qualitative research.[7] In our introductory chapter to *Voice in Qualitative Inquiry*, we wrote:

> The privileging of voice in traditional qualitative research assumes that voice makes present the truth and *reflects* the meaning of an experience that has already happened. This is the voice that, in traditional qualitative research, is heard and then recorded, coded, and categorized as normative and containable data. Given such traditional privileging of voice we ask: How do we go about working the limits of voice? and Why should we be engaged in such a practice? How does putting privileged understandings of voice under poststructural scrutiny result in a positioning of voice as *productive* of meaning—as excessive and unstable voices that surprise us, both pleasantly and uncomfortably, with previously unarticulated and unthought meanings? We

---

[7] Alecia Y. Jackson, "Rhizovocality," *International Journal of Qualitative Studies in Education* 16, no. 5 (2003): 693–710; Alecia Y. Jackson and Lisa A. Mazzei, *Voice in Qualitative Inquiry* (London: Routledge, 2009); Alecia Y. Jackson and Lisa A. Mazzei, "Experience and 'I' in Autoethnography: A Deconstruction," *International Review of Qualitative Research* 1, no. 3 (2008): 299–318; Lisa A. Mazzei, *Inhabited Silence in Qualitative Research: Putting Poststructural Theory to Work* (New York: Peter Lang, 2007); Lisa A. Mazzei, "Desiring Silence: Gender, Race and Pedagogy in Education," *British Educational Research Journal* 37 (2011): 657–69.

assert that in our zeal as qualitative researchers to gather data and make meaning, or to make easy sense, we often seek that voice which we can easily name, categorize and respond to. We argue that a more fertile practice, and one that is advocated in this collection by the authors, is to seek the voice that escapes easy classification and that does not make easy sense. It is not a voice that is normative, but one that is transgressive.[8]

As we read all the data, we were attentive to our own theoretical *and* methodological perspectives on voice, truth, and meaning. We sought "voices" that, even partial and incomplete, produced multiplicities and excesses of meaning and subjectivities. So in fact, rather than seeking stability within and among the data, we were drawn to that data which seemed to be about difference rather than sameness. Given this perspective, Sera's and Cassandra's data were ones we returned to over and over again, and they surprised us with the ways in which they described/inscribed their "experiences." How they seemed to understand how they were positioned – and how they positioned themselves – within a broad range of discursive fields as well as social and material conditions was more nuanced than any of the other first-generation women academics whom we interviewed. In order to work against "sameness" (or resisting the coding imperative to reach "data saturation"), we wanted to emphasize *difference within* Cassandra's and Sera's language-based expressions of subjectivity, power, desire, and so on. In other words, Sera and Cassandra helped us to break open the particular identity of "first-generation academic woman" through their *difference within* the category. Certainly, we can "describe" their difference in categorical ways: Cassandra is black, a full professor, near retirement, physically disabled due to mobility problems, and works in the social sciences. Sera is white, an early-career assistant professor, a single mother, and works in the humanities. Though they grew up in opposite geographical and cultural ends of the USA, and had very different childhood experiences, their trajectories to academia are quite similar. Yet we do not treat these categorical similarities and differences as comparative, correlational, or causal; to do so would remain entrenched in liberal humanist identity-work of centering and stabilizing the subject in conventional qualitative research. Rather, we noticed that, particularly in Cassandra's and Sera's data, they expressed multiplicity, ambiguity, and incoherent subjectivity.

We read Sera's and Cassandra's interview-transcripts-positioned-as-partial-and-incomplete over and over, keeping in mind the theoretical constructs that initiated our project, those constructs that we had encountered as graduate students and that continued to inform our scholarly work (and our non-academic lives) over the past ten to fifteen years. Therefore, as we read the data, the theory was in our selves, but something different happened in the moments of plugging in. We characterize this reading-the-data-while-thinking-the-theory as a moment of plugging in, of entering the assemblage, of making new connectives. We began to realize how plugging in creates a different relationship among texts: they *constitute* one another and in doing so create something new.

This "something new" was how the larger theoretical frameworks dissolved, and what sprouted in the assemblage of our thinking were *people, or theorists*. On some level we could say that Sera constituted Derrida, who constituted Cassandra, who constituted Foucault, who constituted Spivak, and so on. They make each other in the plugging in and create new

---

[8]   Lisa A. Mazzei and Alecia Y. Jackson, "Introduction: The Limit of Voice." In *Voice in Qualitative Inquiry*, edited by Alecia Y. Jackson and Lisa A. Mazzei, 1–13 (London: Routledge, 2009), 4.

ways of thinking about *both theory and data*. Articulation is about making new combinations to create new identities.

The theorists who rhizomatically emerged were Derrida, Spivak, Foucault, Butler, Deleuze, and Barad. Therefore, in this new assemblage of texts, just as we needed to hone in on specific data episodes, we learned that instead of theoretical frameworks (critical theory, poststructuralism), we needed rather to focus more specifically on theorists; and not just on theorists, but *a* specific concept from the theorists who made up part of the assemblage (deconstruction, marginality, power/knowledge). Perhaps these particular theorists bubbled up for us because in our previous work we have positioned them as productive provocation: theorists who open up thought rather than foreclose it. Further, just as we narrowed our focus on the data, we grasped onto these concepts as they were articulated in a certain moment and time in a philosopher's *oeuvre*. We recognize that, for example, Foucault's view of the subject modified as he expanded and deepened his own thinking. So even as we put concepts to work in order to emphasize the processes of social, cultural, and material life and ways of knowing/being, we are careful to locate both theory *and* data.

Therefore, what plugging in requires from a methodological perspective is not limited to merely an intimacy with *both* the data and the theory, nor simply a keen attentiveness to the particularities and situatedness of each. Rather, we believe that plugging in involves at least three maneuvers:

1 putting philosophical concepts to work via disrupting the theory/practice binary by decentering each and instead showing how they *constitute or make one another*;
2 being deliberate and transparent in what analytical questions are made possible by a specific theoretical concept (deconstruction, marginality, power/knowledge, performativity, desire, intra-activity) and how the questions that are used to think with *emerged in the middle* of plugging in; and
3 working the same data chunks repeatedly to "deform [them], to make [them] groan and protest"[9] with an overabundance of meaning, which in turn not only creates new knowledge but also shows the *suppleness of each when plugged in*.

And so, we worked with unstable subjects and concepts-on-the-move that would intervene in a process to diffract, rather than foreclose, thought. We plug in to help extend a thinking at the limit.[10] This then is at least one of our aims, a thinking at the limit of our ability to know, as made possible by these theorists and their concepts at work, these data and their excesses.

---

[9] Michel Foucault, *Power/Knowledge: Selected Interviews and Other Writings: 1972–1977*, translated by Leo Marshall Colin Gordon, John Mepham and Kate Soper, edited by Colin Gordon (New York: Pantheon Books, 1980), 22–23.

[10] In *The Mystical Element in Heidegger's Thought*, John Caputo (1986) writes of Heidegger as "a thinker whose thinking is conducted at the limits of philosophy" (p. 1). Throughout the book, Caputo discusses Heidegger's thinking "post philosophy," as he describes Heidegger as wanting to shake loose of Western philosophy in order "to overcome philosophy and take up the task of thought" (p. 266). Heidegger speaks of the end of philosophy as an end to the rationalities and strictures that limit thought. What he pursues is a transgression of these limits and strictures that opens him to the beginning of thought, or rather, toward the beginning of thought not previously possible because it was outside or beyond the permissible, seeable, hearable limits.

The threshold

Think of a threshold. In architecture, a threshold is in the middle of things. It exists as a passageway. A threshold has no function, purpose, or meaning until it is connected to other spaces. That is, a threshold does not become a passageway until it is attached to other things different from itself. Thresholds contain both entries and exits; they are both/and. A single threshold can be not only an entryway, but also an exit; therefore the structure itself is not quite as linear and definitive as one might think. In other terms, thresholds can denote excess, such as in having a low threshold for pain. The excess of a threshold is the space in which something else occurs: a response, an effect. Once you exceed the threshold, something new happens.

We offer the figuration of the threshold as a way to situate our plugging in, or how we put the data and theory to work in the threshold to create new analytical questions. In the space of the threshold, we became aware of how theory and data constitute or make one another – and how, in the threshold, the divisions among and definitions of theory and data collapse. In our project, we were surrounded by texts: the data, the theory, our memories of the interview process, our shifty selves as researchers, our current interactions with some of the research participants, our own personal and professional knowledge of being women academics (one of us first-generation), and so on. As Deleuze and Guattari wrote, "Machines make thought itself nomadic";[11] therefore, all of these aforementioned texts/literary machines, when plugged in while in the threshold, produced something new, something different from mere themes and patterns generated by coding.

At the very most, we can claim a ground that shifted under our feet as we proceeded through the threshold. We can go to Derrida: "Determined and dated, this is a reading of the work in which I find myself engaged: which therefore is no more my own than it remains arrested here. This too is a situation to be read ..."[12] Our thinking with theory activity can be considered determined and dated. Determined and dated by a particular task that is at once something we do in the present, and infiltrated by traces of past and future readings. Derrida uses an interesting word choice: arrested. Arrested, as a signifier, in its plenitude explodes into multiple meanings if we follow it along some chain of signification: arrest – seize – stop – halt – *to make a brief visit*. Arrest does not simply mean "seize" in its totality, for if we follow the trace, the word is opened up to imply temporality. Thinking with theory as arrested in the threshold, then, can signify *temporary meaning that can escape and transform at any moment* – at moments after more reading, for example (which is part of the shifting ground of the threshold).

So it is in this way that we approached our thinking with theory. The data were not centered or stabilized, but used as brief stopping points and continually transformed, and exceeded, as we used theory to turn the data into something different, and we used data to push theory to its limit. For example, we "read" the same excerpt of data from Cassandra, one of the participants in our interview study, with a power/knowledge reading alongside Foucault, and with a posthumanist performative stance alongside Barad. In the reading with Foucault, the questions that emerged explored how power relations are endowed "with processes which are more or less adjusted to the situation."[13] That is, power relations are

---

[11] Deleuze and Guattari, *A Thousand Plateaus*, op. cit., 24.

[12] Jacques Derrida, *Positions*, translated by Alan Bass (1972; repr. Chicago: University of Chicago Press, 1981), vii.

[13] Michel Foucault, *Power*, translated by Robert Hurley *et al.*, edited by Paul Rabinow, *Essential Works of Foucault 1954–1984, Volume III* (New York: The New Press, 2000), 224.

specific and local to subjects who are in mutual relations with one another. In thinking with Barad, she taught us to be aware of a diffractive reading that emphasizes not how discourses function to produce power relations, but how power relations materialize in the intra-action between/with the material and the discursive.

It is impossible for us to treat our thinking with theory as a full answer because it gets its very identity from what is excluded: we included only a small range of theories, and arrested a specific concept, rather than a body of work, from each theorist. What is central is at the expense of what is marginal (we follow Derrida in this regard: the center always conceals something). We are not merely using the vocabulary of Foucault (power) or Spivak (marginality) or Deleuze (desire), and we resist *forcing* the concepts into our thinking of data. Rather, we are *doing* and *using* the vocabulary and concepts as we push research and data and theory to its exhaustion in order to produce knowledge differently; in this way, we focus on the constitutive and generative aspects of texts. By refusing a closed system for fixed meaning (transferable patterns and themes generated from coding data with reductive language), we engage the threshold as site of transformation.

To transform both theory and data and to keep meaning on the move in the threshold, we crafted a set of analytical questions that we would pursue with the help of each theorist – an image that we experienced as having Butler or Derrida or Spivak reading over our shoulder and asking a series of questions. Again, these are not *the* questions or concepts (any more than first-generation-academic-women is *the* data), but we chose concepts that would help us extend our thinking beyond an easy sense. While we will talk more about what each of the theorists opens up in the chapters that follow, we present here the analytical questions informed by the key concepts that we plugged into the data, including what is to be stretched in our thinking with the concepts.

We noticed a genealogical connection of our movement from one theorist to the next in ways that expand/stretch/distort previous ways of knowing. Derrida helped us account for the silence as trace and as a purposeful and productive way to think about what else participants might be saying in the gap. In thinking voice and silence, Deleuze extended our thinking by complicating the production of silence in an interrogation of what was produced and what was producing what we name a desiring silence. Similarly, a movement to Barad and her theory of intra-action draws on the immanence and vitalism that Deleuze presents in his concepts toward an enactment of processes of becoming that shift to a focus on ontology. Foucault offers a view of power as relational and productive (as opposed to always prohibitive), and Spivak relies on Foucault's power/knowledge combination to posit her perspectives of marginality in the "teaching machine." Spivak takes up Foucault to a point and then brings in Derrida to deconstruct how the teaching machine secures its center by defining marginality in the academy. Butler, too, considers Foucauldian power relations as productive of a performative subjectivity. Continuing on this genealogical bent, Barad draws heavily on the work of Foucault and Butler, but theorizes the relationship between the material and the discursive to what she terms a posthumanist performativity. The following gives an overview of each chapter, or "threshold."

Derrida: *Deconstruction.* Our past encounters with Derrida caused us to reject the signifiers that we rely on as researchers – experience, truth, voice, data. With Derrida, we stay close to the narratives to examine what is produced in the deconstructive moment – the jarring and excessive nature of events that do not fit neatly into categories, nor capture an experience, but that rupture structures and received notions of the academy. Hence the analytic question that Derrida prompts is: *How does the presence of Sera and Cassandra in the* *academy make visible the excesses of race, class, and gender in the event that is deconstruction?* We plug the narratives of Sera and Cassandra into our thinking of deconstruction as the event in an attempt to glimpse the irruptive nature of deconstruction and its effects on these women, their family members, and colleagues in the academy. Places of irruption tear the fabric of what is supposed to be – where language is strained, where meaning is missed, where destabilization occurs, and where excess produces a snagging that resists closure. That is, deconstruction as *always already* happening.

Spivak: *Marginality.* Spivak relies on Foucault's concept of power/knowledge to position the teaching machine (the university) as a vehicle of power/knowledge that seeks to locate and define what counts as authentic inhabitants of the margin. Thus we learn from both Foucault and Spivak how the center (the academy) positions and defines marginality through its constitution of the subject. Spivak takes Foucault's analysis to its limit, and then abandons such focus on the subject to bring in Derrida's deconstruction. Her deconstruction re-positions marginality not as a positive space *outside* of the center, but as constituted *within* the center. Using the domain of the teaching machine (the university), Spivak deconstructs both the center *and* the margin for their paradoxes, predicaments, and constraints, and offers an exploration of: *How is Cassandra outside in the teaching machine?*

Foucault: *Power/knowledge.* The academy is an institutional structure, yet we wanted to think differently about power as merely repressive or prohibitive in such a space. So we went to Foucault to help us think about the relation between power and knowledge: not that one *is* the other ("knowledge is power"), but how they *express* one another. We put to use Foucault's theory of power relations: relations that are unstable, unequal, and produce knowledge about the self. This became salient as we read data about Cassandra and Sera entering the academy as new professors, and through our locating, in the data, manifestations of power/knowledge in their practices as they negotiated power relations and new knowledge about themselves in an as-yet-unknown terrain. We looked to Cassandra's and Sera's practices of power/knowledge to see how they might disrupt historical truths or struggle with (even evade) others' (students, administrators) practices of power/knowledge which seek to contain them. The analytic question for our power/knowledge reading is: *How do power/knowledge relations and practices produce Cassandra's and Sera's multiple subjectivities as they venture into the academy as first-generation professors?*

Butler: *Performativity.* Judith Butler's theory of performativity is central to all of her work that seeks to undo normative categories that place rigid structures on how people live out their lives. Butler's performativity, as it relies more on linguistic action than on the theatrical, explores (and exposes) how gender identities get done (and undone) as a reiterative and citational practice within discourse, power relations, historical experiences, cultural practices, and material conditions. Moving beyond the binary frame set up in language via humanism and structuralism, Butler's theory of gender performativity works to unsettle the stabilizing gender categories that attempt to normalize and regulate people, and accentuates a process of *repetition* that produces gendered subjectivity. This repetition is not a performance *by* a subject, but a performativity that *constitutes* a subject and thus produces the space of conflicting subjectivities. Paradoxically, agency is derived from within this constitution as subjects' performative acts both reproduce *and* contest the foundations and origins of stable identity categories. We build upon Foucault's power/knowledge and Derrida's language theory – and gesture toward Barad in the final data chapter – to explore: *What are the performative acts that (re)produce Cassandra's and Sera's subjectivities as academic* *women?* Performativity gives us a framework to approach the data – and the subject – as decentered, non-foundational, and never fully constituted.

Deleuze: *Desire.* While Derrida had much to say to us about the absent present, we began to brush up against the limits of methodological thinking about voice with Derrida. Derrida helped us consider the trace, the always-already absent present, but failed to help us interrogate why the absent present in the form of silence might be inhabiting the narratives. For Deleuze and Guattari, desire is about production (in a similar way that Foucault's power is productive, and that Butler's subject is produced). Desire's production is active, becoming, transformative. It produces out of a multiplicity of forces that form the assemblage. We desire not because we lack something that we do not have, but because of the productive force of intensities and connections of desires. To turn desire on its head is to open up a consideration of how silences work, and why they persist, because those "speaking" with silence act and are acted upon in a transformative process. Deleuze prompts us to ask: *How does a desiring silence function to keep/maintain/produce smooth social, familial, and professional relations?* In other words, how does desire work, and who does it work for?

Barad: *Intra-activity.* It is the work of Karen Barad and others named as "new materialists" or "material feminists" to ask how our intra-action with other bodies (both human and nonhuman) produces subjectivities and performative enactments not previously thought. We see the work of Karen Barad as an enactment of the ontological shift made by Deleuze in a philosophy of immanence. This is to think of *knowing in being* that is not merely a re-insertion of the material, nor a privileging of the material, but a shaking up of the privileging of the discursive in postmodern thought without a re-centering of the material that preceded the linguistic turn. This fundamental break presented by Barad helps us "fashion an approach that brings the material back in without rejecting the legitimate insights of the linguistic turn."[14] Such fashioning prompts the question: *How do Cassandra and Sera intra-act with the materiality of their world in ways that produce different becomings?*

While we might have ordered the chapters differently (indeed, the sequencing was a vexing task), we have arranged them in such a way as to encourage difference *and* repetition. We view each chapter as a threshold to visit briefly, to arrest a temporary meaning, to emphasize movement. Each threshold is a new opening, a new space, but not disconnected from other thresholds. We have purposefully repeated data segments among chapters to permit a nomadic and rhizomatic reading in the threshold, a reading that does not rely on what has come before (or after), but that encourages a proliferation of thought. Like our encounter in the threshold, we offer these repetitions so that readers might make different sense of the data as it is plugged in again and again with different theorists and their concepts. Repeating the data encourages a reading of texts through one another as we invite readers into the threshold.

Folding and flattening

As we claimed in the first section, "Plugging in," we characterize our thinking with theory as making three moves: 1) disrupting the theory/practice binary by decentering each and instead showing how they *constitute or make one another*; 2) allowing analytical questions that are used to think with to *emerge in the middle* of plugging in; and 3) showing the

[14] Susan Hekman, *The Material of Knowledge: Feminist Disclosures* (Bloomington: Indiana University Press, 2010), 7.

suppleness of both theory and data when plugged in. So what we have practiced is not an attention to one of the various poles in a myriad of binaries: subject/object; data/theory; researcher/researched; but a flattening and attentiveness to how each constitutes the other and how each, as supple, sprouts as something new in the threshold. Such practice incites the provocations to be found in a plugging of theory into data into theory. It also evokes a folding – not just of data into theory and *vice versa* – but also of ourselves as researchers into the texts and into the theoretical threshold. It is a purposeful methodological repetition that prompts practices that are "multiple, simultaneous, and in flux."[15] This practice of folding "is an attempt to begin thinking [differently about data and research] when thought has not yet occurred. That is to say, thought ... which might, through repetition, give birth to something new."[16]

In our plugging of data into theory into data, we did not simply flatten the poles of the binary, but we also began to reconsider the implications of such flattening in this enterprise called qualitative research. Can there be useful knowledge if the traditional categories no longer hold? Consider, for example, the subject. As we practiced folding data, our participants, theorists and their concepts, and ourselves into a threshold, we were continually confronted with the subject. Judith Butler wrote, "In speaking the 'I,' I undergo something of what cannot be captured or assimilated by the 'I,' since I always arrive too late to myself."[17] If the "I" of the participant is always becoming in the process of telling, so too the "I" of the researcher is always becoming in the process of researching, listening, and writing. What might constitute a re-telling and an approach to research that displaces many of the normalizing features of data stories and the subject in qualitative inquiry? In our process of flattening and folding, we do not seek more and more reflexivity that reveals more and more about the researcher's ways of knowing. We seek to unsettle the "I" of both the researcher and researched who is a static and singular subject.

Do we still believe in the subject? Yes, and no. Like St Pierre,[18] we do not adhere to the liberal humanist subject that is an individual person or self. We do try to understand the historical constitution of subjectivity and the entangled production of agency that occurs in the process of intra-action as described by Karen Barad. Barad discusses the "entangled state of agencies"[19] that exceed traditional notions of how we conceive of agency, subjectivity, and the individual. For Barad, "agency is an enactment, not something that someone or something has."[20] Susan Hekman further develops the idea of the subject in what she terms the "'I' of the mangle."

> The "I" is a mangle composed of multiple elements. The social scripts defining subjecthood are a key aspect of that mangle. But the mangle also encompasses a body that is sexed and raced, a body that is located at a particular place in the social hierarchy, and a body/subject that has had a range of experiences. The result may be a subject that fits

[15] Patti Lather, *Getting Lost: Feminist Efforts Toward a Doubled Science* (Albany: SUNY Press, 2007), 4.
[16] Lisa A. Mazzei and Kate McCoy, "Thinking with Deleuze in Qualitative Research," *International Journal of Qualitative Studies in Education* 23 (2010): 505.
[17] Judith Butler, *Giving an Account of Oneself* (New York: Fordham University Press, 2005), 79.
[18] Elizabeth A. St Pierre, "Qualitative Data Analysis after Coding." Paper presented at the AERA Annual Meeting, April 2011, New Orleans, LA, USA.
[19] Karen Barad, *Meeting the Universe Halfway: Quantum Physics and the Entanglement of Meaning* (Durham: Duke University Press, 2007), 22–23.
[20] *Ibid.*, 235.

neatly into the definition of subject the social scripts circumscribe. Or the result may be an "I" who cannot find a script that fits, that resists the scripts available to her/him. In all cases, however, there is no single causal factor determining the subject; the elements of subjectivity intra-act in a complex web.[21]

Our aim here is not to recite a manifesto, but instead to enact a process of data/theory/ writing that is at once and at the same time using, producing, and questioning the practices that are and have been available to us. To embrace, not avoid, the methodological "hot-spots" where difficult situations may exist or erupt. Maggie MacLure alerts us that these hot spots may have much more to teach us than the "static connections that we often assume between self and other, researcher and researched."[22] Karen Barad has this to say:

> The dichotomized positions of realism and social constructivism—which presume a subject/object dichotomy—can acknowledge the situated/constructed character of only one of the poles of the dualism at a time. Realists do not deny that subjects are materially situated; constructivists insist upon the socially or discursively constructed character of objects. Neither recognizes their mutually constitutive "intra-action."[23]

We are purposeful in our choice of folding and flattening to describe our methodological practice that rejects an interpretivist stance and that embraces the mutually constitutive nature of which Barad writes. The "intra-action" that characterized our process was made of re-considering the mutual constitution of meaning as happening in between researcher/ researched; data/theory; and inside/outside. The data and theory are folded into one another whereby this process results in a "new inside of this outside"[24] that occurs in the threshold as described above. We insert ourselves as researchers into the data in a process that Hillevi Lenz Taguchi and Karin Hultman describe as a flattening.[25]

Part of the work of flattening is a move away from a stance toward coding that situates the researcher at a distance from the data. In our view, coding concerns itself with the macro in a move described by St Pierre that is "pedestrian and uninteresting."[26] In the interview study that informs this project, the macro was at some levels predictable, and certainly did not produce new knowledge. For instance, we could present the following so-called major themes and patterns in a writing up of the findings which will not come as a surprise to many, especially those who are women in the academy:

- impostor syndrome
- continuing male privilege (and ignorance of such on the part of many male colleagues)
- double standards in the treatment of men and women

---

[21] Hekman, *The Material of Knowledge*, op. cit., 100–101.

[22] Maggie MacLure, *Qualitative Inquiry: Where are the Ruins?* Keynote presentation to the New Zealand Association for Research in Education Conference, University of Auckland, December 2010, 14.

[23] Karen Barad, "Agential Realism: Feminist Interventions in Understanding Scientific Practices." In *The Science Studies Reader*, edited by Mario Biagioli (New York and London: Routledge, 1999), 2.

[24] Gilles Deleuze, *Foucault*, translated by Sean Hand (1986; repr. Minneapolis: University of Minnesota Press, 1988), 97.

[25] Karin Hultman and Hillevi Lenz Taguchi, "Challenging Anthropocentric Analysis of Visual Data: A Relational Materialist Methodological Approach to Educational Research," *International Journal of Qualitative Studies in Education* 23 (2010): 525–42.

[26] St Pierre, "Qualitative Data Analysis After Coding," op. cit.

- the importance of mentoring.

These themes are not interesting, nor particularly new, not to us anyway. Coding takes us back to what is known, not only to the experience of our participants, but also to our own experience; it also disallows a repetition that results in the production of the new, a production of different knowledge. A focus on the macro produced by the codes might cause us to miss the texture, the contradictions, the tensions, and entangled becomings produced in the mangle as described by Susan Hekman. A focus on the macro pulls us *out* of the threshold – that dynamic space that is always becoming – and locks us into more of a territorialized place of fixed, recognizable meaning. The micro of the folding that we attempt produces a "dynamic and shifting entanglement of relations."[27]

In a return to the threshold, a couple of our analytical questions may be helpful to illustrate the difference between "patterns" that we mention above, and the type of thinking "in the mangle" that the micro produces. For example, Foucault would have us ask, "How do power/knowledge relations and practices produce Cassandra's and Sera's multiple subjectivities as they venture into the academy as first-generation professors?" We know from the data that male privilege continues in the academy, but how are these women recognizable by the disciplinary structures (both material and discursive) that they and their male colleagues inhabit? We know from the data that double standards for men and women continue, but Derrida would have us look for examples of both when and how deconstruction happens by the very fact that these women are in the academy, and how this happening disrupts the institutional structures that seek fixity. How do we understand deconstruction, then, as the event that happens in the mangle of the "I" that is a complex web of factors? These questions, and the others we take up as prompted by the philosophers we are thinking with, produced the possibility of the irruptive emergence of a new concept, rather than a re-production of what is known.

The move away from the macro of coding and into the threshold is what happens when we seek to move away from patterns for the purpose of changing our relationship to theory and data. To plug data and theory into one another in the threshold is to position ourselves as researchers otherwise than merely always-already subject ready to capture and code the experiences of our participants and their material conditions as always-already object. Such a practice of reading diffractively means that we try to fold these texts into one another in a move that flattens our relationship to the participants, the theory, and the data.

A process of mapping as we refer to it here is not for the purpose of providing an outline or a plan to facilitate a movement from point A to point B – from data to theory or theory to interpretation. It is a process that, prompted by Deleuze and Guattari, gets us off the representational hook; as they put it: "Writing has nothing to do with signifying. It has to do with surveying, mapping, even realms that are yet to come."[28] To chart this unnamed and unmapped territory is to deterritorialize data, deterritorialize theory, and deterritorialize our selves. To deterritorialize is to resist the route that is known in the form of tracing – to data, theory, meaning, representation. Tracing puts us back on the path that makes easy sense if we revert to coding; tracing is coding. Mapping, then, results in a flattening and closeness that intervenes to prompt previously unthought questions: What is blocked? What attempts to take root? Which lines survive? To deterritorialize and reterritorialize is to leave

---

[27] Barad, *Meeting the Universe*, op. cit., 224.
[28] Deleuze and Guattari, *A Thousand Plateaus*, op. cit., 5.

the trace, to flatten the hierarchies, and to reterritorialize ways of thinking about data, method, and meaning-making.

Entering the assemblage

Entering the assemblage is a process that can take many forms. We present a map with multiple entryways into which readers plug their own thinking with theory into ours. As stated at the beginning of this chapter, an assemblage isn't a thing; it is the *process* of making and unmaking the thing. It is the process of arranging, organizing, fitting together. So to see it at work, we invite readers into this assemblage and to ask what new territories are claimed as they encounter the process of plugging data into theory into data with us in the threshold.

We have purposefully sequenced the chapters in a way that exploits the connections to be made between and among the theorists we are thinking with. For example, Spivak leans heavily on Foucault for power/knowledge analyses, and subsequently positions herself in relation to Derrida's concept of deconstruction. Continuing on this genealogical bent, Barad draws heavily on the work of Foucault and Butler, but extends the movement from an emphasis on the discursive to enact a material performativity. Barad's work is situated in a body of work by feminists who enact Deleuzian becoming and a material/discursive rewriting of subjectivity.

Similarly, while readers can approach the chapters sequentially and read the book cover-to-cover, some may choose to read nomadically and/or rhizomatically. Deleuze tells us that repetition produces a difference, an effect, emerging from a "production of production."[29] Repetition on our part is not merely a repeating of the same, but a purposeful attempt to resist the "gravity of the circle of recognition and its representations."[30] In order to generate a production of the new, we have presented a purposeful repetition of data chunks among chapters. It is our hope that as readers engage these repeated excerpts over and over, as we did, different provocations will be made as we/you plug the texts into one another. This practice is, as described by Barad, a diffractive reading of one text (data) through another (theory). This is not a careless move, nor a failure to carefully read and edit. It is a purposeful enactment as we invite readers into a process of thinking about how the theoretical concepts that we engage evoke different questions and produce different thought.

When we began this project, one of our aims was to present ways of reading data across multiple theories as a way to add layers of meaning to data for both experienced and novice researchers. Further, as faculty who teach both introductory, general, and advanced qualitative research courses, we found ourselves wanting a text that we could use with students who may be new to this theoretical work, and to provide an entry into new ways of thinking with a new vocabulary. As such, each chapter is preceded by an interlude that indicates what each theorist helps us think that the others do not. We also include what we are naming schematic cues (hooks or gestures, if you will) that readers can hang onto as a brace as they enter this new theoretical terrain. Finally, we end each chapter with an introductory set of

---

[29] Simon O'Sullivan and Stephen Zepke, "Introduction: The Production of the New." In *Deleuze, Guattari and the Production of the New*, edited by Simon O'Sullivan and Stephen Zepke (London, Continuum, 2009), 1.

[30] *Ibid.*

recommended readings, both primary and secondary texts, as well as some suggested research exemplars.

Our treatment of the concepts, the theory, and the data is not meant to be exhaustive. It is meant to be irruptive in an opening of ways of thinking and meaning. We have attempted to present our reliance on theory across the chapters to shake us out of the complacency of seeing/hearing/thinking as we always have, or might have, or will have. We take seriously the following quote from Derrida that speaks to the necessity of theory in qualitative research:

> There should be philosophy across the borders, not only in philosophy proper, but in other fields, such as law, medicine, and so forth. ... We should have philosophers trained as philosophers as rigorously as possible, and at the same time audacious philosophers who cross the borders and discover new connections, new fields, not only interdisciplinary researche[r]s but themes that are not even interdisciplinary.[31]

We are not claiming to be audacious philosophers, but what we are claiming is the possibility of new questions and different ways of thinking research and data, in the time that we call "after coding," as we plug one text into another.

---

[31] Jacques Derrida, *Deconstruction in a Nutshell: A Conversation with Jacques Derrida*, edited and with commentary by John D. Caputo (New York: Fordham University Press, 1997), 7.

Why Derrida?

Deconstruction in a nutshell: "the tension between memory, fidelity, the preservation of something that has been given to us, and, at the same time, heterogeneity, something absolutely new, and a break."[1] In our view, there are many mis-appropriations or mis-understandings of deconstruction. Deconstruction is *not* about dismantling and replacing the dominant signifier in a binary with that which has been subordinated (reversing man/woman to woman/man). Deconstruction is *not* about de-construction and re-construction. Deconstruction *is* about the preservation of traditions through a constant engagement with the tensions and omissions in such a way as to see how the "orthodox, received, dominant interpretation has been produced"[2] without interrogation. Gayatri Spivak describes it as "a way out of the closure of knowledge."[3]

We go to each of the theorists because they help us think something that we cannot think otherwise, or with anyone else. In order for deconstruction to be of use to us as researchers, we must, at Derrida's urging, first begin with knowledge of a literate under-standing of the tradition within/against which we work. Derrida teaches us that all knowl-edge, all constructions are contingent and partial: "The idea is not to jettison the classical discipline [in this case the positivist underpinnings of qualitative research], but to disturb it by way of exploring what systematically drops through its grid and, by so disturbing it, to open it up."[4]

While Derrida's early naming of deconstruction in *Of Grammatology* was concerned with the problem of language and the undoing of texts, he went on in future years to demonstrate that deconstruction is not just about unsettling texts, but can be put to use to unsettle *institutions* in many different contexts. For instance, he wrote about the concepts of justice, hospitality, and democracy in a *putting to work* of deconstruction as illustrated in texts such as *Rogues* (democracy), *Force of Law* (justice), and *Of Hospitality* (politics and ethics). In *Negotiations*, Derrida is quoted as saying that he does not think that nonhierarchical structures exist. One use of deconstruction, then, is to look for the places

---

[1] Jacques Derrida, *Deconstruction in a Nutshell: A Conversation with Jacques Derrida*, edited and with commentary by John D. Caputo (New York: Fordham University Press, 1997), 6.

[2] *Ibid.*, 85.

[3] Gayatri Spivak, "Translator's Preface." In *Of Grammatology* by Jacques Derrida (Baltimore: Johns Hopkins University Press, 1976), lxxvii.

[4] Derrida, *Deconstruction in a Nutshell*, op. cit., 77.

or *events* where deconstruction happens to unsettle such structures and institutions. Derrida claimed not to be "an enemy of hierarchy," but was "simply impatient before the given, stabilized, installed, that is to say, vulgar and dormant forms of hierarchy"[5] whether they be in the institutions of democracy, education, law, and so forth. It is on this later work, with an emphasis on deconstruction as the event, that we focus in this chapter.[6]

And so, what are the underpinnings of qualitative research that Derrida would help the two of us explore? What might we do to put deconstruction to work in a way that "explores the tensions, the loose threads, the little 'openings'"[7] in this tradition that is called qualitative research? Within this inheritance as qualitative researchers is a valorizing of speech, voices heard and recorded.[8] According to Elizabeth St Pierre, we must accept the limits of experience as a metaphysical construct *à la* Derrida and acknowledge that the accounting narrated by our participants cannot secure truth.[9] Such acceptance of limits requires an acknowledgment that speech is no more pure or authentic than other forms of data. It is an acceptance of the tensions and loose threads present in our research narratives that make it impossible to capture a truth or essence in the data. It is being on the lookout for these openings in our transcripts *with* Derrida that present a consideration of moments when deconstruction is happening with our participants.

Might there then be a possibility in the doing of qualitative research, particularly discourse-based research, to trouble our naïve notions of "what it means to mean" and thereby to loosen ourselves from an attachment to a "thereness" to be found in data? For example, as we continued to think about the places of description in Sera's and Cassandra's tellings, we also looked for what was left out, elided, or silenced. Instead of an attachment to a "thereness" in the data only to be found in what was audibly voiced, we could then pursue an attachment to a "thereness" in the data that is only to be found in a reading that transgresses boundaries. Pursuing this transgressive reading results in an articulation of the disjointure between presence and absence, between what is spoken with words and between words, between what absents itself and what presents itself, between what is transparent and what is veiled. In the moments where Cassandra and Sera both obliged and resisted the telling of a linear life story, we try to illustrate with examples how we paid attention not just to the coherence, but to the tensions, inconsistencies, omissions, and moments of destabilization.

In Chapter 2, we demonstrate how we approached the transcripts in an attempt to glimpse the irruptive nature of deconstruction and its effects on Sera and Cassandra, their family members, and colleagues in the academy. Places of irruption tear the fabric of what is supposed to be – where language is strained, where meaning is missed, where destabilization occurs, and where excess produces a snagging that resists a closure. In

---

[5] Jacques Derrida, *Negotiations: 1972–1990*, translated by Martin Joughin (New York: Columbia University Press, 1990), 21.

[6] In the prefatory note written by Richard Kearney to introduce an interview with Jacques Derrida that appears in the book *States of Mind*, he provides examples of Derrida's application of his "'deconstructive' analysis to a wide variety of subjects – literary, scientific, linguistic and psychoanalytic, as well as strictly philosophical." Richard Kearney, *States of Mind: Dialogues with Contemporary Thinkers* (New York: New York University Press, 1995), 157.

[7] *Ibid.*, 76.

[8] For a theoretical and methodological challenge to traditional notions of voice, see the text *Voice in Qualitative Inquiry*, edited by Alecia Y. Jackson and Lisa A. Mazzei (London: Routledge, 2009).

[9] Elizabeth A. St Pierre, "Afterword: Decentering Voice in Qualitative Inquiry." In *ibid.*, 221–36.

Cassandra's interview, she talked about the "very good mentor, who happened to be a white male" who helped her navigate the system when she first arrived at Regional State University by telling her things that were not explicitly stated in the faculty handbook.[10] She also recounted experiences in which white students questioned her competence and a subsequent lack of support that she received from white male administrators. We do not point to the places of inconsistency to refute her stories. We point to the places of inconsistency as a way to exploit the snag and to tear at what is not apparent in a search for the categories and patterns, as discussed in Chapter 1. Further, we are not using deconstruction as traditional ideology critique. We are not using deconstruction merely to expose the hierarchical structures of patriarchy, class inequality, racism, etc. We are using deconstruction to catch sight of how the presence of first-generation women in the academy, specifically the presence of Sera and Cassandra, prevents a closure of knowledge, a disruption of the categories of academic in a way that precludes fixed understandings of both "good behavior" or "transgressive behavior." In other words, deconstruction as *always already* happening. We use deconstruction, then, to help us ask, *How does the presence of Sera and Cassandra in the academy make visible the excesses of race, class, and gender in the event that is deconstruction?*

Schematic cues

Absent presence. The absent presence is that which was never there in a physical or "real" sense, but that which is always already there, preceding our speaking and writing. The absent presence is the trace, of which Derrida writes, that haunts our texts and our tellings. What Derrida illustrates in *Of Grammatology*[11] is that "language works not because there is an identity between a sign and a thing, not because of presence, but because there is a difference, an absence."[12] The task, then, of deconstruction is to keep a watchful eye/ear for that which might otherwise be missed.

Aporia. A signifier that can have many meanings, but often thought of as a puzzle or conundrum; that which proposes a difficulty in logic because it presents evidence for more than one truth. An aporia is a paradox.

Deconstruction. The process of deconstruction results in a destablizing of that which we have unproblematically come to accept. Gayatri Spivak described the process as such: "To locate the promising marginal text, to disclose the undecidable moment, to pry it loose with the positive lever of the signifier; to reverse the resident hierarchy, only to displace [not replace] it; to dismantle in order to reconstitute what is always already inscribed."[13] In other words, the process of deconstruction is a means of exploiting the tensions and inconsistencies with the way things are and the way things have been, not just in language, but in institutions. When Derrida wrote, "There is nothing outside of the text,"[14] he was referring to the fact that "outside" is merely another text, another set of referents and assumptions.

---

[10] For faculty in US universities who are in tenure-track or tenure-stream positions, faculty handbooks provide the criteria against which faculty are evaluated to be granted (or denied) tenure and promotion.

[11] Jacques Derrida, *Of Grammatology*, translated by Gayatri Spivak (1967; repr. Baltimore: Johns Hopkins University Press, 1976).

[12] Elizabeth Adams St Pierre, "Poststructural Feminism In Education: An Overview," *International Journal of Qualitative Studies in Education 13*, no. 5 (2000): 482.

[13] Spivak, "Translator's Preface," op. cit., lxxvii.

[14] Derrida, *Of Grammatology*, op. cit., 158.

There is no external reality, only intertextuality. In "Letter to a Japanese Friend,"[15] Derrida describes the word deconstruction as having imposed itself on him as denoting a disarranging of the construction of words in a sentence. While he might have chosen the word destruction, he was purposeful in not doing so, as destruction was necessarily nihilistic and not what he was intending.

It is important to remember that, no matter the context for deconstruction (whether literary, philosophical, or methodological), the project of deconstruction is to dismantle our preconceived notions and expose the absent presence. The absent presence is that which has been ignored in an attempt to preserve the illusion of truth as a perfectly self-contained and self-sufficient present. For example, Kearney reminds us that "we find Derrida questioning and subverting the traditional priorities of speech over writing, presence over absence, sameness over difference,"[16] man over woman, and so forth. For according to Derrida, "there is nothing thought that cannot be rethought…Even deconstruction itself must be deconstructed"[17] (and so must Chapter 2).

Différance. Because there is no one-to-one correspondence between the words we use and the meanings they intend, Derrida's concept of *différance* refers to the continual deferral of meaning in the play of language. Meaning is always deferred, incomplete, and lacking origin. Derrida sees the sign as a *structure* of difference, marking both absence and presence: "It is because of *différance* that the movement of signification is possible…keeping within itself the mark of the past element…and constituting what is called the present by means of this very relation to what it is not."[18] The sign takes the place of the present thing itself, both meaning and referent; it is the present in its absence, or the absent presence. Derrida writes, "When we cannot show the thing…when the present cannot be presented, we signify, we go through the detour of the sign. The sign, in this sense, is deferred presence… The circulation of signs defers the moment in which we can encounter the thing itself, make it ours."[19] Thus for Derrida the sign is *différance*, that which at once defers presence and moves toward the deferred presence it seeks to reappropriate. In this way, the meaning of the sign is always postponed or deferred. He goes on to argue that *différance* in no way ensures that the deferred presence will return. It is not that the presence remains absent or hidden – it is indefinitely postponed.[20]

Erasure. To put a signifier under erasure is to expose the uncertainty of what that signifier might be or could become, and to open up the traces present (the always-already absent presence). Putting signifiers (such as data, truth, narrative) under erasure is to engage in the process of using them and troubling them simultaneously, rendering them inaccurate yet necessary.

Event. The event as we use it here is the moment of deconstruction. It is a happening that destabilizes fixed structures and understandings. It is deconstruction at work, or the happening of deconstruction in the event that causes a reconstitution of that which has been

---

[15] This letter was first published in *Derrida and Différance*, translated by David Wood and Andrew Benjamin, 1988. We refer the reader to *Counterpath* by Catherine Malabou and Jacques Derrida, where the letter is reprinted with permission, pp. 246–48.

[16] Kearney, *States of Mind*, op. cit., 158.

[17] *Ibid.*

[18] Jacques Derrida, "Différance." In *Margins of Philosophy,* translated by Alan Bass, (1968; repr. Chicago: University of Chicago Press, 1982), 13.

[19] *Ibid.*

[20] *Ibid.*

constructed (fixed) and unproblematically accepted. The event is an actual happening that jars things and pushes them off balance just enough to keep things moving, thus enabling transformation.

Signifier/signified. Signifiers are those symbols or words that we use to designate something. For instance, we use the signifier "data" to designate field notes, documents, and interview transcripts. That to which a signifier refers is known as a signified. According to Derrida, however, there is no one-to-one correspondence between that which we identify and that which is identified, hence his discussion of *différance*.

Presence. That which is there, in front of us. In Derrida's project, and in our project, we critique presence as that which is known to us through accounts given by our participants, as transparent in the words that they speak, and as an unmediated experience "there" to be "gotten" (clearly received and understood).

Sous rature. Translated, it means "under erasure." To put something under erasure is "to write a word, cross it out, and then print both word and deletion. (Since the word is inaccurate, it is crossed out. Since it is necessary, it remains legible.)"[21] The practice of writing under erasure is an outward mark of the contortion and inadequacy of language. To write under erasure is to acknowledge that "the authority of the text is provisional, the origin is a trace; contradicting logic, we must learn to use and erase our language at the same time."[22]

Structuralism. Structuralism is based on the assumption that if social reality has a meaning, there must be a structure – a system of conventions – that make meaning possible. Structuralists view language as a social yet *closed* system of signs that is governed by rules and convention, and that is immune to drastic change through external historical forces or individual agency. Structuralism radically challenged humanist views of language in that it moved the essence of knowledge (and therefore the function of language) from objective to relational; however, it still locates meaning in a stable structure that is *a priori*, inherent, universal, and generalizable. (Readers who are new to poststructural theory may want to refer to Interlude IV on Butler, to read about language in humanism, structuralism, and poststructuralism, before proceeding with Chapter 2.)

Text. For Derrida, there is nothing outside the text. We can think of a text literally in the form of transcripts and books, but to limit the "text" to these spoken or written words is to limit our understanding of what *counts* as data. We then think of the text as the situations and events (in addition to the narratives) that constitute our research sites – that which is communicated. Derrida further elaborated on the question of the text in stating, "If deconstruction really consisted in saying that everything happens in books, it wouldn't deserve five minutes of anybody's attention."[23]

Trace. The trace for Derrida is the always-already absent present understood to be essential to thought and experience. The trace is that which inhabits our language before we use it. Trace, as used by Derrida in the original French, carries with it notions of track, footprint, imprint. The trace then is the absent presence of imprints on our words and their meanings before we speak or write them.

---

[21] Spivak, "Translator's Preface," op. cit., xiv.
[22] *Ibid.*, xviii.
[23] Jacques Derrida as cited in Peter Baker, *Deconstruction and the Ethical Turn* (Gainesville, FL: University Press of Florida, 1995), 16.

Chapter 2

Derrida: Thinking with deconstruction

Deconstruction is neither a theory nor a philosophy. It is neither a school nor a method. It is not even a discourse, nor an act, nor a practice. It is what happens, what is happening today in what they call society, politics, diplomacy, economics, historical reality, and so on and so forth.[1]

Deconstruction happens

The fact that deconstruction cannot refer back to any founding event, the fact that, like mourning, it has no time, is precisely what destines it to roaming or voyaging.[2]

As with each of the theorists we are thinking with in this book, there are many aspects of Derrida's work that we might have pursued. Having narrowed down to a focus on the irruptive nature of deconstruction (instead of, for example, justice, friendship, hospitality), we are specifically interested in the *event* that *is* deconstruction. There are other ways that we might have approached deconstruction; however, for this reading, we are attempting to stay close to deconstruction as the event – not a reading that is *about* the event, but the *actual happening* that jars things and pushes them off balance just enough to keep things moving, thus enabling transformation. Given this focus, we began reading Sera's and Cassandra's interview transcripts "under the influence of deconstruction"[3] to glimpse when deconstruction might be happening. Assuming a deconstructive stance is to both use and trouble categories at the same time. So while we talk about the categories of race, class, and gender, using the only signifiers that we have, we do not do so without caution. Such doing and troubling prompts the following analytic question for our deconstructive reading: *How does the presence of Sera and Cassandra in the academy make visible the excesses of race, class, and gender in the event that is deconstruction?*

When does deconstruction happen? We cannot say with certainty that we can know when deconstruction happens, because it is *always already* happening. Derrida repeatedly tells us that "Deconstruction is not a method or some tool that you apply to something from the outside ... Deconstruction is something which happens and which happens inside."[4] To

[1] Catherine Malabou and Jacques Derrida, *Counterpath: Traveling with Jacques Derrida*, translated by David Wills (Stanford: Stanford University Press, 2004), 225.

[2] *Ibid.*, 227.

[3] Maggie MacLure, "Broken Voices, Dirty Words: On the Productive Insufficiency of Voice." In *Voice in Qualitative Inquiry*, edited by Alecia Y. Jackson and Lisa A. Mazzei, 97–113 (London: Routledge, 2009).

[4] Jacques Derrida, *Deconstruction in a Nutshell: A Conversation with Jacques Derrida*, edited and with commentary by John D. Caputo (New York: Fordham University Press, 1997), 7.

engage a Derridean reading of Sera's and Cassandra's narratives does not mean that we simply deconstruct the text of the interview transcripts merely to locate the inconsistencies, tensions, and failings. It requires that we also "make room for 'the irruptive emergence of a new "concept," a concept which no longer allows itself to be understood in terms of the previous regime'."[5] This new concept is what we encounter in the excesses made possible by Cassandra's and Sera's presence and the trace of an absent presence that haunts their tellings.

Making room for a new concept is the process of engaging Derrida's strategy of the trace.[6] The trace, for Derrida, is the always-already absent present "that is the condition of thought and experience."[7] The trace is that which dwells in our language before we inhabit and use it. Because our language is imbued with the trace, to employ Derrida's strategy permits us to use "the only available language while not subscribing to its premises."[8] Trace, as used by Derrida in the original French, carries with it notions of tracks, footprints, imprints. The trace, then, is the absent presence of sometimes imperceptible imprints on our words and their meanings before we speak or write them. The trace is that which contributes to our being and doing in a tug-of-war with the competing meanings that we both resist and accept – both acknowledged and unacknowledged. If, for example, we use the signifier "academic" without deconstructive scrutiny, then we fail to locate the competing "meanings" attached in a historical sense: for example, male, well educated, father as intellectual, expectation of not only college education but also graduate education. A lack of deconstructive scrutiny means we fail to put the signifier academic under erasure in a move that disallows us both to accept the traces that put Sera and Cassandra in their place, and to trouble the traces in ways that establish their belonging at the same time. Alternatively, putting the signifier academic under erasure means that the competing understandings of what might count as academic to include first-generation women who may have grown up in a lower socio-economic status and thereby had substandard preparation for college are given legitimacy and belonging in the previous club which did not include them.

When Sera was asked to describe some of the most difficult experiences she had when she first entered the academy, she talked about this feeling of being an impostor:

> Yeah. A great deal of intimidation, I guess. But, again, I didn't really chalk it up to being first-generation. I just chalked it up to being not smart. It was like oh, I don't know if I can do this. I'm acting a lot of the time. I feel like that you hear people say fake it until you make it. And I feel like I did a lot of that … Once I had my PhD, I expected myself to be this person I thought I was supposed to be.

Sera's presence in spite of her "impostor" status, and her persistence to become this person that she "thought she was supposed to be," can be read by us as an enactment of putting the signifier academic under erasure, not in a conscious, intentional way, but in an irruptive happening. The imprints of what she thinks she is supposed to be (self-assured, smart, college-ready) always already make and unmake her in ways that serve to both intimidate and motivate. She wants to be self-assured and smart, because that is what is asked of

---

5 Gayatri Spivak, "Translator's Preface." In *Of Grammatology* by Jacques Derrida (Baltimore: Johns Hopkins University Press, 1976), lxxvii.

6 Jacques Derrida, *Of Grammatology*, translated by Gayatri Spivak (1967; repr. Baltimore: Johns Hopkins University Press, 1976).

7 Spivak, "Translator's Preface," op. cit., xvii.

8 *Ibid.*, xviii.

her in an owning of being an academic. Her presence, despite not fulfilling the promise of the multiple traces, serves to present the possibility of irruption and destabilization – adding new imprints to the signifier (academic) that has claimed her and that she claims. Deconstruction happens in the event that produces her interpretation of academic. The trace of what she is "supposed to be" and the unspoken traces of being an impostor are present in a taking on of the signifier academic and all that it portends – thereby presence *in* absence. And what of the signifiers that Sera uses to describe that which she is "supposed" to be? These signifiers both unmake and make her into the self-assured, smart academic that she both is and is making. The expectations, both absent and present in a naming of being smart and not smart, means that the absent presence of being "not smart" haunts the way she begins to see herself as the absence takes on as much importance as the presence.

On the lookout for deconstruction

Deconstruction is always on the move and is therefore purposefully difficult to pin down, so we will use some phrases that offer a glimpse into how deconstruction happens. Deconstruction has to do with what is not present; it destabilizes; it snags; it is what remains to be thought; it is excess. We use the phrase "deconstruction happens" because Derrida was very clear that deconstruction is neither a closed, formulaic method nor a unifying tool, but what Derrida himself called "the experience of the impossible."[9] In the context of a qualitative interview, an "experience of the impossible" would be what haunts truth-telling, understanding, and the arrival of (deferred) meaning. It would be moments when the interviewee recounts disruptions that unsettle what has already been said or remembered. For example, as interviewers, it is impossible for us to anticipate what might unsettle the arrival of (deferred) meaning. It is impossible for us to predict what might interrupt and destabilize the narrations of identity and experience. Nonetheless, how might we as researchers open ourselves to this destabilization, this impossibility, this deconstruction, when deconstruction happens? Deconstruction has to do with traces that are discarded, but that remain nonetheless, traces that therefore make thought possible if we are but to pay attention. The following explanation provided by Sera begins to provide a glimpse of the trace that remains:

> In this past couple of years, I feel like I'm becoming smarter than I ever was when I was trying to figure out [things] so now I'm reading things differently, and I feel like I know a lot. I know more about what I don't know, and I know how to read [scholarly texts] differently.

In this excerpt and the previous one, Sera continues to equate being an academic with being smart. She seems to be conflicted about what constitutes being smart, and the trace confounds with multiple possibilities. The irruption and insertion of a new trace might be reflected in her assertion above, that one mark of being smart is knowing what she doesn't know and knowing how to read in a way that produces questions, not just understanding. Sera is then both disrupting the binary and enacting deconstruction at the same time. Derrida tells us that all knowledge, all constructions are contingent and partial. In this moment, Sera

[9] Jacques Derrida, "Passions: 'An Oblique Offering'." In *Derrida: A Critical Reader*, translated by D. Wood (Oxford, UK: Blackwell, 1992), 200.

is both respectfully inhabiting the tradition by "fake[ing] it until you make it," while at the same time destabilizing it from within by becoming the academic that is both expected and unexpected.

A deconstructive approach to data adheres to "sneaking suspicions that something may be wrong with what we currently believe, while keeping a watchful eye ... that something else, something other, still to come, is being missed."[10] This something else, this other, this search for the other is a purposeful seeking of Derrida's trace. Nothing, according to Derrida, is simply absent or present, "There are only, everywhere, differences and traces of traces."[11] These traces or excesses echo in the text that continues to interrupt and deconstruct the present in its recounting of the past. This trace echoes in both Cassandra's and Sera's telling, in ways that erupt and irrupt through the event that is deconstruction. For example, when asked about her decision to attend college, Sera said that she never had it in mind, and she never thought, "Oh, poor me. I don't get to go to college." She talked about being "shuttled different places" in school, and one of those places happened to be the library on a day when students were filling out financial aid forms. She was accepted to a large state university, and then her grandmother died, "Which sounds really horrible, but she left me $10,000 for college that she had been socking away in her freezer." Sera describes these echoes, these *events*, as "accidents" that led her to be in the right place at the right time in terms of filling out financial aid forms, taking the right tests, being seated outside the department chair's office when an opening came up for a graduate assistant position; but perhaps they are better understood as irruptions. As researchers, we (and they) can overlook these accidents as merely that, or perhaps we can re-read these accidents as moments of something other, something new, of which Derrida wrote, breaking in and presenting the possibility of the tension between what is happening and what is perceived. In our initial conversation with Sera, we likened some of our own episodes of being in the right place at the right time as similar accidents – how does this openness to the excess allow us to re-view both our own and her experiences not as a series of accidents, but as echoes that produce a destabilization, one that permits the irruptive event to occur, producing more/different excesses and deconstructive events? Derrida would say that these events are not accidents, but are in fact irruptions that allow for the possibility of the impossible.

As we will continue to demonstrate with further examples from the interviews with Sera and Cassandra, it is not just that deconstruction happens which is important in our attempts to make sense, it is *what happens* as a result of the deconstructive event. In other words, what is produced by the event that is deconstruction? Where are the places in the narratives in which "Sentences and their words always lead elsewhere than the place we were expecting them"?[12] In the following example, such questioning leads us to re-read the data, not in order to pin down what is relevant to creating the trajectory of Cassandra's career, but to seek a reading that endeavors to understand the moments of deconstruction and what these moments produce. After having earned her master's degree, Cassandra returned to Southern State, a historically black university where she had earned her bachelor's degree. She tells us of the following incident that happened after she had been teaching at Southern State for fifteen years in a position that she enjoyed:

---

[10] Derrida, *Deconstruction in a Nutshell*, op. cit., 73.
[11] Jacques Derrida, *Positions*, translated by Alan Bass (Chicago: University of Chicago Press, 1981), 26.
[12] Hélène Cixous, *Stigmata: Escaping Texts*, 2nd edn (London: Routledge, 2005), x.

[I] was adamant that I didn't need a doctorate. I already had tenure and was quite happy doing what I was doing, but I actually think it was divine intervention in a lot of my life decisions because I just absolutely had no thought whatsoever of doing a lot of the things that I ended up doing, but in the annual reports that they did there every year, they would ask you things like, what are your professional development goals and that kind of thing.

So, I had a standard response, "As funds are made available, I will pursue my doctorate degree," and I said that thinking I was very safe because there were no funds available to do that, and had not been.

They had had a program years earlier, but a lot of people had gotten their doctorate's using that program and then had gone other places to work, so they stopped doing it, and the last year that I did that, which was – would've been '82, I guess, my program chair came into my office a couple of days later and said, "Did you mean what you said on there about going back to school?" and I said, "Yes," and he said, "Well good, because we have funds available," and I was shocked. I was absolutely shocked.

Cassandra describes her "standard response" as "safe." She provides a response that positions her as being cognizant of the need to set professional goals, and yet this so-called safe response ends up creating the possibility for a pivotal deconstructive moment to occur. It is the persistent deferral, in the form of a response that was intended to block or delay any engagement with further professional development, that turns out to be the *key* that produces a response.[13] As researchers, we can witness the happening of deconstruction producing something other than what was intended as it breaks into Cassandra's narrative. It is in and through such destabilizing moments that we glimpse the snag as understood by Derrida. Clearly Cassandra's annual incantation, "As funds are made available, I will pursue my doctorate degree," led elsewhere than the place that she was expecting it to. Our task, then, as researchers is to glimpse what is produced that exceeds meaning and expectations, that provokes a destabilization, and that allows the event of deconstruction to be present in our reading of the data.

How does deconstruction happen? In speaking of the trace that makes meaning possible, Derrida reminds us that deconstruction is "the tension between memory, fidelity, the preservation of something that has been given to us, and, at the same time, heterogeneity, something absolutely new, and a break."[14] When Sera describes her encounters with search committee members who discounted candidates who self-identified as feminist, and then uses herself as an example as not fitting their stereotypical notion of what counts as "feminist," she is riding the tension between preservation of a male-dominated institution and a certain "image" of what constitutes a feminist. Such an evocation of the trace presents the possibility of the break that these voices of feminism(s) can bring to a department.

When we did a search recently, a lot of the people [candidates] identified themselves as a feminist that [were] applying for the job. And I [Sera] had to say it doesn't mean this person is going to be this, this, and this. [But the search committee members said] … no, we're not going to even bring that person in because they are feminist, and I don't want a feminazi working with me. It's going to be a bad fit.

---

13 We thank Maggie MacLure for sharing this insight.
14 Derrida, *Deconstruction in a Nutshell*, op. cit., 6

In returning to this statement by Sera, perhaps she is deconstructing the binary of feminist as bad and nonfeminist as good, or at the very least, inserting an-other trace. This is not to say that she is intentionally doing deconstruction. It is to say, however, that she continues to unsettle and destabilize through her presence and by example. As researchers, we begin to look at the trace as being present in ways that can serve to limit Sera, Cassandra, and other women in the academy. Sera's questioning of her colleagues, and her refusal to let them define "feminist," offers the opportunity to refuse the limits of the trace inhabiting her colleague's definition of feminist. It produces a deconstructive moment that seeks to redefine and reinsert this other trace.

We can also read the above as *différance* in action. In describing Derrida's use of the signifier "*différance*" Spivak tells us that "*différance* invites us to undo the need for balanced equations, to see if each term in an opposition is not after all an accomplice of the other."[15] Tension, Derrida reminds us, is characteristic of everything he tries to do,[16] and so we look for the sources of tension and disruption that signal the deconstructive event. Those moments that signal a dismantling, not of "institutions but some structures in given institutions which are too rigid or are dogmatic or which work as an obstacle to future research"[17] and the possibility of newness. In order for newness to occur, the philosophical culture must remain open to debate that leaves a space for deconstruction. Without an intimate knowledge of the tradition with which one engages, a prying loose is not possible. "Deconstruction presupposes the most intensely cultivated, literate relation to the tradition,"[18] whether that be the tradition of philosophy of which Derrida speaks, or the tradition of the academy. Here, Sera continued to talk about the search process:

> We had decided [who we were going to invite for interviews], we'd gone through [applicants] … And then there was a late person, and I was like this person seems so great. Let's look at this person, too. Oh wait, feminist [as a resistance voiced by committee members]. And I said, "I'm a feminist. I'm not a feminazi. And we really look at all these other great things. She might be very sweet." And it turns out she was. And I'm so glad. But there was definitely that initial [response], "That's not going to work."

Sera knows the tradition, respects the tradition, and she must adhere to the tradition as a matter of survival in her role as an untenured faculty member. Even in her defense of this potential candidate, she is attempting to convince the other search committee members that the potential candidate "might be very sweet." In other words, she may not be an "angry bitch" as read in the trace of feminist held by some. And yet we see her as keeping the tradition open to destabilization through her presence in the form of a deconstructive critique,

---

[15] Spivak, "Translator's Preface," op. cit., lix. Also, Alan Bass has this to say in the Translator's Preface to *Writing and Difference*, "Wherever Derrida uses différance as a neologism I have left it untranslated. Its meanings are too multiple to be explained here fully, but we may note briefly that the word combines in neither the active nor the passive voice the coincidence of meanings in the verb *différer*: to differ (in space) and to defer (to put off in time to postpone presence). Thus, it does not function simply either as *difference* (difference) or as *différance* in the usual sense (deferral), and plays on both meanings at once." (p. xvi)

[16] Derrida, *Deconstruction in a Nutshell*, op. cit., 8.

[17] *Ibid.*

[18] Jacques Derrida, *Negotiations: Interventions and Interviews 1971–2001*, translated by Elizabeth Rottenberg (Stanford: Stanford University Press, 2002), 15.

one that refuses to let others hold onto their understanding of feminist without undergoing deconstructive scrutiny. Despite their efforts, the members of the search committee cannot stop the flow of deconstruction, for if they do, they have fixed meaning and therefore have arrested the play. In other words, they have stopped thought. If Derrida is right about deconstruction, then Derrida does not have the final word on deconstruction.[19] Because Sera challenges a hegemonic idea that her colleagues have of what constitutes a feminist, and is present in ways that contest this image, a destabilization occurs that allows the committee to consider, and ultimately hire, a candidate who proclaims herself as a feminist; hence deconstruction happens. The flow of deconstruction precludes an arrested meaning of what constitutes a feminist and the play of *différance* resumes.

Cassandra, too, is very literate of a tradition in which, in 1997, she became the first African American female to achieve the rank of full professor at Regional State University, a mid-sized comprehensive university of 800+ full-time faculty. She is often asked to serve on diversity committees, and believes that she is "valued for work on diversity committees." She agrees to serve "on a lot of committees all over the campus" because colleagues say that they "need a minority on the committee." She also readily admits the futility in the way university committees function when she describes the process:

> I was in the position of assistant to the provost for women's concerns for a while, and while I was talking to him I told him that one of these days I was gonna write a book called *Games Academicians Play* and he asked me "What did I mean?"
>
> I said, "You form a committee where somebody doesn't really want you to accomplish anything, they form a committee and so you discuss the problem for a year and you come up with the recommendation for improving the situation and then you file a report and then it sits somewhere and then when somebody brings the problem up again you form another committee to study it, and you have several meetings where you discuss it to death and then you form [another committee]."

And yet her service on the committees keeps the tradition open through the deconstructive nature of her presence in the possibility of newness. In response to a question about justice, Derrida responded: "This is what gives deconstruction its movement, that is, constantly to suspect, to criticize the given determinations of culture, of institutions ... to respect this relation to the other as justice."[20] Cassandra more overtly challenges the hierarchy at times, something that she can do as a tenured full professor, by her own admission. We can criticize those who form the committee and file the report in order to "tick the box" of compliance, and yet without the presence of Cassandra or others who bring a different perspective, the possibility of something absolutely new is not possible. In writing of the place of history in deconstruction, Derrida writes: "If the readability of a legacy were given, natural, transparent, univocal, if it did not call for and at the same time defy interpretation, we would never have anything to inherit from it."[21] It is through an inclusion of difference/ *différance* that sources of tension and disruption signal the deconstructive event.

---

[19] John D. Caputo, lecture at Syracuse University, October 11, 2005.
[20] Derrida, *Deconstruction in a Nutshell*, op. cit., 18.
[21] Jacques Derrida, *Specters of Marx: The State of the Debt, the Work of Mourning, & the New International*, translated by Peggy Kamuf (1993; repr. London: Routledge, 1994), 16.

As Cassandra continued to describe her experience with the Provost, she was asked what his response was when she described the process; she said, "I think he just kind of went on to the next topic." When the administrator Cassandra is speaking of changes the topic, is it because he disagrees with her assessment, or is embarrassed by his participation in a system that resists change? What are we to make of the trace present in Cassandra's example? What is present in the absence of a response? Is it a failure to recognize his privilege, or is it a confrontation with privilege? What are the traces present in Cassandra's statement as both inside and outside that demand an acknowledgment and that also produce a failure to respond? To recognize the play of the trace is to admit all of these possibilities at once.

In thinking with Derrida and thinking with deconstruction, we are on the lookout not for what deconstruction is, or for what it means, but for what it produces, what it opens up. We pose these and other questions as we begin to attend to deconstruction as happening in our research settings in ways that produce different practices and knowings. We didn't ask follow-up questions of Cassandra to "get at" what the administrator meant by his silence. We didn't ask her to "explain" his silence. We use the deconstructive questions to create a gap that allows the trace, something other, to insert itself in the crack. We use the deconstructive questions to alert ourselves to the happening of deconstruction.

How can we attend to this happening of deconstruction as researchers? Derrida writes that he is not an enemy of hierarchy in general; he is "simply impatient before the given, stabilized, installed, that is to say, vulgar and dormant forms of hierarchy."[22] There are many instances in our interviews with Sera and Cassandra in which the vulgar hierarchy is present as a reminder of double standards between the genders. Gail Collins[23] writes, in a column entitled "The Crying Game," about the continuing phenomenon among male and female politicians in which men are now seen as sensitive when they cry, whereas women are seen as emotional and volatile. Colleagues in Sera's college (primarily male colleagues) who routinely say that they are unavailable for meetings because they have to pick up children, or attend a school function, are lauded as being a "good" parent, "ideal" spouse, and "caring" individual. This vulgar hierarchy is evidenced when Sera is given the following advice by colleagues:

> And so in my work relationships, I've been told that while on the surface people will say oh lovely that you have kids. Oh that's just wonderful. Even for married people ... say that you need time off because you need to do research, you need time off because you're going to a conference, not [that] you need time off because of spring break for your kids. Okay. Got it.

In the example above, Sera is vulnerable as woman, single parent, and untenured faculty, and yet these sites of vulnerability also portend deconstruction. The above example illustrates that deconstruction does not dismiss identity categories, but it unsettles how these categories seek to stabilize identity and arrest meaning in ways that are limiting.

---

22 Derrida, *Negotiations*, op. cit., 21.
23 Gail Collins "The Crying Game," *The New York Times*, A31, Thursday December 16, 2010. This story was printed shortly after John Boehner succeeded Nancy Pelosi as Speaker of the House in the U.S. Congress. Collins writes about the double standard of the appropriateness for men and women to shed tears in public, men now often valorized for being sensitive, but women still stigmatized for being hysterical.

Deconstruction is not simply a reversal of the binary: good professor/bad professor; male/female; tenured/untenured. Deconstruction is not merely a critique of that meaning which has become arrested, nor a substitution of another truth, but a destabilization that creates a gap that allows the trace, something other, to insert itself in the crack. Woman, single parent, and untenured can be this other that is inserted into understandings of academic, enabling a critique from within the limits of the structure of the binary. What we hope to demonstrate with the above example is the instability of meaning and the categories that attempt to contain and restrain. Deconstruction as we are approaching it, then, is not simply a reversal and re-inscription, but is a search for the irruption and destabilization of seemingly fixed categories. Sera can be a "good professor" in a traditional understanding, and also re-inscribe the signifier with meanings that have previously been on the marginalized side of the binary – woman, first-generation, mother, untenured.

The following sections in this chapter present *possible* irruptions that emerge from the excesses and snags that produce a destabilization. In keeping with our discussion in Chapter 1 of the productive nature of the post-theories that we are taking up in our thinking with theory, we can look for places where deconstruction is occurring: where meaning is missed and destabilization occurs – or, deconstruction as the event.

Deconstruction as destabilizing

We began this chapter by explaining deconstruction not as a technique or method, but as "what happens."[24] This "what happens" *happens* through a process of destabilizing that which craves order, sameness, and hegemony. It is a reading/doing/thinking that requires the continuous opening and exploration of the spaces, passions, and meanings not yet understood or *deconstructed*. This "not method" happens when the difference or otherness that both Sera and Cassandra possess is recognized not as an absence, but as a presence. This critical aspect of difference as presence is the "what happens" when the notion of what *counts* as *normative* is disrupted by difference being given a voice. This "what happens" *happens* when the very presence of these women who "don't belong" serves to transgress and destabilize the "vulgar and dormant forms of hierarchy"[25] that seek to contain not only these women, but also others in the academy (including professors and students who do not adhere to the norm).

To talk about deconstruction as destabilizing is to approach the data in ways that prevent a closure of meaning. It is an unsettling, off-kilter reading/rending/rendering that allows that which is threatening to the order and stability of the hierarchy to emerge. When the administrator of whom Cassandra is speaking in the previous section changes the topic, we pose a series of questions as a way of destabilizing our reading. Derrida writes that "because it [deconstruction] destabilizes the conditions of possibility of objectivity, of the relation to the object, of everything that constitutes an assured subjectivity ... deconstruction proves the impossibility of closure, of totality, of a system or discourse of or on method."[26] What is it about deconstruction as the event that prevents closure? In our thinking with Derrida and plugging our deconstructive questions into the narratives, how

---

[24] Malabou and Derrida, *Counterpath*, op. cit., 225.
[25] Derrida, *Negotiations*, op. cit., 21.
[26] Malabou and Derrida, *Counterpath*, op. cit., 226.

might we seek that which is in the cracks, gaps, aporias that destabilize and open the possibility for change in the following account by Cassandra?

> As I mentioned, I had been brought here to be a mentor to the African-American students and to create courses and programs and so forth to talk about diversity, and so some of the white students felt that I was paying too much attention to the black students and so they wrote these long, very critical letters of me that accused me of reverse discrimination and that I was showing favoritism to the black students because they would come in to my office.
>
> My office is small now, but it was even smaller then. And they [black students] would be sitting all on the floor and everything and we just hung out together. I was a mother figure, that was pretty much the same thing that I did at [Southern State University] so I knew how to work with those students and I knew that [they] need a lot of personal attention. Now there was never a time when I didn't give the same amount of attention to any white student who wanted it.
>
> [Interviewer]: And your door was open to them –
>
> Exactly, my door was open and, but they, – that was an accusation, – it became so huge that it went all the way up through the provost's office and I found myself spending a lot of time writing letters of rebuttal and that kind of thing and eventually the, – some, the university came up with some funding and sent several of us to a conference in Atlanta on racial issues to find solutions to the problem, or something, a very nice conference. I still quote some of the stuff to this day that came out of that. It was very supportive of what I had been doing and –
>
> [Interviewer]: In terms of how you mentor minority students?
>
> Yeah. They spent thousands of dollars for us to go there and I don't know what else came of it, but it made me feel good. But that was a rude awakening, I guess, for me because up until that point I really did think that the university wanted me here to do what I was doing and, but slowly over the course of the next two years I realized that that was not necessarily why I was here. They needed someone to fill that position in that grant and they wanted it to look like they were making an effort.

There are many moments or possibilities for destabilizing in the account given above. We cannot know the long-term effect on the other faculty and administrators, but we can know that this "event" of student protest was not something that could be ignored. As a result of the students' complaints and Cassandra's response, the university decided that the issue was important enough (or embarrassing enough) that some response (other than a silent one) was necessary. When Cassandra said, "I still quote some of the stuff to this day" that came out of the Atlanta conference on racial issues that she attended with colleagues, it serves as an affirmation of what she was already doing. We can't know, but perhaps this event that leads to being sent to the conference produces something new in the form of conversations with students and colleagues – changed pedagogy, or policy discussions. The center is destabilized and her "marginal" practices for mentoring minority students are validated. She is also validated in the publication of a textbook that, after ten years, "has been very well received" and is still producing royalty checks. While we are not so naïve as to assume that radical change might occur given one such instance, we look to deconstruction as *one* way to understand the possibility of something other than what has always been. We look for the creation of a deconstructive space in the academy that fosters the destabilizing moment. According to Derrida,

That is what deconstruction is made of: not the mixture but the tension between memory, fidelity, the preservation of something that has been given to us, and, at the same time, heterogeneity, something absolutely new, and a break. The condition of this performative success, which is never guaranteed, is the alliance of these to newness.[27]

Cassandra and the others still engage in a literate upholding of tradition, and the institution does not fundamentally change, but the structures within do. By her very presence, she continues to destabilize and permit/allow the possibility of deconstruction.

Deconstruction as snag

If deconstruction happens – and deconstruction is always happening, even when we as researchers are too self-absorbed or myopic to notice – then what are we to make of this? Plugging one text into another is very much like this happening of deconstruction; as researchers, we do not start out with themes that we will plug the data into, but must live with the uncertainty that we are unsure of what may emerge until it happens. We could be paralyzed by this potential irruption of deconstruction everywhere, unable to make meaning, unable to discern the disruptive moments in our encounters doing qualitative research. Or, like Derrida, we might relish the exhilaration of missed meanings and destabilizing moments – of voices and identities [and researchers] in trouble.[28]

Trying to shake ourselves loose from the need/desire to fix meaning, to find some stability amidst the unstable nature of this work, we returned to Derrida and the image of the snag in language that he discusses in *Dissemination*: "Dissemination endlessly opens up a *snag* in writing that can no longer be mended, a spot where neither meaning, however plural, nor *any form of presence* can pin/pen down (*agrapher*) the trace."[29] While Derrida's statement is interesting and highly relevant, what is perhaps more interesting is Barbara Johnson's comments as translator on this entire paragraph as it appears in the original text. She describes it as the "most untranslatable in the entire book" and goes on to display the original French, but also to differentiate between Derrida's use of "pin" and that of Lacan: "While Lacan's theory, according to Derrida, aims to 'pin down' the history of a subject, dissemination is what produces an irreducible snag in that project."[30]

To return to the title of Derrida's text, *Dissemination*, what are we to learn if we assume, momentarily, that Derrida accepted, literally *and* intentionally, a denotation of dissemination as producing a proliferation of meaning, as spreading widely and promulgating extensively, thereby preventing a "pinning down"? To do so is to be mindfully aware of the methodological practices and narrative assumptions that attempt to remove the play of the trace, that wish to *mend* the snag, and instead to beckon the specter that is engaged in disrupting, snagging, disseminating, and undoing the structures. Have we, in writing this chapter and poring over data, allowed the snag to be laid bare, or have we instead attempted to repair it and present a mended story, a coherent interpretation that makes easy sense?

[27] Derrida, *Deconstruction in a Nutshell*, op. cit., 6.
[28] Alecia Youngblood Jackson, "Performativity Identified," *Qualitative Inquiry* 10, no. 5 (2004): 673–90.
[29] Jacques Derrida, *Dissemination*, translated by Barbara Johnson (1972; repr. Chicago: University of Chicago Press, 1981), 26.
[30] Barbara Johnson, translator's note in *Dissemination*, *ibid.*, 27.

While, at some level, we are always already trying to make meaning, even as we resist it with language that is "twisted and bent,"[31] we are also trying to snag, to open up, to reveal the imperfections and to purposefully get tripped up on the loose ends. It is our hope that this chapter has succeeded somewhat in achieving an undoing and tangling of loose ends. In writing of the insufficiency of voice as a purveyor of meaning, Maggie MacLure has this to say:

> But the insufficiency of voice – its abject propensity to be too much and never enough – is unavoidable. Voice will always turn out to be too frail to carry the solemn weight of political and theoretical expectation that has been laid upon it. For voice is also tied to idle, frivolous things that tarnish authenticity, weaken trust or block analysis as [sic] least as these are usually conceived ... I want to suggest that, rather than trying to repair or deny these necessary insufficiencies we need methodologies that are capable of dwelling on, and in, those very properties of voice that make it such troublesome material for research ... These insufficiencies, I will suggest, are productive; they allow people to mean more than one thing at a time: to fashion mobile and nuanced readings of situations: to connect with others despite not knowing exactly "who" they themselves are. These mundane qualities of voice also allow people to engage with others without offering to render themselves "transparent," an important facility in the quasi-colonial contexts of research interviewing and observation.[32]

To put deconstruction to work and to permit the frailty and insufficiencies of our data to emerge so that we may "fashion mobile and nuanced readings of situations" is to think with Derrida in ways such that we become attentive, almost obsessed with the snags in the data. These productive snags are the places where imperfections are revealed, where loose ends abound, and where we (and our participants) trip up, catch on an opening, and sometimes stumble. Not only does such an approach allow our participants to not know "exactly 'who' they themselves are," it frees researchers from having to construct a tidy and coherent narrative.

Going back to the data again and again, we are compelled to attend not simply to themes and patterns in the narratives, but to those places of inconsistency, of uncertainty, and of productive rending. Going back to the data in search of the snags is an enactment of thinking with Derrida in the threshold. We eschew efforts to triangulate, verify, affirm, confirm, and substantiate, for to do so is to seek "easy sense." "Making 'easy sense,' while expedient and far less frustrating ... is what happens when we practice our received methodologies, ... ignore the irruptions"[33] and fail to test the limits of our knowing. Making easy sense is what we do when we privilege experience as truth, assume voice to be transparent, and resist the hard work that thinking with theory requires. Such work is not only hard work, but risky work as well. It is work that assumes fallibility and a willingness to declare publicly that we might not, or cannot, know anything with certainty.

There are many snags in Cassandra's narrative, but one that is prominent and pervasive is a continued presence of racism and segregation. She grew up in a segregated small town in

---

[31] Spivak, "Translator's Preface," op. cit., xiv.
[32] MacLure, "Broken Voices, Dirty Words," op. cit., 97–98.
[33] Lisa A. Mazzei, *Inhabited Silence in Qualitative Research: Putting Poststructural Theory To Work* (New York, Peter Lang, 2007), 110.

the southern USA, and was hired at Regional State University to serve as a mentor for minority students, and yet most people in the university and town are white. She tells the following about her quest to find other black people in the town in the early 1990s, and about her father's pride at what she was doing/being as so exceptional:

> I actually could go for days at a time without seeing anybody who looked like me and so, I remember that one Saturday my first semester up here – it was probably in November.
>
> I said, there's gotta be some black people here. I said, I know where they are, because on Saturday afternoons back home I could go to Wal-Mart or K-Mart or a store like that, and see black people, plenty of them, but my home town's 60 percent black, so, I got in my car and I went to Wal-Mart and I didn't see them, and I said there are no black people here. I did find out later that there are a small group living up on the hill. I think my daddy was more impressed by the fact that I was doing something that not too many black people did. That was what he was really proud of.

In describing her father's pride at her "doing something that not too many black people did," the snag trips us up and refuses to let us forget about the persistence of racism and about the isolation that African American and other minority scholars (including scholars of color and those who are gay and lesbian) continue to face in university towns, particularly those located in rural settings or small cities, and that continue to promote exclusivity and segregation even as they attempt to do otherwise. For those of us who have not experienced this isolation, or the feeling of going for days without seeing anyone who looks like us or thinks like us, Cassandra's telling rends the façade of the academy, thus presenting a haunting, uncomfortable presence.

While it is easy to read the instances of sexism, racism, and classism in Sera's and Cassandra's narratives, and those of the other women in our study, such an approach of finding evidence in the transcripts to substantiate these themes does not call attention to the snags; in fact, it often dictates that we overlook the snags. Despite Cassandra's negative experience with white students and colleagues in the academy, what is one to do with the snag when she talks of her "very good mentor, who happened to be a white male" when she first came to Regional State University? She describes her experience with him as follows:

> What he did was he helped me to navigate the system and he would tell me things that were not necessarily written in the faculty manual and so I've basically tried to do the same thing with [my mentee who is not tenured].

We have many examples of racism and sexism from Cassandra's data, and yet, as we re-read this excerpt, we see how this and other snags were ignored, if not in our analysis, then certainly in the interview itself in our not asking a follow-up question that acknowledges the snag. What are we to do with this description of her mentor by Cassandra, both in terms of our research participants and in terms of ourselves as researchers? Why do we, in our role as interviewers, not pursue the snag/contradiction between the traditional hierarchy of the institutions of privilege and a reliance on this same privilege on the part of both Sera and Cassandra to survive and ultimately succeed? Cassandra has certainly had to face much adversity and discrimination, and yet she benefits from the privilege of having not just *any* someone, but a white male someone, who shows her the ropes. Perhaps pursuing the snag makes us uncomfortable in that we may have to acknowledge our own privilege and placement on the "wrong" side of the binary. Hélène Cixous writes about the veils that can serve to mask what we choose not to see, or wish to see; "Not seeing oneself is a thing of peace."[34] Perhaps an unattended snag in this instance may serve the same purpose as Cixous' veil.

There are also snags in Sera's interview that continue to remind us of the different challenges that women in the academy sometimes face, compounded by being a parent, and in her case, a single parent. How Sera is judged differently by colleagues, how perhaps she and Cassandra were hired in part due to their race and/or gender because, as Cassandra tells us, "I'm valued for work on diversity committees," and yet the advice she is given and/or the messages that continue to be dominant in a so-called "enlightened institution of higher education" reveal the inconsistencies in the expectations for men and women academics and the ways in which Sera and Cassandra attempt to *not* call attention to themselves in order to fit in.

Invoking both Derrida's *Dissemination*, and the specters that haunt in the form of the trace that he puts forth in *Specters of Marx*, we think the snag in a way that attempts to get tripped up on that which has been elided or missed. To attend to the snag is to ask ourselves, as researchers, what were the filters (of race, gender) that were censoring the ignored or stuck places voiced by our participants? Why were we unable to cultivate a method of inquiry in response to these snags? How might we re-approach this data, and other of our research projects that more carefully cultivate the snags? One possible understanding, provided by Briggs, is that "the received methodology acts as a hidden filter, blocking our ability to hear what 'they' are saying while allowing the comforting sound of our own preconceptions about language and life to be echoed in the data."[35]

If we consider further how our received methodology has produced us as "good researchers" who are attentive to that which is spoken by our participants, certainly if we are relying on interviews as a primary source of data, then a possible outcome is that we are so focused on what ought to be spoken about that we are left insensible to the voices inhabiting the snags, especially as those snags can be masked when researchers are positioned in such a way that their privilege veils the snag. In keeping with our methodological project for this book, this speaks to an attentiveness to process (plugging in) and what is produced, without it becoming secondary to product (what participants are articulating). Returning, then, to Briggs, a focus on process, or on the snag of Derrida, would have us researchers re-think not only the interview process, but the very nature of data.

To return to the notion of the play of *différance* is to question/consider how the dynamic of an interview encounter, and the subsequent text that might be elicited rather than missed, might be reframed, reshaped, re-imagined if, as researchers, we are to begin intentionally to bring the snags to bear on this enterprise. By that we mean, what if we are to consciously (as much as possible) frame the questions that we ask our participants – the questions that we withhold, the audible responses that we garner, the responses overlooked – as essential

---

34 Hélène Cixous "Savoir." In *Veils*, by Hélène Cixous and Jacques Derrida, translated by Geoffrey Bennington (Stanford: Stanford University Press, 2001), 12.

35 Charles L. Briggs, *Learning to Ask: A Sociolinguistic Appraisal of the Role of the Interview in Social Science Research* (New York: Cambridge University Press, 1986), 125.

aspects of the dialogue that radically affect the outcome of our interviews, whether or not we like to acknowledge them.

Such a move, putting these snags into play, requires an acute awareness that not only permits a listening that has been impossible, but further demands an attentiveness and openness that has been absent. It demands of the researcher a removal of the white noise that serves to deaden and obscure the extraneous sounds. To engage the snags in the doing of qualitative research is to "begin the process of *listening to ourselves listening* with renewed vigor"[36] in order that we might be attentive to the productive, deconstructive moments that have previously been ignored or missed.

As we continue the work of qualitative inquiry, bound by the textual nature of much of the data that we examine, to be alert to the snag as a site of continued productivity is an intentional engagement with deconstruction to open up meaning. If we purposefully seek the snags that trip us up and let ourselves fall, then meanings have the potential of presenting themselves from our view on the floor. If we keep our heads down in order to anticipate the snags, thereby avoiding a fall, we risk a foreclosure of that which is a new concept, as named by Derrida.

Part of the work of being tripped up is to return to the discussion in Chapter 1, in which we resist the presence of experience and the limiting of thought that occurs in the process of pulling apart our data in order to put it back together again. This act of disassembling and reassembling produces a coherent narrative, but a coherent narrative bereft of contradictions. We therefore rely on theory, the snag, to shake us out of the complacency of seeing/hearing as we always have, or might have, or will have. Without theory, we have no way to think otherwise. Rather than representing data by stabilizing it and finding meaning, we want to show the suppleness of truth and meaning. Unless we think with theory, we are bound to pursuing the patterns in our data through a process of coding and categorizing that is supported by a repeated occurrence of a particular phenomena in our data. Thinking with Derrida's theory, on the other hand, produces the possibility of an irruptive moment that will serve to point us to that which resides outside/within the significant chunk of the data that has previously been left out, ignored, not counted. Deconstruction as *always already* happening.

Thinking with deconstruction

Thinking with Derrida's deconstruction offers a way to consider how the excesses of gender, race, and class function to destabilize institutional norms of the academy in a happening of deconstruction as the event. We followed Derrida's claim that there is "nothing outside the text" and therefore looked at the "texts" of the institutions inhabited by Sera and Cassandra. We were guided by Gayatri Spivak's description of the process of deconstruction as a "way out of the closure of knowledge."[37] We approached the tellings of Sera and Cassandra and their institutional settings in order to locate the inconsistencies, to pry loose the fixed categories (academic, gender, race), to insert the trace (first generation), to seek the snag, all in an effort to dismantle what is always already inscribed. We used the process of deconstruction as a means of exploiting the tensions and inconsistencies with the way things are and the way things have been (not just in language, but in the academy) in order to open up that which Derrida refers to as the impossible – that which is yet to come. We used

---

[36] Mazzei, *Inhabited Silence*, op. cit., 91.
[37] Spivak, "Translator's Preface," op. cit., lxxvii.

deconstruction to ask both how we can unsettle the structures of the academy, and how we can unsettle the sedimented practices of qualitative research.

More on deconstruction

The following texts are offered not as *the* texts to consult, but as providing an entry point for those who are new to the writings of Derrida and would like to learn more about deconstruction. We list the secondary texts first as a continuation of the "schematic cues" presented in the interludes, which readers can use as a brace as they enter this new theoretical terrain. Following the secondary texts are suggested entry points for approaching the writings of Derrida, and finally, research exemplars that illustrate additional examples of *thinking with* deconstruction.

Secondary texts

Derrida, Jacques. *Deconstruction in a Nutshell: A Conversation with Jacques Derrida*. Edited and with a commentary by John D. Caputo. New York: Fordham University Press, 1997.
Spivak, Gayatri. "Translator's Preface." In *Of Grammatology* by Jacques Derrida. Baltimore: Johns Hopkins University Press, 1976.
St Pierre, Elizabeth Adams. "Poststructural Feminism in Education: An Overview," *International Journal of Qualitative Studies in Education* 13, no. 5 (2000): 477–515.

Primary texts

Derrida, Jacques. *Of Grammatology*, translated by Gayatri Spivak. Baltimore: Johns Hopkins University Press, 1967/1976.
——*Margins of Philosophy*, translated by Alan Bass. Chicago: University of Chicago Press, 1972/1982.
Malabou, Catherine and Jacques Derrida. *Counterpath: Traveling with Jacques Derrida*, translated by David Wills. Stanford, CA: Stanford University Press, 2004.

Research exemplars

MacLure, Maggie. "Broken Voices, Dirty Words: On the Productive Insufficiency of Voice." In *Voice in Qualitative Inquiry: Challenging Conventional, Interpretive, and Critical Conceptions in Qualitative Research*, edited by Alecia Y. Jackson and Lisa A. Mazzei, 97–113. London: Routledge, 2009.
Mazzei, Lisa A. "Silent Listenings: Deconstructive Practices in Discourse-Based Research," *Educational Researcher* 33, no. 2 (2004): 26–34.
——*Inhabited Silence in Qualitative Research: Putting Poststructural Theory to Work*. New York: Peter Lang, 2007.

Interlude II

Why Spivak?

We begin this interlude with a quote from Terry Eagleton: "There must exist somewhere a secret handbook for post-colonial critics, the first rule of which reads: 'Begin by rejecting the whole notion of post-colonialism.'"[1] Eagleton is gesturing toward Gayatri Spivak, whose deconstructive project is a critique of postcolonialism. We turn to Gayatri Spivak from Derrida because she uses deconstruction to critique that which she inhabits: the field of post-colonialism. Spivak doubts that the field of postcolonial studies in the academy can "fight imperialism" because it simply allows the indigenous elite to claim what she deems a "spurious marginality."[2] Although Spivak herself is a member of this indigenous elite, she uses deconstruction to expose how "marginality" is re-claimed, who re-claims it, and what becomes *valued* via such re-claiming. Spivak writes,

> The political claims that are most urgent in decolonized space are tacitly recognized as coded within the legacy of imperialism: nationhood, constitutionality, citizenship, democracy, socialism, even culturalism.[3]

Spivak goes on to write that what are being re-claimed are "regulative political concepts" that have been inherited from Western Europe; thus she rejects postcolonialism as an adequate referent for the times because decolonization has not happened.

We go to Spivak because, as we read Cassandra's data, we came upon many instances in which Cassandra spoke about discriminatory practices in the academy, and how she both resisted and complied with normalizing tendencies of the "teaching machine." Cassandra's data provoked our thinking about margins and minorities in academia, but we wanted to think differently about margin/center politics. In some feminist literature (e.g. bell hooks, Audre Lorde), the margin is positioned as a radical space separate from the center; the margin is a positive, creative site of resistance that minorities can inhabit to secure their difference. This critical way of thinking about margins is based mostly on identity politics, essentialism, and what Spivak terms "ethnic fetishism." While we do not doubt the use of margins as a positive space, we found Spivak's deconstruction of "marginality" to be a more nuanced and complex consideration of margin/center politics *in academia*.

---

[1] Terry Eagleton, *Figures of Dissent* (London: Verso, 2003), 158.
[2] Gayatri Spivak, *Outside in the Teaching Machine* (New York: Routledge, 1993), 277.
[3] *Ibid.*, 281.

Spivak relies on Foucault's concept of *puissance/connaissance* (power/knowledge) to position the teaching machine (the academy) as a vehicle of power/knowledge that seeks to locate and define what counts as authentic inhabitants of the margin. Thus we learn from both Foucault and Spivak how the center (the academy) positions and defines marginality through its constitution of the subject. Spivak takes Foucault's analysis to its limit and then abandons such focus on the subject to bring in Derrida's deconstruction. Spivak's deconstruction enables us to think about neither the center nor the margin as bounded space; she writes, "As the margin or 'outside' enters an institution or teaching machine, what *kind* of teaching machine it enters will determine its contours."[4] Her deconstruction re-positions marginality not as a positive space *outside* of the center, but as constituted *within* the center. Using the domain of the teaching machine (the university), Spivak deconstructs both the center *and* the margin for their paradoxes, predicaments, and constraints, and offers an exploration of the question: *How is Cassandra outside in the teaching machine?*

Schematic cues

Catachresis. Spivak takes hold of the word catachresis to incite a deconstruction of post-colonialism's claim to academic marginality. A catachresis is a "concept-metaphor without an adequate referent."[5] Any "master word" that attempts to represent (in foundational fashion) a group would be catachrestic; for example, women. Or, in Spivak's project, post-colonials. The relationship between the concept-metaphor and the referent is arbitrary, imposed, and loaded with *différance*: such is catachresis.

Center. Derrida insisted that every structure has been given a center – a point of presence, an origin – in order to organize it and limit its "play," its transformation. He writes, "The entire history of the concept of structure … must be thought of as a series of substitutions of center for center, as a linked chain of determinations of the center."[6] Derrida names these determinations, or signs, "Being as presence": essence, existence, substance, subject, consciousness. A transcendental signified, in its essence, "would refer to no signifier, would exceed the chain of signs, and would no longer itself function as a signifier"; it would become a sign itself.[7] The idea of a transcendental signified shuts down all possibilities of multiple meaning and keeps binaries in rigid form, pushing the other term – the signified's difference that gives it its identity – to marginal status.

Colonialism. Childs and Williams explain that colonialism is "the settling of communities from one country in another" with an organized interference in its culture, and that colonialism must be distinguished from imperialism, which is the "extension and expansion of trade and commerce under the protection of political, legal, and military controls."[8]

Deconstruction. Spivak's deconstructive project is a persistent critique of what she inhabits. She sets to work Derrida's deconstruction, explaining that Derrida examines "how texts of philosophy, when they established definitions as starting points, did not attend to the fact

---

[4] *Ibid.*, ix.

[5] *Ibid.*, 60.

[6] Jacques Derrida, *Writing and Difference*, translated by Alan Bass (1966; repr. Chicago: University of Chicago Press, 1978), 279.

[7] Jacques Derrida, *Positions*, translated by Alan Bass (1972; repr. Chicago: University of Chicago Press, 1981), 20.

[8] Peter Childs and Patrick Williams, *An Introduction to Post-Colonial Theory* (New York: Prentice Hall, 1997), 227.

that all gestures involved setting each defined item off from all that it was not."[9] In other words, deconstruction looks for what is concealed, repressed, or pushed away within the maneuvering processes of the center. Thus Spivak's deconstruction of academic marginality is "a suspicion that what is at the center often hides a repression."[10] Elsewhere, she writes that "the named marginal is as much a concealment as a disclosure of the margin, and where s/he discloses, s/he is singular."[11] That is, the double-bind of the margin is to at once conceal or erase in an effort to name or essentialize, yet that which is concealed will always return to disrupt the singular. It is in this way that deconstruction works for Spivak: not to resolve the double-bind, but to be in-between.

Marginality. In all her writing about postcolonial marginality, Spivak references college and university settings, not "subaltern projects of literacy or pedagogy of the oppressed,"[12] nor is she referring to the "revolutionary or resistant marginal in metropolitan space."[13] Spivak is concerned with "the valorization of marginality in universities, such that there is an over-zealous drive to locate, represent, and inhabit the margins."[14] She resists the easy placement of academic postcolonials on the academic margins because those who claim both "postcolonialism" and "marginality" are doing so from a position of being in-between *both; Spivak adheres to a refusal of either postcolonialism or marginality as pure, universal space.*

Postcolonialism. Spivak insists that postcolonialism is a "future anterior, something that will have happened, if one concerned oneself with the persistent crafty details of the calculus of decolonization."[15] In other words, Spivak is suspicious of the term "postcolonialism" because she is doubtful that decolonization (or "stripping away the material effects and structures of the colonial power"[16]) has happened in all places and for all time. She explains, "To imply that postcoloniality is a step beyond colonialism is the new immigrant's reactive and unexamined disavowal of the move (however justified) away from the post-colonial scene to embrace the American dream – the civilizing mission of the new colonizing power."[17]

Puissance/connaissance. Spivak borrows this power/knowledge doublet from Foucault. *Puissance/connaissance* is traditional, received, inherited power structures and knowledge formations that are imposed by structural conditions. Put another way, *puissance/ connaissance* is imposed from above or outside, rather than constructed or created in daily practices. (Also see the "Knowledge" schematic cue in Interlude III.)

---

[9] Gayatri Spivak, *A Critique of Postcolonial Reason: Toward a History of the Vanishing Present* (Cambridge, MA: Harvard University Press, 1999), 423.

[10] Gayatri Spivak, *In Other Worlds: Essays in Cultural Politics* (New York: Routledge, 1988), 104.

[11] Spivak, *A Critique of Postcolonial Reason*, op. cit., 173.

[12] Gayatri Spivak, "Teaching for the Times." In *Dangerous Liaisons: Gender, Nation, and Postcolonial Perspectives*, edited by Anne McClintock, Asmit Mufti, and Ella Shohat (Minneapolis: University of Minnesota Press, 1997), 468.

[13] Spivak, *Outside in the Teaching Machine*, op. cit., 64.

[14] Childs and Williams, *An Introduction to Post-Colonial Theory*, op. cit., 173.

[15] Spivak, "Teaching for the Times," op. cit., 469.

[16] Childs and Williams, *An Introduction to Post-Colonial Theory*, 227.

[17] Spivak, "Teaching for the Times," 478.

Chapter 3

Spivak: Thinking with marginality

There can be no universalist claims in the human sciences. This is most strikingly obvious in the case of establishing "marginality" as a subject-position in literary and cultural critique.[1]

Spivak's deconstructive project is a persistent critique of what she inhabits. Perhaps her most "famous" line to sum up deconstruction is: "This impossible 'no' to a structure, which one critiques, yet inhabits intimately, is the deconstructive philosophical position."[2] An example that Spivak offers for grasping onto the "impossible no" of deconstruction is the following:

> The making of an American is defined by at least a desire to enter the "We the People" of the Constitution. One cannot dismiss this as mere "essentialism" and take a position against civil rights, the Equal Rights Amendment, or the transformative opinions in favor of women's reproductive rights. We in the United States cannot not want to inhabit this rational abstraction.[3]

It is impossible to say a full "no" to a structure that creates the very life that we have, and it follows that resistance and critique are never transcendent, but reside in the middle of things. According to Spivak, deconstructionists do their work from within (from an intimacy with the structure); it is that very within-ness that enables critique of the limits of the structure, or how it limits life. Structures themselves are not as stable as they appear, yet they do define and regulate people's ways of living. So, for Spivak, it is up to the deconstructionist to determine the contours of a structure and to take a position that is "in the middle, but not on either side."[4] For her deconstructive work, Spivak relies on Derrida, who writes,

> The movements of deconstruction do not destroy structures from the outside. They are not possible and effective, nor can they take accurate aim, except by inhabiting those structures. Inhabiting them *in a certain way*, because one always inhabits, and all the more when one does not suspect it. Operating necessarily from the inside, borrowing all

---

[1] Gayatri Spivak, *Outside in the Teaching Machine* (New York: Routledge, 1993), 53.

[2] *Ibid.*, 60.

[3] Gayatri Spivak, *A Critique of Postcolonial Reason: Toward a History of the Vanishing Present* (Cambridge, MA: Harvard University Press, 1999), 172.

[4] Leon de Kock, "Interview with Gayatri Chakravorty Spivak: New Nation Writers Conference in South Africa," *Ariel: A Review of International English Literature* 23, no. 3 (1992): 39–40.

the strategic and economic resources of subversion from the old structure ... the enterprise of deconstruction always in a certain way falls prey to its own work.[5]

For example, Spivak explains that "the everyday here and now named 'postcoloniality' is a case of [deconstruction]."[6] More specifically, Spivak is concerned with "the valorization of marginality in universities, such that there is an over-zealous drive to locate, represent, and inhabit the margins."[7] Spivak resists the easy placement of academic postcolonials on the academic margins because those who claim both "postcolonialism" and "marginality" are doing so from a position of being in-between *both*; Spivak adheres to a refusal of either postcolonialism or marginality as pure, universal space. That is, Spivak herself claims access to the center, or to the culture of imperialism, and to social and academic elitism. As well, she is placed (pushed? forced?) into the margin by those who view her as Other, or by those who position her as one-of-us-with-cultural-particularities. She cannot not want to inhabit either space (the "impossible no") because of what each provides: Spivak insists that "the academy is an important apparatus of upward class mobility,"[8] and her ethnicity enables a particular positioning in the academy that benefits her in terms of recognition by others (such as through elite speaking and teaching engagements). Yet she *fully* inhabits neither the center nor the margin as she participates in the deconstruction of each.

Spivak takes hold of the word *catachresis* to incite a deconstruction of postcolonialism's claim to academic marginality. A catachresis is a "concept-metaphor without an adequate referent."[9] Any "master word" that attempts to represent (in foundational fashion) a group would be catachrestic; for example, women. Or, in Spivak's project, postcolonials.[10] The relationship between the concept-metaphor and the referent is arbitrary, imposed, and loaded with *différance*: such is catachresis. Spivak sets up "postcolonial marginality" as catachrestic by asserting that

> the political claims that are most urgent in decolonized space are tacitly recognized as coded within the legacy of imperialism: nationhood, constitutionality, citizenship, democracy, even culturalism ... What is being effectively reclaimed is a series of regulative political concepts ... which were written elsewhere in the social formations of Western Europe.[11]

That is, academic postcolonialists *use the language of colonialism* to define the margin; there is no historical reference *from within postcolonialism* to describe its condition. Spivak clarifies that the inadequate referent does not make postcolonialism *less* important or *less* urgent;

---

[5] Jacques Derrida, *Of Grammatology*, translated by Gayatri Spivak (Baltimore: Johns Hopkins University Press, 1997/1967), 24.

[6] Spivak, *Outside in the Teaching Machine*, op. cit., 60.

[7] Peter Childs and Patrick Williams, *An Introduction to Post-Colonial Theory* (New York: Prentice Hall, 1997), 173.

[8] Spivak, *Outside in the Teaching Machine*, 294.

[9] *Ibid.*, 60.

[10] In poststructuralism, all of language could be considered catachrestic. See note 22 on p. 297 of *Outside in the Teaching Machine*: catachrestic master-words are "misfits only if the ordinary use of language is presupposed to have fully fitting cases. Thus 'to fit' is itself a catachresis and points to a general theory of language as catachrestical that must *be actively marginalized in all its uses*." [emphasis ours]. Spivak uses catechresis in the most narrow sense.

[11] Spivak, *Outside in the Teaching Machine*, 60.

rather, postcolonialism-as-a-catachresis switches on deconstruction. This, of course, does not solve the problem or erase the concept for something new; rather, it attempts to expose the paradoxes, predicaments, and constraints of the term (or, its catachresis). For Spivak, positioning "postcolonialism" as catachrestic in a deconstructive project "can show us the negotiable agenda of a cultural commitment to marginality, whereas ethnicist academic agendas make a fetish of identity."[12] That is, deconstruction might reveal the paradox of "identity fetishes" because ethnicity can never be a pure, essentialized space. It follows, then, that claims to marginality are also negotiable. Spivak eschews reliance on ethnic identities, victimhoods, or historical/philosophical claims to emancipation and oppression that define a positive space of marginality in the academy. Spivak spells it out for the indigenous elite (a group to which she belongs): "'postcoloniality,' far from being marginal, can show the *irreducible margin in the center*."[13] Put differently, so-called postcolonials who claim marginality do so from *within*, *not removed from*, the center. Spivak refers to this particular "impossible no" as outside in the teaching machine.

How is Cassandra outside in the teaching machine? Thinking with Spivak's deconstruction of marginality exposes how Cassandra is never purely "in" the center, nor "in" the margin, nor simply moving between each. Rather, Cassandra is *outside in* and therefore exposes the "irreducible margin in the center." This excerpt from Cassandra's interview speaks to being outside in the teaching machine:

> Being the only African-American in a lot of settings, I felt a lot of pressure to fit in because people seemed to want that from me. I was on a lot of committees all over the campus because sometimes when I would refuse they would say, "But Cassandra, we need a minority on the committee." So, I ended up spending a lot of time doing that kind of thing and I guess I just felt like that I was, and I still do to this day, I have an on mode and an off mode. My off mode is when I'm being myself and my on mode is when I'm doing what I feel I need to do professionally in order to fit in. But then there are other African-Americans here who might not relate to me on the same level of my same experience; just because we share the same race doesn't mean that we share the same culture. I'm small-town rural. Southern and Pentecostal. And so, all of those things give me a very unique kind of perspective. It's kind of hard for everybody to fit neatly into that kind of little pocket.

Cassandra is positioned as marginal by others who desire her "blackness" in the center. "Being professional," according to Cassandra, is giving the *appearance* that she is inhabiting the margin and turning on Spivak's "identity fetish" via tokenism. That is, Cassandra's "on mode" was when she was positioned in the margins as the token black woman on academic committees and giving others what was needed for them to position her as belonging to academia. Yet Cassandra pointed out that she never purely inhabited that space, or as Derrida put it, she "inhabits in a certain way."[14] Cassandra professed that she is not only African-American but also small-town rural, southern, and Pentecostal; therefore academia's "fetish" for her blackness is foiled: she is other things, too. She herself is irreducible to one identity, and thus is the margin, too. Cassandra shows the "irreducible margin in the center" because

---

[12] *Ibid.*, 65.
[13] *Ibid.*, 63 [emphasis added].
[14] Derrida, *Of Grammatology*, op. cit., 24.

she is at once part of the academic elite and part of what gets defined as marginal in academia; Cassandra is outside in the teaching machine.

Margins and centers in the teaching machine

To further explicate how Cassandra is outside in the teaching machine, we use Spivak's deconstruction of margin/center politics in the academy. Spivak's "teaching machine" is the elite university; following Foucault, she describes a teaching machine as the "aggregative apparatus of Euro-American university education, where weapons for the play of power/ knowledge as *puissance/connaissance* are daily put together, bit by bit, according to a history rather different from our own."[15] Her point is that the academy relies on *traditional* and inherited power structures and knowledge formations to function: doing things the same way because 1) they have always been done that way, and 2) they secure power hierarchies. It follows, then, that Spivak's teaching machine (the academy) is an institutional center that uses force fields to create boundaries around, and make visible, (irregular) lines of knowing and ways of doing and not doing.[16] As an apparatus of *puissance/connaissance*, the academy-as-center wants an identifiable margin: wants to generalize it, wants to name it, wants to secure it through *separation*. The machine's center desires to secure what (or whom) is marginal in a way that often maintains the center's own *puissance/connaissance*.[17]

What are the ways of doing and not doing at Cassandra's institution, Regional State University? How does the teaching machine attempt to secure its *puissance/connaissance* via identifying its margins? Spivak explains that "as the margin or 'outside' enters an institution or teaching machine, what *kind* of teaching machine it enters will determine its contours. Therefore the struggle continues, in different ways, after the infiltration."[18] When Cassandra entered Regional State University in 1992, she was hired specifically as an African-American woman academic to recruit and mentor African-American students in her area of specialty:

> What I was told at the time was that they needed someone here to teach and enhance diversity, and they had gotten a very large grant that allowed them to bring in minority (primarily African-American) students to get their master's degree in [*my area of academic specialty*]. They wanted someone to serve as their mentor and also to develop a course and some programs that would promote diversity within the profession, so that's what I came here to do.

However, over the years she came to the realization that she was "hired as a token." She went on to explain:

> I really did think the university wanted me here to do what I was doing, but slowly over the course of the next two years I realized that that was not necessarily why I was here. They needed someone to fill that position in that grant and they wanted it to look like they were making an effort.

---

[15] Spivak, *Outside in the Teaching Machine*, 53.
[16] *Ibid.*, 36–37.
[17] We thank Stephanie Daza for helping us to think about this point.
[18] Spivak, *Outside in the Teaching Machine*, ix [emphasis in original].

The center of the white institution shaped the contours of Cassandra's marginality. Cassandra entered an institutional center that was predominantly white in terms of faculty and students, a mid-sized comprehensive university that had never promoted a black woman to full professor. Cassandra took seriously her role as a mentor and used similar practices with minority students (such as open-door policies that welcomed students into her office for "hanging-out time") to those she had been using for decades before at Southern State University, a historically black state university. However, Cassandra explained that white students wrote "long, very critical letters that accused [her] of reverse discrimination and that [she] was showing favoritism to the black students." The accusations went all the way up to the university's provost's office, and Cassandra wrote letter after letter of rebuttal. The case was resolved in Cassandra's favor, but at the conclusion of the event, the university sent a group of faculty to what Cassandra described as a "conference in Atlanta on racial issues to find solutions to the problem." Cassandra said that she felt justified, after attending the conference, in terms of her mentoring choices with minority students.

The contours of marginality are visible here in Cassandra's practices of mentoring because her practices work to validate the center's *puissance/connaissance*: a grant culture that requires such tokenism. Yet, in this scenario, no longer was the margin (tokenism) institutionally convenient for the center, because of white students' responses; tokenism is only institutionally convenient if practices by those who are tokens do not disrupt the norm. Cassandra's mentoring (mothering) practices infiltrated the center and caused disruption, yet not enough disruption to decolonize. Those who inhabited the center clamped down on the process and responded in a way that secured its *puissance/connaissance* by sending Cassandra and her colleagues to a professional conference on racism. Thinking with Spivak's deconstruction of marginality exposes that the teaching machine's response is one that reifies colonial thinking and practices: following proper channels of communication for complaints and rebuttals, relying on hierarchical power structures to solve problems, sending faculty off to a conference in hopes of changing behavior (or to superficially quell the complaint).

It might seem obvious to claim that Cassandra was defining a positive marginal space for minorities, one that valorizes the particular needs of a minority group. Yet Spivak contends that the fabrication of "clinging to marginality"[19] rests not on ethnic identity, but on value. If so-called marginality rests only, or primarily, on identity, then what gets missed is how *the academic center attempts to validate its own values*. The academic center regulates what is taught, what is read, what is tested (and the margin does the same, taken up in the next section). Spivak argues for a move away from identity to value-coding, to show how the margin exists not as a group of authentic people, but as a negotiated space of value-codings and differentials. Value-coding in the academy, and therefore the establishment of the center and the margin, is based not on persons or things, but on the currency of knowledge. The teaching machine's colonizing response to Cassandra's situation exposes how the center values a particular type of teaching and mentoring. Are Cassandra's mentoring practices marginal because she is black? A woman? Spivak would claim that we cannot solve such complexity based on authentic identity; instead, the question to pose is how the center, through colonization, governs what practices are valued.

[19] *Ibid.*, 9.

Collision and collusion of margin and center

Spivak's deconstruction of marginality is to make visible the collision and collusion of the center and the margin. That is, deconstruction calls out the ways in which a particular teaching machine assures and validates its own center by shaping the contours of its margins. Furthermore, the margin itself, too, is "involved in the construction of a new object of investigation – 'the third world,' 'the marginal' – for institutional validation and certification."[20] Spivak goes on:

> One has only to analyze carefully the proliferating but exclusivist "Third World-ist" job descriptions to see the packaging at work. It is as if, in a certain way, we [*postcolonialists*] are becoming complicitous in the perpetration of a "new orientalism."[21]

Spivak is convincing in her argument that academic marginality has been delineated by *both* the center *and* the margin via a teaching machine (academic disciplines such as literary, ethnic, and cultural studies) that "determine and overdetermine its conditions of representability."[22] So as Fanon and Said become The Representatives of Colonial Discourse (Spivak's 1988 examples), Spivak critiques: "The study of colonial discourse ... has blossomed into a garden where the marginal can speak and be spoken, even spoken for."[23] The teaching machine is a centering apparatus of colonization in that it recognizes a select, elite group as its margin; the teaching machine's center attempts to define authentic academic marginality – or the "*center*" *of the margin*. Yet the margin (the aspiring elite – a group of which Spivak claims membership), perhaps "unwillingly or unwittingly,"[24] colludes with the center and supports the certainty of authentic marginality. What are the local forces at work *within the margins* to claim and to ensure such legitimacy? In literary production, Spivak refers to instances in which certain literary styles emerge as the only ones that are "ethnically authentic": the example she offers is "magical realism" becoming paradigmatic in Third World literature, particularly Latin America. She is blatant in her reasoning: "The radicals of industrialized nations want to *be* the Third World."[25] That is, claims to Third World marginality are negotiated *within* the margins and serve to monumentalize "ethnically authentic" styles and characteristics of the margins. According to Spivak, this negotiation obscures the center's role in establishing the margin; it is almost as if the center stands aside and concedes, "Yes, claim your identity. Claim your identity, but stay *over there*, out of our way. Claim your identity that is different, but don't disrupt our norms." The "rupture" to which Spivak refers is decolonization. Yet Spivak sees no process of decolonization in the case of magical-realism-as-Third-World-literary-style; rather, the problem is that the consolidation of recognizable styles in literary criticism "boringly repeats the rhythms of colonization."[26] The colonized colonize themselves.

Cassandra colluded with the teaching machine's center when she identified her own teaching and mentoring "style" with African-American students as having a certain essence:

---

[20] *Ibid.*, 56.
[21] *Ibid.*
[22] *Ibid.*
[23] *Ibid.*
[24] *Ibid.*, 57.
[25] *Ibid.*
[26] *Ibid.*, 58.

My office is small now, but it was even smaller then. And they [black students] would be sitting all on the floor and everything and we just hung out together. I was a mother figure, that was pretty much the same thing that I did at [Southern State University] so I knew how to work with those students and I knew that [they] need a lot of personal attention.

Cassandra's use of "those students" signifies that, through her mentoring practices, she is producing, for the center, a contained version of what it "means" to be a black teacher and a black student at a white university. This data excerpt illustrates Cassandra's own collusion with the center to define an authentic margin, and is an example of a neo-colonial center (the academy) "fabricating its allies by proposing a share of the center in a seemingly new way (not a rupture but displacement)."[27] The displacement occurs by the center offering support for Cassandra's practices by hiring her for a specific reason; not firing her in response to student complaints; and yet sending everyone to a conference on racism that Cassandra said validated her practices: "I still quote some of the stuff to this day that came out of that. It was very supportive of what I had been doing." So in this data example, the margin and the center collide and collude to produce what is valued. Perhaps what is valued by this particular teaching machine is not only certain types of teaching and mentoring styles that are easily attributed to pure ethnic identities, but also maintaining proper channels of communication and solving problems. In this instance, the margin contains a center (a black mentoring "style" that is valued because it maintains difference), and the center gets re-centered (or validated) by the margin. The production of marginality is a double-movement of "the local and the overall" that results in "no single, unified form of appearance."[28] If there is a margin *in* a center, and a center *in* a margin, then each one constantly makes and re-makes the other.

An impossible no

To be outside in the teaching machine is to say an "impossible 'no' to a structure, which one critiques, yet inhabits intimately."[29] We have explored various margin/center politics in Cassandra's data, and we have pointed out ways in which Cassandra is outside in the teaching machine, or how she critiques that which she inhabits. Spivak is forceful in her claim that the teaching machine centers the marginal by giving status to an aspiring elite. Cassandra, having grown up in the 1950s as a young black girl in a poor farming community in the segregated south with parents who were not educated past eighth grade, cannot *not* want the upward mobility offered via the teaching machine; during her interview, Cassandra said,

The dreams and hopes that a lot of middle-class colleagues had were not things that I had at that time [upon entering the academy as a professor]. Part of my responsibilities as I saw them from a cultural perspective at that time were to help my family, and so a lot of my funds were channeled into helping them as opposed to trying to save money for a house or that kind of thing.

[27] *Ibid.*, 57.
[28] *Ibid.*, 76.
[29] *Ibid.*, 6.

So Cassandra inhabits a structure that offers her a way of life that is different from working in tobacco and cotton fields from "sunrise to twilight." Cassandra never transcends her historical and cultural background; her background *enables* her "impossible no." Cassandra explained,

> This is my thirty-ninth year in university teaching and I really feel like I am such a misfit for academic culture. I don't know how I lasted in the culture, because I don't fit in neatly with what you would generally think of as being academic, the academic culture. In terms of when I'm sitting around with people and the kinds of things that they love to talk about and they get excited about certain topics. Even though I'm located in [*this unit of the university*], I was never trying to be an educator. I was trying to be a [*practitioner in my field*]. I fell into being an educator. So, a lot of the theories, or the philosophies, and so forth that would be of interest to people who are true educators would probably not be of that much interest to me. My focus and my research and my writing and my practice have been delivery of services to people who are from culturally diverse backgrounds, and I don't know of anybody else here on campus who does that.

When Cassandra entered the teaching machine, the contours of her marginality were formed: she was hired as an African-American woman to recruit minorities into her disciplinary field. Yet being outside-in (a margin within the center) produces her as refusing much of the centering activity of the academy, centering activities such as: publish or perish; stay focused on theory as opposed to practice; represent ("speak for") minorities on committees. Cassandra, rather than fitting neatly into what she describes as academic culture (or the center), emphasizes the practitioner side of her profession in her work at the university. She recognizes the teaching machine's (centering) imperative to produce scholarship, and so she wrote a textbook that outlines practical applications of the "services" that her academic discipline provides. Cassandra works in the community with poor, rural, culturally diverse families by providing therapeutic/rehabilitation services; describing how to best implement these services became the topic of a textbook that she authored. Being outside in the teaching machine enabled Cassandra to achieve promotion to full professor and tenure by asserting a *differentiated value* to the center. So while Cassandra inhabits the center, she inhabits *in a certain way, as the margin-within*. And that positionality reveals the irreducible margin *in* the center.

Cassandra can never fully be outside or inside. She can never be outside her own marginality: what gets inserted *into* the margin are her history and her culture of a black, rural, southern upbringing, and that (marginal) history and culture, too, subsequently get integrated *into* the center via her scholarship. Cassandra focuses her academic life on providing services to families in her present community that, in many ways, resemble families in her hometown community. As Spivak says in an interview,

> This is a classic deconstructive position, in the middle, but not on either side, and unable to solve a problem by taking either side, but on the other hand solving it situationally, and not for ever ... Deconstructive imperatives always come out of situations; it's not situationally relative, but they always come out of situations.[30]

---

[30] de Kock, "Interview," op. cit., 39–40.

So it is from a position of being in the middle – of being at once produced by the margin *and* the center – that Cassandra says the "impossible no." She inhabits the center as marginal – but inhabits the margins *as* the center (an "aspiring elite" who is also a cultural minority). It is from this unique position that she is able to both dwell in and critique the structure of the teaching machine.

Thinking with marginality

Thinking with Spivak's marginality offers a complex and nuanced account of margin/center politics in the academy (the teaching machine). Strategies of power and techniques of knowledge (*puissance/connaissance*) combine to reproduce an "old scenario of empowering a privileged group or a group susceptible to upward mobility as the authentic inhabitants of the margin."[31] In this way, the teaching machine's center identifies the margin via "an economic principle of identification through separation."[32] When the center assures its own validation through separation, the margin becomes coded and valued for what it delivers: authenticity, essence, recognition (such as when Cassandra was hired as a token). Yet Spivak makes important arguments against this linear, one-way positioning: 1) the margin, too, can be complicit in securing its own definition and therefore cannot be a positive space of decolonization in the academy; and 2) the margin has its own center and thus can function to bring differentiated values to the center (or, re-centering the center in the academy).

If "the most serious critique in deconstruction is the critique of things that are extremely useful, things without which we cannot live,"[33] then exposing the paradoxes of marginality gives useful insights into mechanisms of centering: centers do not always hold, and centers are not uniquely monolithic as purely defined space. The same can be said of marginality, according to Spivak. Certainly, entering the academy has provided Cassandra with mobility that she may have never imagined in the 1950s as a young black girl living in a rural, segregated farming community in the southern USA. Cassandra residing in the teaching machine is something that she cannot not want, yet "to think about the danger of what is useful" is the lesson of deconstruction.[34] Deconstruction teaches about the impossibility of Cassandra saying "no" to the academy, and instead invites an analysis of the counterintuitive: How does she say no, and how does she not say no? And how does this happen outside-in margin/centers that constantly make one another? These are the Spivakian questions that have given us the most provocation for our "thinking with marginality."

More on marginality

The following texts are offered, not as *the* texts to consult, but as providing an entry point for those who are new to the writings of Spivak and would like to learn more about marginality and Spivak's deconstruction. We list the secondary texts first as a continuation of the "schematic cues" presented in the Interlude, which readers can use as a brace as they enter

---

[31] Spivak, *Outside in the Teaching Machine*, 59.
[32] *Ibid.*, 55.
[33] *Ibid.*, 4.
[34] *Ibid.*, 10.

this new theoretical terrain. Following the secondary texts are suggested entry points for approaching the writing of Spivak, and finally, research exemplars that illustrate additional examples of *thinking with* marginality.

Secondary texts

Childs, Peter and Patrick Williams. *An Introduction to Post-Colonial Theory*. New York: Prentice Hall, 1997.

Morton, Stephen. *Gayatri Chakravorty Spivak*. New York: Routledge, 2003.

Varadharajan, Asha. *Exotic Parodies: Subjectivity in Adorno, Said, and Spivak*. Minneapolis: University of Minnesota Press, 1995.

Primary texts

Spivak, Gayatri C. *In Other Worlds: Essays in Cultural Politics*. New York: Routledge, 1988.

——*Outside in the Teaching Machine*. New York: Routledge, 1993.

——*A Critique of Postcolonial Reason: Toward a History of the Vanishing Present*. Cambridge, MA: Harvard University Press, 1999.

Research exemplars

Chakraborty, Mridula Nath. "Everybody's afraid of Gayatri Chakravorty Spivak: Reading Interviews with the Public Intellectual and Postcolonial Critic," *Signs: Journal of Women in Culture & Society* 35, no. 3 (2010): 621–45.

Shetty, Sandhya and Elizabeth Jane Bellamy. "Postcolonialism's Archive Fever," *Diacritics* 30, no. 1 (2000): 25–48.

Tarc, Aparna Mishra. "In a Dimension of Height: Ethics in the Education of Others," *Educational Theory* 56, no. 3 (2006): 287–304.

Why Foucault?

In the context of our research, the purpose of a power/knowledge reading is to explain how the cultural and material practices of Cassandra and Sera, as first-generation women faculty, combine power and knowledge to produce their subjectivities. Certainly, the hierarchical power structures in the academy are visible and practiced in terms of rank and responsibilities, and these power structures may seem repressive and unshakable. Yet Foucault's theory of power *relations* offers a different way to analyze the struggles that Cassandra and Sera expressed in their interviews as first-generation women faculty. We use Foucault's theory of power because, as he clarifies, "I've never claimed that power was going to explain everything ... for me, power is what needs to be explained."[1] Therefore a Foucauldian power analysis helps us to explain the multiple (rather than one-way) functions of power in the academy as Cassandra and Sera enter as assistant professors: how power is exercised and its effects. Taking this perspective of power as a relation – as always, moving and circulating among people – also enables a different analysis of knowledge: how knowledge is an *effect* of power. Thus Foucault's power/knowledge doublet captures how people's actions are local reactions and responses, even struggles and resistances, and are temporarily embedded within specific, and shifting, relations of power. Therefore power and knowledge constantly articulate one another in the practices of people. This reciprocal relationship between power and knowledge led to Foucault's reversal of the popular belief that they are identical, as in the common statement "knowledge is power." Foucault explains, "When I read ... the thesis, 'Knowledge is power,' or 'Power is knowledge,' I begin to laugh, since studying their *relation* is precisely my problem. If they were identical, I would not have to study them ... The very fact that I pose the question of their relation proves clearly that I do not *identify* them."[2]

In formulating his power analytics, Foucault's stance is an inversion of traditional interpretive questions such as "What is power?" and "Where does power come from?" These traditional questions are ontological and metaphysical: they lead to searches for essences and origins. Foucault inverted this mode of analysis and investigated *the productive effects of power as it circulates through the practices of people in their daily lives.* Foucault's strategy was to study the deployment of power, a deployment that makes visible how the subject is

---

[1] Michel Foucault, *Power*. Translated by Robert Hurley *et al.*, edited by Paul Rabinow. *Essential Works of Foucault 1954–1984, Vol. III* (New York: The New Press, 2000), 284.

[2] Michel Foucault, *Politics, Philosophy, Culture: Interviews and Other Writings of Michel Foucault, 1977–1984* (New York: Routledge, 1990), 43.

constructed through social relations and cultural practices. These relations and practices are not simple projections of a central power (institutional or legal).[3] Rather, Foucault showed that power's existence is local, capillary, and reaches "into the very grain of individuals, touches their bodies and inserts itself into their actions and attitudes, their discourses, learning processes and everyday lives … *within* the social body rather than *from above* it."[4] Foucault acknowledged that power could exist in unequal and ill-coordinated relations, but even these relations have reciprocal movements that define "innumerable points of confrontation, focuses of instability, each of which has its own risks of conflict, of struggles, and of an at least temporary inversion of power relations."[5] These relations produce effects that are inscribed into the entire power network, including subjects who are invested in particular networks of relations.

Cassandra's and Sera's practices and the production of their subjectivity as they negotiated their entry in higher education were effects of a network of social, material, cultural, and power relations within discursive fields. This network, as it connects and disconnects, regulates and produces certain conditions (or rules) for living in the world. The analytic question for our power/knowledge reading is: *How do power/knowledge relations and practices produce Cassandra's and Sera's multiple subjectivities as they venture into the academy as first-generation professors?*

Schematic cues

Discourse/discursive fields. Bové does not define discourse, but explains how discourse functions, thus: "Discourse provides a privileged entry into the poststructuralist mode of analysis precisely because it is the organized and regulated, as well as the regulating and constituting, functions of language that it studies: its aim is to describe the surface linkages between power, knowledge, institutions, intellectuals, the control of populations, and the modern state as these intersect in the functions of systems of thought."[6] The social structures and processes that shape our subjectivities are situated within discursive fields, where language, social institutions, subjectivity, and power exist, intersect, and produce competing ways of giving meaning to and constructing subjectivity. Reflecting certain values, competing discourses emerge within discursive fields, and the language and practices of these discourses give rise to an individual's conflicting subjectivities.[7]

Knowledge. In writing about knowledge, Foucault makes an important distinction between *savoir* and *connaissance* (both words reference "knowledge"). He used the word *savoir* to signify *constructed* knowledge about oneself, knowledge that is produced in experience and relations with others. This constructed knowledge – *savoir* – is active and captures a subject's process of modification and transformation. *Savoir* is a practice of knowledge that not only defines, but also changes the way a subject participates in the

---

[3] Michel Foucault, *Power/Knowledge: Selected Interviews and Other Writings: 1972–1977*. Translated by Leo Marshall, Colin Gordon, John Mepham and Kate Soper, edited by Colin Gordon (New York: Pantheon Books, 1980), 201.

[4] *Ibid.*, 39.

[5] Michel Foucault, *Discipline and Punish: The Birth of a Prison*. Translated by Alan Sheridan (New York: Vintage Books, 1979), 27.

[6] Paul A. Bové, "Discourse." In *Critical Terms for Literary Study*, edited by F. Lentricchia (Chicago: University of Chicago Press, 1990), 54–55.

[7] Chris Weedon, *Feminist Practice and Poststructural Theory*, 2nd edn (Oxford, UK: Blackwell, 1997).

world. *Connaissance* is also the action of making intelligible knowable objects, yet *connaissance* maintains the stability of the subject.[8] Rather than actively inquiring and constructing knowledge through social practices, a subject receives *connaissance*. *Connaissance* is didactic, received knowledge (such as family values) and is most visible in constructions of self/Other, where a fixed self is defined by its Other (e.g. man/woman).

Power: structural and relational. In a 1976 lecture,[9] Foucault critiques conventional notions of repressive power by distinguishing between juridical and economic (or Marxist) theories of power. Juridical power is understood as a right, a commodity, and something that is transferable; therefore it can be abused by those who are "in" authority (such as an absolute monarch or a dictator), and can be opposed (by proletariat revolt or political usurpation). Economic power is also conceived as a possession that is used for domination in relations of production and class. These understandings of economic power as having a stable origin – as something that one has and exerts over others – assume, also, that power can be overthrown so that dominated subjects can free their imprisoned nature and recover their authentic selves which have been lost through systematic, oppressive social and material conditions of poverty and labor.

Foucault critiques not only the idea of power as a possession, but also the belief that those who "have" power intentionally control and wield power over subjects with no agency.[10] Foucault argued that this view of power as intentional is limited because it runs the danger of homogenizing and essentializing subjects as having universal characteristics, rather than recognizing the fluid and relational fields that construct subjectivity.[11] One way in which this works is that juridical and economic theories of power assume a dualism – oppressor/oppressed – that defines subjects as monolithic entities and ignores the subtle ways in which power operates.[12] Furthermore, the objective of analyzing repressive power involves a search for "real" or "underlying" power, which implies a notion of fixed, transcendental power. This view of repressive power disregards the freedom and agency of people and the ways in which they resist within and against relations of power to transform their lives.

Foucault formulates a notion of power that is more than simply prohibitive or repressive (he posits that even restrictions are a form of productive power). Foucault is convincing when he details, "What makes power hold good, what makes it accepted, is simply the fact that it doesn't only weigh on us as a force that says no, but that it traverses and produces things, it induces pleasure, forms knowledge, produces discourse."[13] Productive power is not its own entity, as something to be taken and given away. Power forms a chain that relies on relations (even those that are restrictive) to advance, multiply, and branch out deeply

[8] Foucault, *Power/Knowledge: Selected Interviews,* op. cit., 256.

[9] *Ibid.*, 88.

[10] Foucault did not deny that there are instances of domination when relations of power are asymmetrical or temporarily fixed. His idea of domination was not the global kind in which one person or one group dominates another, but the "manifold forms of domination that can be exercised within society. Not the domination of the King in his central position, therefore, but that of his subjects in their mutual relations." (Foucault, *Power/Knowledge: Selected Interviews,* op. cit., 96.) Domination is not one form of repression that is wielded by one person over a multitude of people, but is made of "polymorphous techniques of subjugation."

[11] Thomas S. Popkewitz and Marie Brennan (eds), *Foucault's Challenge: Discourse, Knowledge, and Power in Education* (New York: Teachers College Press, 1998), 18.

[12] *Ibid.*

[13] Foucault, *Power/Knowledge: Selected Interviews,* op.cit., 199.

into social networks.[14] Foucault defined four facets of power in order to illustrate this complexity: 1) as a multiplicity of force *relations*; 2) as *processes* of struggles that transform, strengthen, or reverse the relations; 3) as a *support* in which many relations intersect and form either a chain or various cleavages of disjunction and contradiction; and 4) as *strategies* in which power crystallizes and is embodied in the mechanisms and practices of social life.[15]

Power/knowledge. In Foucault's earlier archeological studies (e.g. *The Archeology of Knowledge*), he was interested in the relationship between truth and knowledge – the conditions necessary for statements of knowledge to become the truths that we live by. Through his early analyses emerged the problematic of power/knowledge, as he, in retrospect, postulated that the formation of knowledge occurred within relations of power. His studies of power/knowledge in *Discipline and Punish* and the first volume of *A History of Sexuality* are centered on the functions of power as it produces knowledge and particular types of knowable subjects (such as the criminal and the pervert, respectively). In other words, how people are understood, or how knowledge is constructed about people, is a function of power – thus the intricate relationship among power, knowledge, and the subject.

The Subject. Foucault was trained in philosophies that valued the primacy of the subject, particularly phenomenology, and much of his work consists of methodological and epistemological reactions to phenomenology. In phenomenology, reflective subjects give meaning to the world. Subjects' expressions are assumed to be self-evident and clearly present to the consciousness of the meaning-maker. Furthermore, a subject's expression is transcendental in that it exists as an origin, an ideal, and an essential truth that is the foundation for meaning; it reflects, here and now, a pure meaning that is uncontaminated by any exteriority that would challenge its claims to truth. A phenomenological subject is present to (or conscious of) its decisions, actions, and values, and therefore expresses meaning that is coherent, intentional, and transparent. Foucault's questioning of the subject is a departure from certain structural projects that searched for origins and that assumed an essential meaning behind a phenomenon, an ultimate truth to be uncovered/discovered. These structural projects also assumed a subject that existed both beyond and ahead of its own construction. For Foucault to critique the subject, he inverts traditional modes of analysis. Foucault does not analyze the subject through its descriptions of lived experience that are self-evident and clearly present to the consciousness of the subject (and therefore reflect a stable, coherent meaning). Instead, Foucault studies the subject in its obliqueness, "not in the continuity of its self-consciousness, but in the *discontinuity* of its shifting forms, in the different interrogations to which it is submitted, and in the ways in which its interiority is hollowed out."[16]

Subjectivity. Poststructural theories of subjectivity posit a notion of the "self" as a site of disunity and conflict that is always in process and produced within power relations. Weedon defines subjectivity as "the conscious and unconscious thoughts and emotions of the individual, her sense of herself, and her ways of understanding her relation to the world."[17]

[14] Michel Foucault, *The History of Sexuality. Volume 1: An Introduction*. Translated by Robert Hurley (New York: Vintage Books, 1980), 42.

[15] *Ibid.*, 92–93.

[16] Garth Gillan, "Foucault's Philosophy." In *The Final Foucault*, edited by J. W. Bernauer and D. M. Rasmussen (Cambridge, MA: MIT Press, 1994), 37 [emphasis ours].

[17] Weedon, *Feminist Practice and Poststructural Theory*, op. cit., 32.

Subjectivity is not stable, but is constructed in relationships with others and in everyday practices. A woman's subjectivity is not stabilized or essentialized by identity categories (race, class, gender) because her ways of existing in the world can shift depending on social relations, historical experiences, and material conditions. For example, a white, heterosexual, middle-class Christian woman may have a specific sense of herself and may therefore behave in certain ways when she is with other white, heterosexual, middle-class Christian women; however, when she is in the company of others who are very different from her, her sense of self may temporarily shift in response to those specific relational demands. Her self, then, is never stable but is constantly shifting in response to particular situations and conditions, and notions of subjectivity capture this active process of taking up certain subject positions in an ongoing process of "becoming" – rather than merely "being" – in the world.

Chapter 4

Foucault: Thinking with power/knowledge

> What makes power hold good, what makes it accepted, is simply the fact that it doesn't only weigh on us as a force that says no, but that it traverses and produces things, it induces pleasure, forms knowledge, produces discourse.[1]

The academy is an institutional structure, yet we wanted to think differently about power as merely repressive or prohibitive in such a space. Foucault's analytic strategy was to study the deployment of power, a deployment that makes visible how the subject is constructed through social relations and cultural practices. These relations and practices are not simple projections of a central power (institutional or legal).[2] Rather, Foucault shows that power's existence is local, capillary, and reaches "into the very grain of individuals, touches their bodies and inserts itself into their actions and attitudes, their discourses, learning processes and everyday lives ... *within* the social body rather than *from above it*."[3] So we went to Foucault to help us think about power as productive and relational: power relations that are unstable, unequal, and produce knowledge about the self. We also found useful Foucault's unique connection of power and knowledge: not that one *is* the other ("knowledge is power"), but how they *express* one another. This became salient as we read data about Cassandra and Sera entering the academy as "new" professors and our locating, in the data, manifestations of power/knowledge in their practices as they negotiated power relations and new knowledge about themselves in a then-unknown terrain. We looked to Cassandra's and Sera's practices of power/knowledge to see how they might disrupt historical truths or struggle with (even evade) others' practices (students, colleagues, administrators) of power/knowledge which seek to contain them. The analytic question for our power/knowledge reading is: *How do power/knowledge relations and practices produce Cassandra's and Sera's multiple subjectivities as they venture into the academy as first-generation professors?*

The challenge of conducting a power/knowledge reading is that Foucault never created a method of analysis or template that would be transferable to our work (or even to his own future work). Foucault warns, "What I've written is never prescriptive either for me or for others – at most it's instrumental and tentative."[4] He called his methodological approaches

---

[1] Michel Foucault, *Power/Knowledge: Selected Interviews and Other Writings: 1972–1977*. Translated by Leo Marshall, Colin Gordon, John Mepham and Kate Soper, edited by Colin Gordon (New York: Pantheon Books, 1980), 199.

[2] *Ibid.*, 201.

[3] *Ibid.*, 39.

[4] Michel Foucault, *Power*. Translated by Robert Hurley *et al.*, edited by Paul Rabinow. *Essential Works of Foucault 1954–1984, Vol. III* (New York: The New Press, 2000), 240.

"gadgets," and encouraged researchers to use these "gadgets" as "thinking tools," transforming them to suit the purposes of their individual projects.[5] Neither was Foucault interested in developing a theory of power that would obligate analysts to deduce it, to reconstruct its beginnings, and to discover its stable, hidden rationality. Instead, Foucault argued that if power is a cluster of relations, then "the only problem is to provide oneself with a grid of analysis which makes possible an analytic of relations of power."[6] An analytics of power, therefore, is concerned with power's multiple functionings – how it is exercised and its effects – within specific networks of relations.

Foucault, arguing against structural and repressive modes of power, theorizes that power relations exist only when the field of possibilities is open and people may react to each other in various ways.[7] Foucault explains that power becomes possible through the "moving substrate" of unequal, yet unstable, local relations. By relations, Foucault means

> a relationship in which one person tried to control the conduct of the other ... These power relations are thus mobile, reversible, and unstable. It should also be noted that power relations are possible only insofar as the subjects are free. If one were completely at the other's disposal and became his thing, an object on which he could wreak boundless and limitless violence, there wouldn't be any relations of power. Thus, in order for power relations to come into play, there must be at least a certain degree of freedom on both sides.[8]

As a network of relations, power is "constantly in tension, in activity," and power relations are made of various points of instability that produce multiple sites and modes of resistance.[9] In this way, "there are no relations of power without resistances; the latter are all the more real and effective because they are *formed right at the point* where relations of power are exercised."[10]

Because power is embedded in relationships rather than existing merely as a possession that is wielded over others, focusing solely on "who exercises power over whom" is a limited investigation. Instead, Foucault teaches us to be more concerned with questions such as: "If power is exercised, what sort of exercise does it involve? In what does it consist? What is its mechanism?"[11] We learn from Foucault that locating who exercises power and on whom is fundamental to power analytics, but in order to map power relations, or to show power at work, it is also imperative to ask, "How does it happen?" Foucault advises,

---

[5] Foucault, *Power/Knowledge: Selected Interviews*, op. cit., 65.

[6] *Ibid.*, 199.

[7] As Foucault wrote, "Where the determining factors saturate the whole there is no relationship of power; slavery is not a power relationship when man is in chains;" he argued that analyzing a state of domination involves locating how and where resistance organizes, not the nature or essence of the domination. Michel Foucault, "The Subject and Power." In *Michel Foucault: Beyond Structuralism and Hermeneutics*, edited by Hubert L. Dreyfus and Paul Rabinow (Chicago: University of Chicago Press, 1982), 212.

[8] Michel Foucault, *Ethics: Subjectivity and Truth* (New York: The New Press, 1994), 292.

[9] Michel Foucault, *Discipline and Punish: The Birth of a Prison*. Translated by Alan Sheridan (New York: Vintage Books, 1979), 26.

[10] Foucault, *Power/Knowledge: Selected Interviews*, 142 [emphasis ours].

[11] *Ibid.*, 89.

Even if we reach the point of designating exactly all those people, all those 'decision-makers,' we will still not really know why and how the decision was made, how it came to be accepted by everybody, and how it is that it hurts a particular category of person.[12]

Foucault's work reminds us to study the *functions and effects* of power, not its origin.

Inversions

In formulating his power analytics, Foucault's inquiring stance is an inversion of traditional interpretive questions such as "What is power?" and "Where does power come from?" These traditional questions lead to searches for stable definitions, ontological essences, and foundational origins. Foucault inverts this mode of analysis, and instead investigates the productive *effects* of power as it circulates through the practices of people in their daily lives, studying "power at its extremities ... in its more regional and local forms."[13] So as we approached our power/knowledge reading of Cassandra's and Sera's interview data, we discerned the circulation of power among local relations: Cassandra, Sera, their colleagues, their students, their mentors, their administrators, and so on. We glommed onto those moments in the data where power was kept on the move among Cassandra and her others, as well as Sera and her others, and then we attempted to describe the mechanisms and technologies that enabled power relations. That is, when Cassandra and Sera struggled with/against power, how were they themselves vehicles of power? How did power operate on, through, and from them? To do this, we had to stay close to their practices (as re-membered and re-told by them in the interview) to explain how they themselves were vehicles of power, keeping power on the move. We followed Foucault and, rather than analyzing power from the point of view of its internal rationality, we looked to the data and analyzed power relations as something that circulates within and among the practices of people:

> Power is employed and exercised through a net-like organization. And not only do individuals circulate between its threads; they are always in the position of simultaneously undergoing and exercising this power. *Individuals are the vehicles of power, not its points of application* ... It is already one of the prime effects of power that certain bodies, certain gestures, certain discourses, certain desires, come to be identified and constituted as individuals. The individual is an *effect* of power and the *element* of its articulation.[14]

In this way, a power/knowledge reading is not concerned with the inherent meaning of practices. It is not always possible to know the origins or intentions of practices; therefore, the intentions of the subject are implicated in a power/knowledge reading. We are in agreement with Foucault when he argues, "People know what they do; they frequently know why they do what they do; but what they don't know is what what they do does."[15]

---

[12] Michel Foucault, *Politics, Philosophy, Culture: Interviews and Other Writings of Michel Foucault, 1977–1984* (New York: Routledge, 1990), 103–4.

[13] Foucault, *Power/Knowledge: Selected Interviews*, 96.

[14] *Ibid.*, 98 [emphasis ours].

[15] Dreyfus and Rabinow, *Michel Foucault: Beyond Structuralism and Hermeneutics*, op. cit, 187.

For example, consider this moment from Cassandra's interview in which she attempted to "make sense" of her power relations with students and colleagues in reference to her teaching and mentoring. She said,

> I know that that happens to people, probably several other people even within the College because students do things like that, but the interesting thing for me is I never know whether it's because I'm black or whether it's because I'm a woman or whether it's because it's both. There is this phenomenon that has been written about in some of the feminist literature, and it's specifically black feminist about the "double whammy." And so in my case, I don't know what's happening ... I find myself questioning as to whether they would do it to some of my colleagues.

We use this excerpt to illuminate that thinking with Foucault's relations of power is not about seeking the inherent meaning of practices. Even for Cassandra, finding meaning or attributing cause is not possible: we can never know people's intentions, and intentions exceed subjects' practices in terms of the *effects*. While practices may be planned and coordinated with aims and objectives, the overall effect may exceed any intention of the subject. In other words, according to Foucault, there is not a rational subject presiding over practices; the rationality of practices is found in the relations in which they are inscribed.[16] Therefore practices take on significance not for their truth value or inherent meaning, but for the ways in which they disrupt or sustain relations of power and advance knowledge. Analyzing practices from this perspective makes visible the power networks that enabled certain practices and therefore ensured their significance. Such cultural and material practices, then, are responsive interpretations of the situation at hand. People interpret their situations to both accommodate them and struggle against them to disrupt, contest, and re-signify.[17] Therefore analysis in a power/knowledge reading does not uncover hidden meaning because cultural and material practices are already interpretations. A power/knowledge reading involves *interpretations of interpretations*, which are found in the significance of cultural practices.

In our thinking with Foucault's power/knowledge, we read the initial struggles of Cassandra and Sera as new professors with an eye toward power relations that were "constantly in tension, in activity," and that expressed both control and freedom. We characterize the power relations among Cassandra and Sera and their students, administrators, colleagues (and so on) as moving around in the discursive field of higher education in which there were specific expectations and intelligible practices of teaching and mentoring, grounded in the mores of their respective universities. We attend to their practices as responsive (rather than intentional) while temporarily embedded in specific relations of power. And we notice how Cassandra and Sera are vehicles of power: how power worked on, through, and from them (rather than power ceasing in order simply to oppress or empower either of them once and for all).

Mapping power relations

Cassandra was aggressively recruited to her current institution, Regional State University, in 1992. Cassandra said that the university needed someone to "teach and enhance diversity,

---

[16] Michel Foucault, *The History of Sexuality. Volume 1: An Introduction*. Translated by Robert Hurley (New York: Vintage Books, 1980), 95.

[17] Dreyfus and Rabinow, *Michel Foucault: Beyond Structuralism and Hermeneutics*, xxvii.

and they had gotten a very large grant that allowed them to bring in minority, primarily African-American, students to get their master's degree in [my area of academic specialty] and they wanted someone to serve as their mentor and also to develop a course and some programs that would promote diversity within the profession, so that's what I came here to do." So in 1992, Cassandra was hired into Regional State University as an African-American woman academic at the level of associate professor to recruit and mentor African-American students in her area of specialty – a role that she had filled for fifteen years at Southern State University, a smaller, historically black university. Cassandra, then, entered Regional State, a university that was predominantly white in terms of faculty and students, a mid-sized comprehensive university that, as of 1992, had never promoted to full professor an African-American woman. Cassandra herself had been educated, as an undergraduate student in the late 1960s, at Southern State University, and she had returned to that state university to teach while completing her master's and doctoral degrees. Cassandra explained that she took seriously her role as a mentor and used practices with minority students (such as open-door policies that welcomed students into her office for "hanging out time") similar to those she had been using for many years before at Southern State, where she had begun her academic pursuits and firmly established herself as an effective teacher.

In the discursive field of the predominantly white university, Regional State, Cassandra was caught up in a web of power relations and practices that were constantly in tension. This was visible in Cassandra's description of a group of white students' responses to her mentoring of minority students. Cassandra explained the white students wrote "long, very critical letters that accused me of reverse discrimination and that I was showing favoritism to the black students." Cassandra said,

> My office is small now, but it was even smaller then and they [the black students] would be sitting all on the floor and everything and we just hung out together. I was a mother figure, that was pretty much the same thing that I did at [Southern State University] so I knew how to work with those students and I knew that [they] need a lot of personal attention. Now there was never a time when I didn't give the same amount of attention to any white student who wanted it.

The accusations travelled all the way up to the university's provost's office, and Cassandra wrote letter after letter of rebuttal. That particular case was resolved in Cassandra's favor, yet power relations stayed on the move. In her interview, Cassandra described constant power struggles with students. Power worked on, through, and from Cassandra and particular students as they were in continuous struggles with one another to produce and negotiate the "definition" of good teaching, learning, and mentoring at the predominantly white university. These power relations, as temporarily embedded within the particular discursive field of Regional State University, produced practices that were responses which made visible the power networks.

Cassandra described the practices of power, inscribed in relations, in her interview. She explained that a group of her students accused her of incompetence. The students wrote long letters to her Dean, and again, she had to write a rebuttal and the case was dismissed. She recounted many events during which students challenged her knowledge base during class by asking her "simple," "obvious," and "factual" questions. She said, "It was if they felt that I hadn't even read the book, that I wouldn't know the answer to that question that they were asking, which I thought was rather stupid. I would answer the question – but there would be those little things that they would put out there, especially earlier in the semester, to kind of see if I knew what I was talking about." These uneven practices of students challenging Cassandra (with her in turn having to justify her teaching) became more elaborated by students when they involved colleagues. She explained that some students have "actually gone to my colleagues and told them what I said [in class] and asked them what they thought about it." She went on to describe that students admitted verifying information from Cassandra's class with another professor:

> Most of the time they would support me, but there would actually be sometimes that my colleagues would disagree with what I said, even though it was on a topic where I was considered the expert, and they were not. I would never challenge their expertise in their area, but they would say, 'I don't agree with that.' And the students would then feel that I obviously didn't know what I was talking about because Dr. So and so didn't agree with me.

Cassandra's descriptions of her struggles with students and colleagues at Regional State University illustrate that there is no single source of power that may have oppressed her; power relations are endowed "with processes which are more or less adjusted to the situation."[18] That is, power relations are specific and local to subjects who are in mutual relations with one another. In the discursive field of Southern State University (the historically black institution where she began her career), Cassandra was certainly caught up in power struggles; yet the ones described above are unique to the discursive field of Regional State University. Cassandra, as a first-generation black woman professor, was caught up in power relationships with white students and white colleagues who attempted to control not only her actions, but also her subjectivity. They continually attempted to position her as less knowledgeable, and in the data excerpts above, power swirls about in the students' and colleagues' practices of challenging her knowledge and authority in the field. The individuals (Cassandra, students, colleagues) are vehicles of power via their practices of control. As Foucault describes, power "is everywhere; not because it embraces everything, but because it comes from everywhere"; it is not a consolidating and invincible unity or structure, but a repetitious and self-producing effect of mobile, strategical practices and relations within particular social networks.[19]

If we follow Foucault in thinking with power/knowledge, we shift our aim away from attempts to capture the meaning of the past and/or to understand the terminal point of the present in terms of the past (a linear or causal analysis). Alternatively, mapping power is to take up what Foucault called "the little question: 'What happens?'"[20] and analyze the social, cultural, and material practices in which power is productive. So rather than going after meaning, we map power by locating manifestations of power in present practices within current situations: where they arose, how they took shape, and their social effects (not their implicit meaning).[21] We have mapped the location of power relations within the discursive field of Cassandra's current teaching institution of higher education, and we have described the techniques of those power struggles in terms of accusations and rebuttals. We continue

[18] Foucault, *Power*, op. cit., 224.
[19] Foucault, *The History of Sexuality. Volume 1: An Introduction*, op. cit., 93.
[20] Michel Foucault, "The Subject and Power," op. cit., 217.
[21] Dreyfus and Rabinow, *Michel Foucault: Beyond Structuralism and Hermeneutics.*

to move away from the meaning of practices by now turning to one of the *effects* of practices of power: knowledge.

Knowledge and power/knowledge

Foucault uses the word *savoir* to signify constructed knowledge about oneself, knowledge that is produced in experience and relations with others. This constructed knowledge – *savoir* – is active and captures a subject's process of modification and transformation. *Savoir* is a practice of knowledge that not only defines, but also changes the way a subject participates in the world. What was most interesting to Foucault was how it is possible for subjects to understand themselves in relation to others, and how subjects use knowledge constructed within relations and practices to transform themselves.[22] Foucault's reading of Nietzsche directs him toward this understanding of *savoir*:

> There is knowledge only in the form of a certain number of actions that are different from one another and multifarious in their essence – actions by which the human being violently takes hold of a certain number of things, reacts to a number of certain situations, and subjects them to relations of force. This means that knowledge is always a certain strategic relation in which man [*sic*] is placed.[23]

Knowledge becomes an effect of these strategic relations, and because relations are fluid and contingent, knowledge is partial and situated. Knowledge neither reflects reality nor exists prior to relations. Knowledge is an *activity* that produces subjects and the ways in which they interact within and against their social and material worlds. A knowing subject, then, is an acting subject. Cassandra, caught up in a power network with particular students and colleagues, was continually forced to engage in practices such as defending her disciplinary expertise; these practices of *savoir* defined not only her participation in the power relations, but also how she understood herself in relation to others. In this way, both Cassandra's responses and the students' and colleagues' assertions are practices of power/knowledge.

In his effort to develop a relation between power and knowledge, Foucault is careful to explain that power and knowledge do not exist in simple opposition to encourage or restrict one another. They merge and become visible as forms of power/knowledge in cultural and material practices within specific conditions. So each time students challenged Cassandra's mentoring style, or sought out a colleague to "test" her teaching competence, they produced particular knowledge about Cassandra. As a vehicle of power, too, Cassandra kept power on the move by refusing the produced knowledge of her as inadequate or unqualified. In each practice, power and knowledge merged. Knowledge was formed by activity that is in itself a practice of power, and power was exercised by the distribution or restraint of knowledge. They expressed, rather than mirrored, one another.[24]

---

[22] *Ibid.*, 257.

[23] *Ibid.*, 14 [emphasis ours].

[24] For example, in volume one of *The History of Sexuality*, Foucault explains that various practices of power in medical, educational, and psychological observations about children's sexed bodies produced certain knowledge about children's sexuality. In turn, this knowledge of children's sexuality was distributed and restrained by doctors, families, psychologists, and educators who, in relations of power, took charge of children's sexuality to control and even to eradicate it.

Knowledge (like power) is not a possession, but something produced in subject (trans) formation. "Knowledge is not made for understanding; it is made for cutting," Foucault insists.[25] This "cutting" can be activity used to destabilize what seem to be fixed truths and foundational knowledge, such as Cassandra's practices of power/knowledge (letters of rebuttal in defense of her teaching and mentoring) that "cut through" students' produced "truths" about her. "Cutting" – resistance, criticism, struggle, dispersion – performs this work through the appearance of "particular, local, regional knowledge, a differential knowledge incapable of unanimity and which owes its force only to the harshness with which it is opposed by everything around it."[26] In other words, "cutting" works to produce Cassandra as a knowing subject in particular ways, and in response to specific power/knowledge practices.

Power produces things, such as knowledge, subjectivity, and resistance. Cassandra's descriptions of teaching and mentoring, caught up in power relations with students, colleagues, and administrators in the academy, illustrate how power and knowledge combine to produce something different. Cassandra's power/knowledge reactions were local, embedded in specific relations of power, and used at times to destabilize, resist, and transform. Now, we turn to an analysis of how *savoir* was produced through Cassandra's practices of power; or the ways in which her participation in the world of the academy was redefined and changed.

In her interview, Cassandra said that she was content at the small, historically black institution "playing the teacher/mentor role." However, making the move to a larger university with what she defined as "unwritten scholarship expectations" resulted in Cassandra writing a textbook that "has been very well received." She went on to say,

> The book is ten years old, but I still keep getting these checks and so that has opened up all kinds of doors for me in terms of name recognition and in terms of offers to do conferences and things. And I've become, in some circles, the go-to person for an answer to that kind of thing, and so when people ask certain kinds of questions they either email me or they will call me to do conferences. I had an opportunity to do one video tape on that kind of a topic and so it just really made me feel good about carving out my little niche and doing well in that professional endeavor.

Cassandra explained that she "used to have a very, very low self-concept," but that writing an academic book has helped her to be "less affected" when a student or colleague challenges her expertise. This description of Cassandra's responsive practices of power/knowledge exposes the conditions that shape their possibility and acceptance at a given time. Importantly, these conditions involve a multiplicity of discourses and power relations that occur simultaneously and operate through complex networks. That is, Cassandra's writing a textbook was an unpredictable power/knowledge practice in response to discursive institutional expectations and pressures. Yet her writing, as a power/knowledge practice, formed a new power network in which she was temporarily embedded. This new power chain moved through her to produce a different way of responding to challenges from students and colleagues regarding her expertise.[27] More confident, or "less affected," ways of dealing with

---

[25] Michel Foucault, "Nietzsche, Genealogy, History." In *The Foucault Reader*, edited by Paul Rabinow (New York: Pantheon Books, 1984), 88.

[26] Foucault, *Power/Knowledge: Selected Interviews*, 82.

[27] We thank Kate McCoy for this insight.

accusations became available via this unpredictable power/knowledge relay – one that produced not only a new power dynamic, but also resistance (in the form of "knowledge for cutting"). Something new – *savoir* – is produced for Cassandra to take up and use when students and colleagues attempt to position her as someone with little legitimacy for academic life. Therefore power/knowledge is a perpetual and reciprocal (rather than causal) relationship in which power creates and accumulates knowledge, and knowledge induces effects of power.[28] Thus power/knowledge practices cannot be determined in advance, nor do power/knowledge networks remain stable; they are *responsive* ways of behaving that become possible within other relations or situations of power/knowledge. And they produce unpredictable effects, such as subjectivity.

We learn from Foucault that power/knowledge relations and practices are "continuous and uninterrupted processes which subject our bodies, govern our gestures, dictate our behaviors ... subjects are gradually, progressively, really and materially constituted through a multiplicity of organisms, forces, energies, materials, desires, thoughts."[29] An indispensable aspect of a power/knowledge reading, then, is disentangling the complex production of subjectivity as an effect of power/knowledge relations and practices. Just as subjects do not possess power or knowledge, neither do they possess fixed identities that are self-referential. A power/knowledge reading of the effects of cultural and material practices within relations illustrates how subjects are in a double-process of being produced as well as transforming themselves.

Power/knowledge and subjectivity

Because power relations are too subtle and too complex to produce knowledge that is established as stable truth, power/knowledge practices within relations of power do not produce a subject who progresses through history in a linear fashion with a stable, coherent identity. Instead, power relations produce subjects who exceed their own identities, subjects who can never know in advance the effects of power relations embedded in their cultural practices. As Foucault explains, for power to produce a subject, the production would be "the destruction of what we are as well as the creation of a completely different thing, a total innovation."[30] This idea of a "total innovation" points to Foucault's concept of power/knowledge as *practice* and how this practice produces subjectivity.

If we follow Foucault and accept that the subject can be conceived differently from one who is either "transcendental in relation to the field of events or runs in its empty sameness throughout the course of history,"[31] then our purpose in thinking with power/knowledge entails an analysis of the subject's "actual destruction, its decomposition, its explosion, its conversion into something else."[32] In the interview data, we noticed moments of "destruction, explosion, conversion" in Cassandra's and Sera's subject positions, and we situate those transformations in power/knowledge relations within which Cassandra and Sera are temporarily forced. The ways in which power/knowledge plays out as they encounter the academy as first-generation professors enables the production of something new and different.

[28] Foucault, *Power*, xvi.
[29] *Ibid.*, 74.
[30] *Ibid.*, 275.
[31] Foucault, *Power/Knowledge: Selected Interviews*, 117.
[32] Foucault, *Power*, 247.

Sera began her first years as a new assistant professor at Prairie College. This particular university was caught up in a discursive field in which teaching accountability in higher education was measured and evaluated by students, and according to Sera, "they [administrators] were very serious" regarding the evaluations. In this discursive field, what "counted" as good teaching was linked directly to objective, numerical rankings. This discursive field produced techniques for surveillance by anonymous bodies (unnamed students) that regulated and produced professors' subject positions. Sera said,

> Once I had my PhD, I expected myself to be this person I thought I was supposed to be. And I was in this horrible, horrible – I was in the very, very wrong place for me. Not only did I feel like I didn't know enough to be a professor, even though I just went through seven years of all of this deep learning and deep thinking, I knew that if a student asked me a question, I still might not know the answer.

Sera went on to explain that at Prairie, as a professor she was expected to achieve high scores on her teaching evaluations. She clarified, "If you didn't hit it [top evaluation scores] all the way down, not only did the chair come and make an appointment with you to talk about those places where you didn't hit it, but you had to write up a strategy for how you were going to deal with bringing that 4 up to a 5 or that 4.5 up to a 5."

This discursive field of surveillance and evaluation enables power/knowledge practices (teaching evaluations by students) that produce and regulate knowing subjects. Sera's comment, "I expected myself to be this person I thought I was supposed to be" is a response to the power/knowledge relations and practices of the academy that produce her as an expert. Yet in this particular discursive field, the technocratic, evaluation-driven accountability structures in the academy incite a power/knowledge relay through all people involved, and produce Sera as what she describes as a professor who "didn't know a lot of stuff." She added, "And so they [students] would play with me a little bit about it." She said that with faculty and students there was always "niceness on the surface," but went on to say,

> I was talking to a student, and then he said something that seemed very nice, and he smiled. And I thought oh, that's cool. And then maybe an hour later, I thought he was totally insulting me, and I couldn't read it. I didn't know. And then after I had seen that, I started really noticing it in just the interactions with students. I had a student come up to me and say why do you have to be so expository. And she stormed out of the class. And I went and looked up the word expository. I mean, I just had no idea what she was talking about and what she wanted from me.

Sera's descriptions of power relations between her and her students is not of power as a possession that is transcendent to the discursive field in which it is temporarily located. Rather, Sera is caught up in multiple power relations within the academy: between her and students *and* between her and institutional evaluation structures that attempt to position her as someone who is supposed to "know enough" to *be* a professor. Multiple and disperse power/knowledge practices, that appear superficially "nice," in the same discursive field produce Sera as someone who does not quite "fit in" to the structure.

Furthermore, according to Foucault, other historical conditions that involve a multiplicity of discourses and power relations can occur simultaneously and operate through complex networks. Therefore Sera's history as a first-generation college graduate and academic, her growing up in "poverty and struggle," the instability of her childhood home life, the lack of savvy concerning all aspects of undergraduate and graduate college life as a student, exist not as foundational experiences or stable contexts. Rather, they serve as discursive constraints that make up a larger network of power/knowledge in which Sera constantly navigates as she is produced *and* as she attempts to create new *savoir*. It is in this dynamic that Sera emerges as a split subject: as one who is subjected to power/knowledge, but also one who is offered a range of subject positions from which to choose. Cassandra, too, expressed multiple subjectivities in response to power/knowledge demands; for example, the discursive fields of two different academic institutions were vying for Cassandra's subjectivity: one historically black, that emphasized particular ways of teaching and mentoring; the other predominantly white, that refused her mentoring style and expected scholarly production as a measure of success.[33] These competing discursive fields offered Cassandra a range of conflicting subject positions and produced Cassandra not as a stable subject, but as one who converted into *something else*.

This "something else" points to the relations among power, knowledge, and subjectivity. Foucault's important question about the subject is, "Might there not be experiences in which the subject might be able to dissociate from itself, sever the relation with itself, lose its identity?"[34] Foucault's later work on power/knowledge and the subject is focused on that question: how subjects transform themselves, or create new knowledge about themselves and their worlds, within relations of power. However, this "transformation" is not subjects' transcending any sort of core identity; rather, the "transformation" is explosion, excessiveness, incoherence, a refusal of containment. While Cassandra was produced, through power/knowledge practices, as scholarly within one discursive field, she was at once multiply produced as an expert *and* as discriminatory regarding teaching and mentoring minority students within two conflicting discursive fields. The question remains: how is it possible for subjects to transform themselves in relation to others (construct subjectivity) via knowledge produced within power relations and practices?

Sera, too, offers insight into the double move of being produced by power/knowledge relations and practices, and her responding to the ensuing range of subject positions that are enabled by discourse. In her interview, she discussed how, by the end of her two-year tenure at Prairie College, she had a "following of students" who were part of the Prairie College "underground." As she put it, there were "a bunch of students [whose] parents were making them be there, and they were partying. I could make these comments [in class], and they would just crack up." She continued by saying, "I was definitely starting to gain some comfort there. And a comfort in my role as trying to figure out how I was going to say that I didn't know the answer without saying, 'I don't know the answer.' So figuring out ways to do that." So Sera's subjectivity, too, shifted within relations of power/knowledge to produce different *savoir*: a practice of knowledge that not only defines (temporarily), but also changes the way a subject participates in the world. Sera describes "new" power/knowledge practices that produce a different subject position in this way:

> I guess what I'm seeing now is that I like the academic life more than I – like I see myself doing this work for a long time. I know people struggle with, well, I could make

[33] We thank Fran Huckaby for this insight.
[34] Foucault, *Power*, 248.

a bunch of money in industry or I could be a consultant. And maybe it's because I feel comfortable here and because I feel like I'm really learning a lot right now. Every morning, what I like to do is drink a cup of coffee and read an article or read a chapter or something. And I love that. And I'm getting a little bit better at public speaking stuff in terms of like teaching a class face-to-face or [online]. So I guess I'm feeling like this is fine and the life seems like a good life.

Sera's practices of power/knowledge – relationships with "underground" students as well as reading and learning more about her discipline – take on significance for how they disrupt relations of power and advance knowledge. The "cutting" practice of *savoir* is evident here in that Sera's responsive strategies to power/knowledge practices that attempt to contain her produce her as a split subject. Neither Sera nor Cassandra may ever completely escape power relations that produce them as "not good enough" for the academy; yet as vehicles of power, their own responsive (however indirect) practices of power/knowledge produce different conditions that allow more freedom and make room for new ways of interacting with the world.

Thinking with power/knowledge

We used Foucault's theory of power/knowledge to think with so that we could explain how the cultural and material practices of Cassandra and Sera, as first-generation women faculty, combine power and knowledge to produce their subjectivities. The analytic question for our power/knowledge reading was: *How do power/knowledge relations and practices produce Cassandra's and Sera's multiple subjectivities as they venture into the academy as first-generation professors?* Rather than analyzing how Cassandra and Sera possessed power, or were "empowered" by others (as receivers), we were interested in how power was kept on the move among them in relations with students, families, colleagues, and administrators as they entered the academy.

We located, in the data, manifestations of power/knowledge in practices within current situations, and explained where they arose, how they took shape, and what were their social effects (not their implicit meaning). For this reading, power/knowledge practices arose as both Cassandra and Sera negotiated power relations with students and administrators who attempted to define and contain their teaching and mentoring. The power relations took shape in a net-like organization, in local contexts, that functioned to keep power circulating. Because a power/knowledge reading is an effort to interrogate the rationality of the present,[35] we looked to Cassandra's and Sera's practices of power/knowledge to see how they might have disrupted historical truths or struggled with (even evaded) others' (students, administrators) practices of power/knowledge which sought to contain them. These struggles and evasions within power relations produced different knowledges and subjectivities that, in turn, made their academic lives into that which (temporarily) sustains.

More on power/knowledge

The following texts are offered, not as *the* texts to consult, but as providing an entry point for those who are new to the writings of Foucault and would like to learn more about

[35] Foucault, *Power/Knowledge: Selected Interviews*, 242.

power/knowledge. We list the secondary texts first as a continuation of the "schematic cues" presented in the Interlude, which readers can use as a brace as they enter this new theoretical terrain. Following the secondary texts are suggested entry points for approaching the writing of Foucault, and finally, research exemplars that illustrate additional examples of *thinking with* power/knowledge.

Secondary texts

Popkewitz, Thomas S. and Marie Brennan (eds). *Foucault's Challenge: Discourse, Knowledge, and Power in Education*. New York: Teachers College Press, 1998.
Rajchman, John. *Michel Foucault: The Freedom of Philosophy*. New York: Columbia University Press, 1985.
Sawicki, Jana. *Disciplining Foucault: Feminism, Power, and the Body*. New York: Routledge, 1991.

Primary texts

Foucault, Michel. *Discipline and Punish: The Birth of a Prison*. Translated by Alan Sheridan. New York: Vintage Books, 1979.
——*The History of Sexuality. Volume 1: An Introduction*. Translated by Robert Hurley. New York: Vintage Books, 1980.
——*Power/Knowledge: Selected Interviews and Other Writings: 1972–1977*. Translated by Leo Marshall, Colin Gordon, John Mepham and Kate Soper, edited by Colin Gordon. New York: Pantheon Books, 1980.
——*Power*. Translated by Robert Hurley *et al.*, edited by Paul Rabinow. *Essential Works of Foucault 1954–1984, Vol. III*. New York: The New Press, 2000.

Research exemplars

Howley, A. and R. Harnett. "Pastoral Power and the Contemporary University: A Foucauldian Analysis." *Educational Theory* 42 (1992): 271–82.
Huckaby, M. Francyne. "Researcher/Researched: Relations of Vulnerability/Relations of Power." *International Journal of Qualitative Studies in Education* 24, no. 2 (2011): 165–83.
Jackson, Alecia. "Multiple Annies: Feminist Poststructural Theory and the Making of a Teacher." *Journal of Teacher Education* 52, no. 5 (2001): 386–97.

Why Butler?

Critique is understood as an interrogation of the terms by which life is constrained in order to open up the possibility for different modes of living; in other words, not to celebrate difference as such but to establish more inclusive conditions for sheltering and maintaining life that resists models of assimilation.[1]

Judith Butler's theory of performativity is central to all of her work that seeks to undo normative categories that place rigid structures on how people live out their lives. Butler's performativity, as it relies more on linguistic action than on the theatrical, explores (and exposes) how gender identities get done (and undone) as reiterative and citational practices within discourse, power relations, historical experiences, cultural practices, and material conditions. Moving beyond the binary frame set up in language via humanism and structuralism (man/woman), Butler's theory of gender performativity works to unsettle the stabilizing gender categories that attempt to normalize and regulate people, and accentuates a process of *repetition* that produces gendered subjectivity. This repetition is not a performance *by* a subject, but a performativity that *constitutes* a subject and thus produces the space of conflicting subjectivities. Paradoxically, agency is derived from within this constitution as subjects' performative acts both reproduce *and* contest the foundations and origins of stable identity categories. As Butler develops her theory from *Gender Trouble* to *Undoing Gender*, she explores "livability" through various philosophical frameworks: "The difference between *Undoing Gender* and *Gender Trouble* probably has to do with my sense that a livable life does require recognition of some kind and that there are occasions in which names do sustain us, that there's a sustaining function of the name."[2]

Butler's theory of performativity draws from Foucault's theory of power relations, Hegel's phenomenology, Althusser's theory of interpellation, Spinoza's ethics, and Adorno's and Nietzsche's theories of morality. Butler's theory of gender requires *normative identity categories* to make its point about performativity. In relation to our research project with first-generation academic women, we examine the numerous identity and ideological categories that emerged in Cassandra's and Sera's data and expose the discourses and power relations that regulate, make intelligible, and make *normative* the categories that subjected them. There are identity categories all over the interview data that we collected with Cassandra and Sera: first-generation, academic, woman, black, white, poor, and so on. Other social scientists

---

[1] Judith Butler, *Undoing Gender* (New York: Routledge, 2004), 4.
[2] Judith Butler, "Conversation with Judith Butler III." In *Judith Butler in Conversation: Analyzing the Texts and Talk of Everyday Life*, edited by Bronwyn Davies (New York: Routledge, 2008), 141.

(even qualitative researchers!) may want us to show causal or correlational relationships in and among the data. For example, one approach might be to ask, "Are Cassandra's and Sera's behaviors and/or choices attributed to their gender? Or their race? Or their class?" Performativity, however, claims neither a sovereign nor an intentional subject who behaves or makes choices by their own volition. Butler, following Derrida, explains that "intentions *do* exist, that's not the problem; it's just that intention is not the ground of discourse, it's not the foundation of discourse ... Derrida asks us how we are to locate intention within the field of discourse, which is not the same as doing away with it altogether."[3] That is, the question is not, "What does the subject intend?" Rather, the question is, "How does discourse foreclose the field of what can be intended or said?"[4] Put another way, language-as-a-social-practice does not *reflect* the intention (or action) of the individual; language *produces* the discursive possibilities of performance and therefore "the doer" becomes an effect of that language. Given such a perspective on language and subjectivity, the analytic question for this chapter is: *What are the performative acts that (re)produce Cassandra's and Sera's subjectivities as academic women?*

Schematic cues

Agency. From a humanist perspective, agency is something possessed by humans and is seen as the ability to act on or act in the world. To ascribe "agency" to someone is to imply that one is a voluntary actor making choices that are willed rather than determined. The agency of the subject in a poststructural paradigm is an enactment, not something that an individual possesses. Butler writes that "gender is not a performance that a prior subject elects to do, but gender is performative in the sense that it constitutes as an *effect* the very subject it appears to express."[5] There is neither a prior intention nor a "doer *behind* the deed" of performativity.[6]

Humanism and language. Humanism draws from Rationalist philosophers of the seventeenth century who claimed that knowledge of the world is mediated by innate structures, and these innate structures lead us to the universal, unchanging structure of reality. Philosophers such as Descartes[7] set out to formulate clear, rational principles that could be organized into a system of truths from which accurate information about the world could be deduced. The Cartesian vanity of one clear Truth (one way of thinking about and hence being in the world), and of things/people having their own true and unchangeable essence or form, fueled the definitions of other "humanisms" that have proliferated in the past three centuries. Enlightenment humanism of the eighteenth century defined the essence of "man" as a rational, reasoning individual and the center, creator, and dominator of meaning, truth, freedom, and reality.[8] Kant's theories of radical individualism and rational judgment privileged *a priori* knowledge as clear and true; Kant believed that we have a capacity to

---

[3] Judith Butler, *Judith Butler in Conversation*, op. cit., 190.

[4] *Ibid.*

[5] Judith Butler, "Imitation and Gender Insubordination." In A. Garry and M. Pearsall (eds), *Women, Knowledge, and Reality: Explorations in Feminist Philosophy*, 2nd edn (New York: Routledge, 1996), 380.

[6] Judith Butler, "For a Careful Reading." In *Feminist Contentions: A Philosophical Exchange* (New York: Routledge, 1995), 134.

[7] René Descartes, *Discourse on Method and Meditations on First Philosophy*. Translated by D. A. Cress (1637; repr. Indianapolis: Hackett, 1998).

[8] Isaac Kramnick (ed.), *The Portable Enlightenment Reader* (New York: Penguin, 1995).

possess knowledge without an appeal to experience.[9] For example, "man is free" is an *a priori* judgment because the idea of freedom is connected to all "men" even before we have experience of what "man" or "freedom" is. Such is the designation of essence, in which objects conform to the rationality of the mind, and the mind is structured so that it imposes its way of knowing upon its objects without contamination by the senses or by experience. This concept of humanism (as metanarrative) was fully articulated in the nineteenth century, and remains a powerful shaper of identity and existence today; accordingly, it follows that the constant theme of *essentialism* can be used as a definition of humanism.[10] The word "humanism" refers to something essential and universal, with a defining quality that is shared by everyone, regardless of race, class, gender, history, or culture; "it is a condition, timeless and localized."[11] A humanist view of language searches for stable, coherent meanings and origins of things – the essence of the "thing itself" that is out there, objective, waiting to be perceived. Thus the word *identity* is a humanist signifier in that it evinces an essential nature that stabilizes meaning about people who belong to a particular identity category, such as woman. Butler's theory of performativity works against views of humanist identity.

Sign systems. Saussurean semiology, as a structuralist project, is interested in isolating language as a stable, well-defined system whose internal relations between words could be scientifically analyzed.[12] Ferdinand de Saussure[13] rejects a humanist version of language as a list of terms corresponding to a list of things, as ideas existing independently of words; instead, Saussure defines language – *langue* – as the whole linguistic system, a social structure into which individuals are born that makes their speech *possible*. In his semiology, Saussure isolates the structure and analyzes linguistic units, which he claims are dual in nature, and calls them *signs*. According to Saussure, signs are made up of the *signifier* (word – written or spoken) and the *signified* (idea or concept), and chains of signs make language. Saussure claims that signs do not have an essential, intrinsic meaning, but derive meaning from their relationship to other words in the system; this is a negative relationship, where signs get their meaning from *what they are not*. Saussure writes, "In a sign, what matters more than any idea or sound associated with it is what other signs surround it ... In isolation, [signs] are nothing: the opposition between them is everything," and he believes that the entire mechanism of language is based on these oppositions.[14] Saussure makes this conclusion based on his first principle of the sign: it is arbitrary; there is no natural connection between the signifier and the signified. Weedon provides an excellent example: "It is not anything intrinsic to the signifier 'whore' that gives it its meaning, but rather its difference from other signifiers of womanhood such as 'virgin' and 'mother'."[15] For Saussure, meaning is not out there to be discovered by our minds; meaning is conceptual and generated by the arbitrary structures of language.

[9] Robert Audi (ed.), *The Cambridge Dictionary of Philosophy* (Cambridge, UK: Cambridge University Press, 1999).

[10] Tony Davies, *Humanism* (London: Routledge, 1997).

[11] *Ibid.*, 32.

[12] Simon Clarke, *The Foundations of Structuralism* (Brighton: Harvester Press, 1981).

[13] Ferdinand de Saussure, *Course in General Linguistics.* Translated by Robert Harris (1915; repr. La Salle: Open Court, 1986).

[14] *Ibid.*, 118, 120.

[15] Chris Weedon, *Feminist Practice and Poststructural Theory*, 2nd edn (Oxford: Blackwell, 1997), 23.

Structuralism and language. Humanism suffered severely when structuralism took hold and brought with it the provocative slogan "the death of the subject." Structuralism is a way of analyzing the world in terms of locating and describing permanent, closed structures. Viewing language as a structure, Saussure[16] broadens the concept of language from mere nomenclature or something intrinsic to individuals: both of these perspectives ignore the social and structural aspect of the linguistic sign. With this rejection of the rationality and the individuality of language, Descartes' statement "I think, therefore I am" is revised to "I do not speak, I am spoken." In this way, "structuralism kicks away the twin pillars of humanism: the sovereignty of rational consciousness, and the authenticity of individual speech ... Thought and speech, which for the humanist had been the central substance of identity, are located elsewhere, and the self is a vacancy."[17] Saussure writes that language is a stable structure that we "inherit," that we are "incapable of changing," and that we have "no choice but to accept."[18] In this way, the individual speaker disappears and is absorbed by the structure (hence "the death of the subject"). Saussure[19] emphasized the social – not individual or external – aspect of language: meaning is derived from a *shared value* of a sign that is not intuitive but *constructed* through the shared language. Reality, then, is produced by the language we have at our command (and that commands us, in the structuralist view). In this way, rules that organize, regulate, and normalize language do the same with identity; this organization and regulation is what Butler's theory of performativity is working within and against.

Poststructuralism and language. Both structuralism and poststructuralism share the basic assumption that language is not a medium for expression – that language produces rather than reflects reality. Each theory emphasizes the social nature of language and the arbitrariness of the sign. However, poststructural theories of language *radicalize* some of the basic tenets of structuralism. For one, poststructuralism critiques ahistorical, inherent, coherent structures (as defined by structuralists) that possess stable centers, origins, and foundations. Poststructural theories of language *reconstruct* structural centers as unstable, contingent, situational, and historical. Derrida posits that every structure has been given a center – a point of presence, an origin – in order to organize it and *limit* its "play," its transformation.[20] When a structure's center limits its margins, meaning is closed off, and the signified becomes transcendental. For example, a transcendental signified for the signifier "woman" would make "woman" the same everywhere for all time. A transcendental signified shuts down all possibilities of multiple meaning and keeps binaries in rigid form, pushing the other term – the signified's difference that gives it its identity – to marginal status. In rejection of transcendental signs with meaning that is self-identical and self-present, poststructuralism seeks to liberate the signifier and to open up signs, to cut meaning loose, and to keep that difference (and therefore meaning) at play. To keep meaning at play, poststructuralism posits that signifieds are not simply the product of the difference between *two* signifiers, but the spin-off of a potentially *endless* play of signifiers.[21] By dividing the signifier from the signified, claiming there is no unified, stable distinction between the two (as Saussure would have it), poststructuralism posits that the meaning of a signified is never

---

[16] Saussure, *Course in General Linguistics*, op. cit.

[17] Davies, *Humanism*, op. cit., 60.

[18] Saussure, *Course in General Linguistics*, 72.

[19] *Ibid.*

[20] Jacques Derrida, *Of Grammatology*. Translated by Gayatri Spivak (1967; repr. Baltimore: Johns Hopkins University Press, 1997).

[21] Terry Eagleton, *Literary Theory: An Introduction* (Minneapolis: University of Minnesota Press, 1982).

fully present or fixed; instead, there is a constant deferral of meaning, leaving traces of other signifiers and signifieds that had to be excluded for the sign to be itself. This is the work of language, constructing (not reflecting) meaning through the process of what Derrida calls *différance* – an invented word which combines the meanings of "to differ" and "to defer" (see Interlude I) – to name this unfolding of difference.[22]

---

[22] Jacques Derrida, *Margins of Philosophy*. Translated by Alan Bass (1968; repr. Chicago: University of Chicago Press, 1982).

Chapter 5

Butler: Thinking with performativity

> Power acts on the subject in at least two ways: first, as what makes the subject possible, the condition of its possibility, and second, as what is taken up and reiterated in the subject's "own" acting ... The conditions not only make possible the subject but enter into the subject's formation. They are made present in the *acts* of that formation and in the *acts* of the subject that follow.[1]

Judith Butler's theory of performativity is central to all of her work that seeks to undo normative categories that place rigid structures on how people live out their lives. Butler's performativity, as it relies more on linguistic action than the theatrical, explores (and exposes) how gender identities get done (and undone) as a reiterative and citational practice within discourse, power relations, historical experiences, cultural practices, and material conditions. Moving beyond the binary frame set up in language via humanism and structuralism (man/woman), Butler's theory of gender performativity works to unsettle the stabilizing gender categories that attempt to normalize and regulate people, and accentuates a process of *repetition* that produces gendered subjectivity. This repetition is not a performance *by* a subject but a performativity that *constitutes* a subject and thus produces the space of conflicting subjectivities. Paradoxically, agency is derived from within this constitution as subjects' performative acts both reproduce *and* contest the foundations and origins of stable identity categories.

Therefore the goal for this chapter is to elaborate both Cassandra's and Sera's performativity. What we, as qualitative researchers, find illuminating and exciting about thinking with performativity is how it makes visible the constitution of the subject with/in conflicting and simultaneous, yet temporal, contexts. In this way, performativity offers a way out of stable, humanist binaries and instead emphasizes the doing and undoing of gender constituted through repetition; that is, gender as an *effect* of practice. The effects of gender practices point to the performative dimension of gender, as opposed to gender as a mere performance: "Gender is not a performance that a prior subject elects to do, but gender is performative in the sense that it constitutes as an *effect* the very subject it appears to express."[2] There is neither a prior intention nor a "doer *behind* the deed" of performativity.[3] That is, people do not choose their gendered identities; gender gets produced as people repeat

---

[1] Judith Butler, *The Psychic Life of Power: Theories in Subjection* (Stanford: Stanford University Press, 1997), 14.

[2] Judith Butler, "Imitation and Gender Insubordination." In *Women, Knowledge, and Reality: Explorations in Feminist Philosophy*, edited by Ann Garry and Marilyn Pearsall (New York: Routledge, 1996), 380.

[3] Judith Butler, "For a Careful Reading." In *Feminist Contentions: A Philosophical Exchange* (New York: Routledge, 1995), 134.

themselves. People do not take on roles to act out as in a performance; *people become subjects through repetition.* Gender, then, is a verb, a doing – not a doing *by* a subject, but a performative doing that "constitutes the identity it is purported to be ... the very 'expressions' that are said to be its results."[4] Butler clarifies,

> For a performative to work, it must draw upon and recite a set of linguistic conventions which have traditionally worked to bind or engage certain kinds of effects ... This power of recitation is not a function of an individual's *intention*, but is an effect of historically sedimented linguistic conventions.[5]

The analytic question for this chapter is: *What are the performative acts that (re)produce Cassandra's and Sera's subjectivities as academic women?*

Consider this example from Cassandra's interview:

> [Relationships] started changing even when I was an undergrad because people that I was really close with during my high school years – well, the relationship changed because it was as if I had to prove that I didn't think that I was better than they were. It wasn't because I was doing anything differently, it was because their perception of me was different. So I found myself being like a chameleon because I would try to act like the way that I had always acted when I was around them. And I would talk the way that I'd always talked when I was around them, and then when I went back to college I would fit back in the mold there.

Cassandra goes on to say that she does "this flip-flop kind of thing all the time" with hometown family, friends, and people in the community who are either not college-educated or, if they are, not of the academy. She explained that she does linguistic *and* bodily things like "speak the local dialect" and "try as much as possible to fit in" to keep up social relations at home. "Speaking the local dialect" and using other behaviors to "fit in" are citational practices that take up the norms of the culture and produce Cassandra as an effect of the performance. Yet these performatives do not *fully* constitute her because there was another "mold" to fit into when she went back to college. Therefore the repetition never looks the same, never exhausts its performative possibilities, and therefore "constitutes and contests the *coherence* of that 'I'."[6] Cassandra did not mention how these performative acts made her feel (bewildered, betrayed, comforted – or a bit of each), but she did say, "I know that I'm being successful because – pretty much they'll say things like, they call me Jane there, my middle name. They say, 'That Jane, she ain't changed a bit.'" She also explained, "Sometimes when I'm doing my workshops I tell people that I am actually a multicultural individual. There are different roles that I play in different settings and I've learned how to slip out of one and slip into the other one very easily." Cassandra's slipping subjectivities is performative in Judith Butler's use of the concept: the iterative process of making and unmaking subjectivity that produces her as an unfinished product of discourse and power. Cassandra's subjectivity – or what she describes as her "flip-flopping" – is not simply playing or performing a role. Instead, who-she-is-in-the-moment is produced by – and bound to – particular discourses (the academy, her southern hometown) and relations of power (her

---

[4] Judith Butler, *Gender Trouble: Feminism and the Subversion of Identity* (New York: Routledge, 1990), 25.
[5] Butler, "For a Careful Reading," op. cit., 134.
[6] Butler, "Imitation and Gender Insubordination," op. cit., 376 [emphasis ours].

friends, her family). Cassandra does not emerge as a stable subject; she neither fully gives in to the normative categories that attempt to contain her, nor does she completely refuse them. Her gender cites the normative constraints of her social world, and with each different repetition, her subjectivity gets made again.

Sites of necessary trouble

Butler writes that identity categories are "sites of necessary trouble" because they are out of control to *fully* signify: what is excluded always returns to disrupt its meaning.[7] For example, when Cassandra's performativity excludes what she might deem her academic ways of behaving when she is at home with her family, other expressions of her subjectivity are always silent, erased, hidden – perhaps to herself, but mostly to others. It becomes compulsory, then, for Cassandra's performativity to emerge as "provisional," an "error" or a "mistake."[8]

Butler explains that, as sites of trouble, identity categories are normative (and troubling) because they attempt to regulate people through a process of interpellation, a linguistic act of *hailing*, or calling an individual that initiates her into subjected status and therefore into "a certain order of social existence."[9] This hailing (or, "Hey, you!") is an act of forming the subject to comply with and obey the laws of its domain. Conformity is the anticipated outcome, a compulsion that regulates and governs the norms of identity formation and intelligibility. In her theory of performativity, Butler extends Althusser's linguistic interpellation to assert that interpellation can function without a subject's acknowledgment, or "turning around" to respond to the "Hey, you!"; that is, "the linguistic constitution of the subject can take place without a subject's knowing."[10] An example of this is how Cassandra is still interpellated by her home community even when she is away at the university; her family maintains an expectation of Cassandra that incites her into the circuit of recognition when she returns home. Butler also extends Althusser's linguistic interpellation to include bodily acts, which "give rise to language ... language carries bodily aims, and performs bodily deeds that are not always understood by those who use language to accomplish certain conscious aims."[11] Put simply, Cassandra can say one thing, but do another with her body – and *vice versa*. Therefore conformity (as a response to interpellation) can be full of paradox and excessiveness – the very conditions of performativity.

Cassandra gives an account of this paradoxical conformity when she explains how others "expect" her to "be" an academic by pressuring her to achieve in the areas of teaching and scholarship, when she would rather focus her work on providing professional, therapeutic services in her discipline to the community; she sees herself as more of a practitioner than a scholar. In the following passage, she explains how she is being hailed into the social norms of the academy:

---

[7] *Ibid.*, 372.

[8] *Ibid.*, 372–73.

[9] Judith Butler, *Bodies that Matter: On the Discursive Limits of "Sex"* (New York: Routledge, 1993), 121.

[10] Judith Butler, *Excitable Speech: A Politics of the Performative* (New York: Routledge, 1997), 33. Butler goes on to write, "Interpellation is an address that regularly misses its mark, it requires the recognition of an authority at the same time that it confers identity through successfully compelling that recognition. Identity is a function of that circuit, but does not preexist it. The mark interpellation makes is not descriptive, but inaugurative. It seeks to introduce a reality rather than report on an existing one." (p. 33).

[11] Judith Butler, *Undoing Gender* (New York: Routledge, 2004), 199.

This is my thirty-ninth year in university teaching and I really feel like I am such a misfit for academic culture. I don't know how I lasted in the culture, because I don't fit in neatly with what you would generally think of as being academic, the academic culture. In terms of when I'm sitting around with people and the kinds of things that they love to talk about and they get excited about certain topics. Even though I'm located in [this unit of the university], I was never trying to be an educator. I was trying to be a [practitioner in my field]. I fell into being an educator. So a lot of the theories, or the philosophies, and so forth that would be of interest to people who are true educators would probably not be of that much interest to me. My focus and my research and my writing and my practice have been delivery of services to people who are from culturally diverse backgrounds and I don't know of anybody else here on campus who does that.

Normative, compulsory rules in academia persist in Cassandra's language when she uses phrases such as "true educators," and as she describes academic culture as equated with philosophy and theory. Cassandra inhabits and names the structures that attempt to hail her into citational practices, yet these recitations *not only* reproduce *but also* contest the norms. Butler explains that norms

are called into question and reiterated at the moment in which performativity begins its citational practice. One surely cites norms that already exist, but these norms can be significantly deterritorialized through the citation. They can also be exposed as non-natural and nonnecessary when they take place in a context and through a form of embodying that defies normative expectation.[12]

Cassandra's acts produce her as a particular type of professor who, in some ways, conforms to academic expectations, yet the conformity also produces that which is altered.[13] That is, repetitions of norms are not always identical repetitions; they do not come back to the same. Each repetition produces something different, which is a condition of performativity. So even though Cassandra's acts cite and repeat the category of scholar and academic, the expressions – or the results – of her performativity also defy expectation: "My focus and my research and my writing and my practice have been delivery of services to people who are from culturally diverse backgrounds and I don't know of anybody else here on campus who does that." Cassandra's point is that, paradoxically, the normalizing conditions of the academy have produced a resistant "doing" of scholarship, teaching, and service, a doing that Cassandra described as tightly integrated and seamless. Performativity highlights the ways in which Cassandra-as-practitioner is produced as an effect of the performance; she does not "choose" to integrate her teaching, scholarship, and service. It is the integration, that *depends on and cannot exist without* normative constraints of what counts as "true educator," that makes Cassandra.

Cassandra continued to talk about identity categories as "sites of necessary trouble" in the following excerpt:

Being the only African American in a lot of settings, I felt a lot of pressure to fit in because people seemed to want that from me. I was on a lot of committees all over the campus because sometimes when I would refuse they would say, "But Cassandra, we need a minority on the committee." So, I ended up spending a lot of time doing that

[12] *Ibid.*, 218.
[13] We thank Susanne Gannon for drawing our attention to this point.

kind of thing and I guess I just felt like that I was, and I still do to this day, I have an on mode and an off mode. My off mode is when I'm being myself, and my on mode is when I'm doing what I feel I need to do professionally in order to fit in. But then there are other African-Americans here who might not relate to me on the same level of my same experience; just because we share the same race doesn't mean that we share the same culture. I'm small town rural. Southern and Pentecostal. And so, all of those things give me a very unique kind of perspective and so it's kind of hard for everybody to fit neatly into that kind of little pocket.

When Cassandra said, "People seemed to want *that* from me," the "*that*" is a troubling site of African-American-ness, signalling an essence to a category laden with norms. Cassandra's performative acts of "on and off modes," and doing what she "needs to do professionally" in order to fit in (or not), produce her gender and race subjectivity as an *effect* of the performance. When Cassandra is called by administrative structures to be a token minority in a setting, conformity is incomplete (and, perhaps, paradoxical and excessive) because, as she put it in an earlier excerpt, "just because we share the same race doesn't mean that we share the same culture." The act of interpellation is very real, as Cassandra attested, and the effect of interpellation is that norms seem to keep the "I" coherent and continuous within and among certain persons having particular identities (e.g. black women). However, Cassandra's "flip-flops" and moves between her "on and off modes" are citational practices that make up her performative acts. That is, she responds to interpellation via *uneven* repetitions, using social practices of language. When Cassandra sits in on diversity committee meetings, she is, in effect, conforming to academic structural norms that require only her presence. Other performative aspects are expressed that disrupt "the neat little pocket" of African-American-ness: small town, rural, southern, Pentecostal. In thinking with Butler, we follow her idea that "through the practice of gender performativity, we not only see how the norms that govern reality are cited but grasp one of the mechanisms by which reality is reproduced *and* altered in the course of that reproduction."[14] This enables a reading of Cassandra's performativity as showing how academic norms are reproduced, in that she sits in on meetings that compel her presence and she does what she needs to do to "fit into" academic culture. Yet norms are contested and altered via citational practices that resist those norms, such as practices that produce different ways of Cassandra understanding herself and how she embodies what she perceives as her "roles" at the university.

Performativity and agency

We have shown moments in which Cassandra describes her compulsion to "fit in" as a first-generation academic woman. That Cassandra repeats the category is a condition of her performativity, as Butler describes. Yet the citational practices that compel a "fitting into" an identity category do not imply that Cassandra is locked into that category; on the contrary, as Butler notes, "it is precisely the repetition of that play [taking up an identity] that establishes as well the instability of the very category that it constitutes."[15] This repetition never looks the same, never exhausts its performative possibilities, and therefore "constitutes and contests the *coherence* of that 'I'."[16]

---

[14] Butler, *Undoing Gender*, op. cit., 218.
[15] Butler, "Imitation and Gender Insubordination," 375.
[16] *Ibid.*, 376 [emphasis ours].

It may be that many early career faculty members feel intimidated or insecure in their first academic appointments, regardless of their first-generation status, gender, race, ethnicity, culture, or socio-economic background. As we have stated elsewhere, however, we are not attempting to capture the essence of what it means to "be" a first-generation academic woman, nor are we interested in making causal or correlational attributions to first-generation academic women's experiences. To do either would be to center the subject rather than seeking to open up categories and expose their constitution. That is, by centering the subject, we would privilege (and run the risk of essentializing) one aspect of their identity (race, class, gender) instead of emphasizing the first-generation academic woman's performative distinctiveness. Cassandra echoes our refusal to reduce her(self) to one category in order to "make sense" of the times when students complain about her teaching when she says,

> The interesting thing for me is I never know whether [students complain about my teaching] because I'm black or whether it's because I'm a woman or whether it's because it's both. There is this phenomenon that has been written about in some of the feminist literature, and it's specifically black feminist about the "double whammy." So in my case, I don't know what's happening when students do things like that. I find myself questioning as to whether they would do it to some of my colleagues. They do do it to some of my female colleagues from time to time, but I don't know that they've ever done it to any of my male colleagues.

Cassandra is articulating a crucial aspect of Butler's later theorization of performativity via her work in *Undoing Gender* and *Giving an Account of Oneself*: the paradox of agency. Butler asserts, "If I have any agency, it is opened up by the fact that I am constituted by a social world I never chose. That my agency is riven with paradox does not mean it is impossible. It means only that paradox is the *condition* of its possibility."[17] As Cassandra explains, she is positioned by others in multiple ways that leave her perplexed. Rather than attributing meaning, Cassandra names the social worlds and categories that are not of her choosing, yet those are the ones that make her a viable subject: they are the conditions of her existence and make her life livable or not. They are conditions that confer *recognition*.

Building on Foucault and Hegel, Butler offers this theory:

> The Hegelian tradition links desire with recognition, claiming that desire is always a desire for recognition and that it is only through the experience of recognition that any of us becomes constituted as socially viable beings.[18]

Butler goes on to elaborate this idea, arguing that desire for recognition is in actuality a site of *power*, where who gets to be recognized, and by whom, is governed by social norms. Furthermore, Butler maintains, the choice to be recognized (or not) within the constraints of normativity is a condition of agency in the doing, and undoing, of subjectivity. Butler continues,

---

[17] Butler, *Undoing Gender*, 3 [emphasis ours].
[18] *Ibid.*, 2.

The "I" that I am finds itself at once constituted by norms and dependent on them but also endeavors to live in ways that maintain a critical and transformative relation to them. This is not easy, because the "I" becomes, to a certain extent unknowable, threatened with unviability, with becoming undone altogether, when it no longer incorporates the norm in such a way that makes this "I" fully recognizable … I may feel that without some recognizability I cannot live. But I may also feel that the terms by which I am recognized make life unlivable. This is the juncture from which critique emerges …[19]

What does academia want that produces Cassandra as recognizable and unrecognizable in various domains? *What does academia want* that constitutes Cassandra's life as both viable and unviable? In previous data excerpts, Cassandra is recognized in various ways through her performative acts: fitting into her hometown community, fitting into college culture, not fitting into the scholarly world of academia, not meeting normative expectations of teaching. Each of these performative acts of exposure effects recognition, loss, survival, estrangement.

To further explore the question *What does academia want of Cassandra and Sera?* we turn to data excerpts that expose various degrees of (un)recognizability and how desire for recognition produces performative acts that constitute Sera's and Cassandra's paradoxical freedom. Both Sera and Cassandra were interpellated – or hailed – by their students' expectations of "good teaching" in the academy. Though they teach at different institutions, they each encountered regulatory discursive and social norms in their early years as professors; they were called into "a certain order of social existence" by those students who were already (temporarily) embedded in the culture of higher education – a culture that Sera and Cassandra were part of, yet had not fully conformed to. Sera described some of her first years of teaching in this way:

> [There was] a great deal of intimidation, I guess. But, again, I didn't really chalk it up to being first-generation. I just chalked it up to being not smart. It was like oh, I don't know if I can do this. I'm acting a lot of the time. You hear people say fake it until you make it. And I feel like I did a lot of that. Especially when I was teaching classes, and I had no idea what I was talking about. But I would write it on the board, and students would ask a question. And I would say well, these are the four things. But I couldn't explain them at all at first for a while. And then being a faculty member was this whole different weird thing.

Sera went on to explain that the first institution, Prairie College, where she began her career as an assistant professor was a "very, very wrong place" for her. She had attended public schools and universities for compulsory and higher education. Yet Prairie College is considered a niche institution: a "small, rather conservative, church-affiliated, liberal arts place."[20] Prairie College accepts about 50 per cent of its applicants, and the 2014 freshman class of almost 700 students entered with an average 1,773 SAT score (national average is 1,510). Tuition and fees are $30,000 per year to attend the private college.[21] Sera gave an account of how she was surrounded by "home school students" who constantly tested her

---

[19] *Ibid.*, 4.
[20] This description comes from a long-time resident of the area.
[21] Data taken from the college's website.

knowledge and expertise; she said, "I would be in class, and students would say stuff to me. I mean, I felt like they knew, and looking back now I can say I felt like they knew that I didn't know a lot of stuff. And so they would play with me a little bit about it." Sera characterized her first years of teaching at Prairie College as never feeling like she knew enough to be a professor and never quite meeting her own, as well as others', expectations of someone with a PhD:

> I had a student come up to me and say why do you have to be so expository. And she stormed out of the class. And I went and looked up the word expository. I mean, I just had no idea what she was talking about and what she wanted from me ... Students would raise their hand and say is that an analogy or a simile? And I wouldn't know the difference.

Linguistic or discursive interpellation is an attempt to pull or put someone in "their place" – or force them into subjection based on discursive and social norms. Butler claims that interpellation is not descriptive; it is inaugurative: "[Interpellation] seeks to introduce a reality rather than report on an existing one; it accomplishes this introduction through a citation of existing convention ... Its purpose is to produce its social contours in space and time."[22] Prairie College attempted to interpellate or inaugurate Sera into its norms via strict teaching accountability measures. According to Sera, "they [administrators] were very serious" regarding the evaluations. What "counted" as good (normative) teaching was linked directly to objective, numerical rankings. These norms produced techniques for interpellation by anonymous bodies (unnamed students) that first initiated, then regulated, professors' subject positions. Sera said,

> Once I had my PhD, I expected myself to be this person I thought I was supposed to be. And I was in this horrible, horrible – I was in the very, very wrong place for me. Not only did I feel like I didn't know enough to be a professor, even though I just went through seven years of all of this deep learning and deep thinking, I didn't – I knew that if a student asked me a question, I still might not know the answer.

Sera went on to explain that, at Prairie, she was expected to achieve high scores on her teaching evaluations. She clarified, "If you didn't hit it [top evaluation scores] all the way down, not only did the chair come and make an appointment with you to talk about those places where you didn't hit it, but you had to write up a strategy for how you were going to deal with bringing that 4 up to a 5 or that 4.5 up to a 5."

What academia wanted of Sera (via student expectations) was for her to be a recognizable subject: a demand for confidence, unwavering certainty, broad and deep knowledge of her field, and the ability to stimulate students with intellectual challenges. Sera's students, who come from privileged socio-economic class backgrounds and rigorous college-preparatory programs in high school, have specific requirements for "good teaching" that position Sera as unrecognizable and therefore living an unviable academic life. The process of interpellation by the governing norms of Prairie College (as expressed by students and administrators) created conflicting and undoubtedly bewildering subjectivization for Sera.

---

[22] Butler, *Excitable Speech*, op. cit., 33–34.

Cassandra, too, was interpellated by the teaching norms of the public institution during her early career as an assistant professor. Though Cassandra attended large, public, flagship state universities for graduate school, she earned her undergraduate degree at Southern State University, a small, historically black, land-grant university. She also taught at that same university for fifteen years before pursuing her doctorate, and then again for four years after completing her PhD. Cassandra accepted a position at Regional State University (where she has taught since 1992) after she was aggressively recruited. Cassandra described it this way:

> What I was told at the time was that they needed someone here to teach and enhance diversity, and so, they had gotten a good – a very large grant that allowed them to bring in minority, primarily African-American students, to get their master's degree in [my field] and they wanted someone to serve as their mentor and also to develop a course and some programs that would promote diversity within the profession, and so that's what I came here to do.

Even though Cassandra had almost two decades of teaching experience in higher education, and even though there were what she described as "vibrant black communities" at the predominantly white universities of her graduate training, she said, "It was a whole different ballgame when I came here to [Regional State University]."

Cassandra said that she would "go for days without seeing someone exactly like" her, and was shocked at the absence of black people at Regional State. Yet she believed in her mission, loved "going to work every single day," and was therefore profoundly "disappointed" within her first year:

> I had been brought here to be a mentor to the African-American students and to create courses and programs and so forth to talk about diversity, and so some of the white students felt that I was paying too much attention to the black students and so they wrote these long, very critical letters of me that accused me of reverse discrimination and that I was showing favoritism to the black students because they would come in to my office … They would be sitting all on the floor and everything and we just hung out together. I was a mother figure, that was pretty much the same thing that I did at [Southern State University] so I knew how to work with those students and I knew that you need a lot of personal attention. Now there was never a time when I didn't give the same amount of attention to any white student who wanted it. But it became so huge that it went all the way up through the provost's office and I found myself spending a lot of time writing letters of rebuttal and that kind of thing.

Butler teaches us that "if the schemes of recognition that are available to us 'undo' the person by conferring recognition … then recognition becomes a site of power by which the human is differently produced."[23] Cassandra was "undone" by her others through the governing norms and practices that recognize "proper" teaching and mentoring. Cassandra, while recognizable in a way that gave her a sense of belonging at a historically black institution, was rendered unrecognizable at Regional State University – to the point of her scrambling for survival, for recognition. Cassandra's being forced to "give an account of

---

[23] Butler, *Undoing Gender*, 2.

herself"[24] was a performative response: the writing of letters made her into a different subject. It is not that Cassandra, as a sovereign subject, "chose" to write letters of rebuttal; rather, her citational practice emerged as a refusal of norms – as resisting conformity – and *produced* her agency. Cassandra, as constituted by a social world not of her choosing (power relations with students who accused her of discrimination), paradoxically was re-constituted as recognizable when the unlivable situation was resolved. The performative act is not Cassandra writing the letters of rebuttal, but the letters of rebuttal "writing" Cassandra.

In these two preceding examples, social practices within regulatory regimes attempt to force Sera and Cassandra into subjectivization that keeps them identical to other professors in the academy; this could be one answer to the question *What does academia want of Sera and Cassandra?* The hailings are repeated, and Sera and Cassandra may feel compelled to "fit in," yet their compulsory repetitions are never complete. Rather, their repetitions function to construct illusory origins of identity categories that can continually be made, unmade, and re-made.[25] Their citational practices open up "the possibility of different modes of living,"[26] and these "different modes of living" are performative practices that produce agency. As performative, they are bound to constraints in which they are produced:

> If I am someone who cannot *be* without *doing*, then the conditions of my doing are, in part, the conditions of my existence. If my doing is dependent on what is done to me or, rather, the ways in which I am done by norms, then the possibility of my persistence as an 'I' depends upon my being able to do something with what is done with me.[27]

Cassandra and Sera are "done by norms" in ways that produce the persistence of their performativity, or the production of their subjectivity. Consider Sera, who was unrecognizable to a group of her others (well-educated, privileged students) but who then, within conditions that remained outside herself, was produced as a more viable subject:

> And then by the end of it, and I was [at Prairie] for two years, I had a following of students because there was, as I learned, there was definitely a [Prairie] underground. There was a bunch of students that their parents were making them be there, and they were partying. I could make these comments, and they would just crack up. And then I would meet people within the university, you know, because I grew up like sitting next to the juke box in bars while my parents were drinking and in different places because they weren't together. So there were a lot of people that I met in university settings that were what I consider my people. Like oh, I can swear with this person, I can just be who I am with these people. And there were enough of those that I felt like I could find a comfortable place to be.

---

24 See Butler's book of the same title. Giving an account of oneself is not simply narrating a story but, as interpellated beings, we are called to give an account to answer for ourselves in the face of a query or accusation.
25 Butler, "For a Careful Reading."
26 Butler, *Undoing Gender*, 4.
27 *Ibid.*, 3.

What does academia want of Sera in this instance? What do these norms – not of her choosing, but within which she is constituted – do to her? Rather than being intimidated, insecure, and attempting to go unnoticed, Sera (within discursive constraints) began to find ease in her teaching by being okay with "not knowing the great answers." Sera said, "I love just reading things and talking with people and talking with students and trying to explore [questions] like, What are some possibilities there that don't exist? and Where can we go with this?" So Sera does not "choose" to put together an academic self whom she details as smart, who reads seriously, and who actively contributes to her profession. Rather, the acts of reading and having recognition conferred on her do something else to and for Sera: they produce her as a subject who has not transcended the norms, but who lives a flourishing life within constraints that will always attempt to interpellate her back into conformity. However, with each citational act, the question *What does academia want of Sera?* will crack, loosen its hold and open up. The failed repetition signals the undoing of the category (or the question, in this instance).

We learn from thinking with Butler's performativity that Sera's subjectivity can be fashioned only from what produces her. That is, Sera cannot stand outside the discourse that constitutes her, but agency emerges from within discourse. To rework categories is to challenge the historicity of them, to expose the falsehood of their origins. Agency, then, "is implicated in what it opposes."[28] Put another way, Butler writes,

> Indeed, this "I" would not be a thinking, speaking "I" if it were not for the very positions that I oppose, for those positions, the ones that claim that the subject must be given in advance ... are already part of what *constitutes* me.[29]

So it is only *because* of the seemingly tight boundaries around categories such as "gender," "class," "first-generation," and "academic" that Sera's subjectivity emerges not as a "fixed 'thing'" but as an intersection of those categories and thus "negotiated, open, shifting, ambiguous – the result of culturally available meanings and the open-ended, power-laden enactments of those meanings."[30]

Cassandra, too, was unmade and remade through performative acts. Because Cassandra viewed herself as someone in the academy who provided professional, therapeutic services to the community, she combined her passion for service with the expectations of the academy in terms of research and writing; she wrote a textbook that has "opened all kinds of doors" for her in terms of "name recognition and offers to do conferences." She said, "I've become, in some circles, the go-to person for an answer." Cassandra went on to explain:

> [It has] really made me feel good about carving out my little niche and doing well in the profession. So even if someone challenges me, I'm not at all affected the way that I would've been prior to having done these kinds of things ... I'm not afraid to say, "I don't know the answer to that." And then I will either say, "I will try to find out for you" or "Perhaps you could go to this particular source." ... I've come to the point that

---

[28] Butler, "For a Careful Reading," 137.

[29] Judith Butler, "Contingent Foundations: Feminism and the Question of 'Postmodernism'." In *Feminists Theorize the Political*, edited by Judith Butler and Joan Scott (New York: Routledge, 1992), 9 [emphasis ours].

[30] Dorrine Kondo, *Crafting Selves: Power, Gender, and Discourses of Identity in a Japanese Workplace* (Chicago: University of Chicago Press, 1990), 24.

I can say, "I don't know" and not feel bad about not knowing because I always felt, for many, many years, for most of my life, actually, that I just couldn't say that. I've gotta, I've gotta know. I'm supposed to know, but now I can say "I don't know" and I don't feel bad about it.

Cassandra did not write a textbook with the intention of achieving recognizability from her peers. In performativity, the question is: *What did writing the textbook do to Cassandra?* She could not have predicted or anticipated the effects of textbook-writing, yet textbook-writing made Cassandra into someone with a more livable life. The textbook-writing-with-unintended-effects produced new subjectivities for Cassandra, just as Sera's practice of "reading deeply" in her field produces her as someone different and enables her to describe herself as "intellectual:"

> The intellectual is somebody that's always thinking about things deeply and those connections and cares to do that kind of stuff. I love just reading things and talking with people and talking with students and trying to explore like what are some possibilities there that don't exist and where can we go with this.

Agency, in performativity, while a "strategic, provisional" reaction, is not an intentional response. Butler explains that the "I" does not precede the performative identity; repetition (or the failure to repeat) *creates* the "I." Cassandra's and Sera's subjectivities are *effects* of their practices. Sera and Cassandra are constituted – not determined, or given in advance – which Butler describes as a condition of agency and freedom. That is, if subjects are constantly reproduced, then they are never fully constituted. The "I" is not locked down, and agency is produced within the possibilities of reconfiguring the "I." Butler explains,

> That this is a repeated process, an iterable process, is precisely the condition of agency within discourse. If a subject were constituted once and for all, there would be no possibility of a reiteration of those constituting conventions or norms. That the subject is that which must be constituted again and again implies that it is open to formations that are not fully constrained in advance. Hence, the insistence of finding agency as resignification.[31]

Thinking with performativity

In thinking with Butler's theory of performativity, we were able to explore the question: *What are the performative acts that (re)produce Cassandra's and Sera's subjectivities as academic women?* In this chapter, we looked to those performative acts to expose the nuances of how subjectivity is produced via a paradoxical process of doing *and* undoing gender (and other "identity" categories). Thinking with performativity shows how Sera and Cassandra emerge as constituted (but not determined) and therefore vulnerable to continual resignification. "First-generation academic woman" is not a signifier that is merely imposed upon Cassandra and Sera as individuals; in a double-move of subject production, it is a signifier that becomes heavy with multiple and contradictory meanings in social, historical, and political spheres (including academic, familial, and other spheres imbued with power relations).

---

[31] Butler, "For a Careful Reading," 135.

More on performativity

The following texts are offered, not as *the* texts to consult, but as providing an entry point for those who are new to the writings of Butler and would like to learn more about performativity. We list the secondary texts first as a continuation of the "schematic cues" presented in the Interlude, which readers can use as a brace as they enter this new theoretical terrain. Following the secondary texts are suggested entry points for approaching the writing of Butler, and finally, research exemplars that illustrate additional examples of *thinking with* performativity.

Secondary texts

Butler, Judith. *Judith Butler in Conversation: Analyzing the Texts and Talk of Everyday Life.* Edited by Bronwyn Davies. New York: Routledge, 2008.
Kondo, Dorrine. *Crafting Selves: Power, Gender, and Discourses of Identity in a Japanese Workplace.* Chicago: University of Chicago Press, 1990.
Weedon, Chris. *Feminist Practice and Poststructuralist Theory.* Malden: Blackwell, 1997.

Primary texts

Butler, Judith. *Gender Trouble: Feminism and the Subversion of Identity.* New York: Routledge, 1990.
——*Excitable Speech: A Politics of the Performative.* New York: Routledge, 1997.
——*Undoing Gender.* New York: Routledge, 2004.

Research exemplars

Boucher, Geoff. "The Politics of Performativity: A Critique of Judith Butler." *Parrhesia* 1 (2006): 112–41.
Jackson, Alecia Y. "Performativity Identified." *Qualitative Inquiry* 10, no. 5 (2004): 673–90.
Secomb, Linnell. "Words That Matter: Reading the Performativity of Humanity through Butler and Blanchot." In *Judith Butler in Conversation: Analyzing the Texts and Talk of Everyday Life*, edited by Bronwyn Davies. New York: Routledge, 2008.

Why Deleuze?

One of the hallmarks of the writing of Deleuze and Guattari is their creation of a new language. They stretch language and its possibilities by intentionally using words to connote something other than what we ordinarily take them to mean, as a way to interrupt and rupture our ways of thinking. Deleuze does this through a creation of concepts that "reach beneath the identities our world presents to us in order to touch upon the world of difference that both constitutes and disrupts those identities."[1] Concepts expressed with words like *rhizome* or *desire* can be so easily appropriated without sufficient attention to the radical shift in thinking and the nature of ideas that each portends. As described by Philip Goodchild, "Deleuze and Guattari's writing ... instead of directly throwing aside theoretical norms, ... offers a whole range of digressions and alternatives that carry thought elsewhere, shattering the coherence of hegemonic discourses."[2] Such an emergence of thought and subjectivity can only occur, according to Deleuze, with signs and images that have never before appeared in the same way in a process of becoming.

Eve Tuck describes her first encounter with Deleuze and Guattari's collaborative work *Anti-Oedipus* as "dizzying, and not quite pleasant." She writes that "this text challenged and challenges me because it is concurrently conceptual and literal."[3] We experienced a similar encounter when our initial readings prompted the following questions: What was all this talk of bodies, without organs of all things, and fluids, and flows, and cuts? How could we shake ourselves free of the image of a *literal* body with no organs, and glimpse what Deleuze and Guattari might be saying? In reading Deleuze, and reading about Deleuze, we began to catch a fleeting glance of the notion that, when Deleuze and Guattari conceived the "body without organs," they did so in an attempt to enact thinking without a subject and to confront our reliance on essential objects or material representations to understand and explain. To take the metaphor seriously, in other words, to try to conceive of a literal body without organs, was to return to our interpretive roots and to miss the point entirely. And then we stumbled across a passage in which Deleuze maintained that it was only out of nonsense that thinking could occur. Was it perhaps a failure to understand that pushed us against the limits of interpretive ways of knowing toward a recognition of those limits that were binding and disallowing productive resistances? We were constantly

---

[1] Todd May, *Gilles Deleuze* (Cambridge: Cambridge University Press, 2005), 19.
[2] Philip Goodchild, *Deleuze & Guattari: An Introduction to the Politics of Desire* (London: Sage, 1996), 2.
[3] Eve Tuck, "Breaking up With Deleuze: Desire and Valuing the Irreconcilable," *International Journal of Qualitative Studies in Education* 23, no. 5 (2010): 636.

having to remind ourselves of this use of words to mean different things in a way that was deterritorializing. While maddening, it pushed us in the direction of our current methodological project of interrupting sameness – or so we imagined.

While Derrida had much to say to us about the absent present, we began to brush up against the limits of methodological thinking about voice with Derrida. Derrida helped us consider the trace, the always already absent present, but failed to help us interrogate why the absent present in the form of previously unthought voices might be inhabiting the narratives. Because Deleuze's philosophy is one of immanence, he helps us focus not on the question of what is there, but on what is being produced. For Deleuze and Guattari, desire, for example, is about production. Desire's production is active, becoming, transformative. It produces out of a multiplicity of forces which form the assemblage. We desire, not because we lack something that we do not have, but because of the productive force of intensities and connections of desires.

If desire circulates in ways that produce the unexpected, then we go to desire to examine the unexpected silences in the narrative accounts given by Sera and Cassandra, to ask how desire is functioning to maintain sameness and privilege through the production of a silence – a silence that we name and talk about in Chapter 6 as a *desiring silence*.[4] To turn desire on its head is to open up a consideration of how silences work, and why they persist, because those *speaking* with silence act and are acted upon in a transformative process. Thinking with this notion of desire as productive calls us to ask: What are the competing forces, intensities, and interests (privilege, status, ability to maintain sameness) with which we approach the conversations with Sera and Cassandra through the lens of desire? What are the desiring machines that we and they are plugging into and that are plugging into them/us to produce this desiring silence?

Given this focus, while in the threshold with Deleuze, Cassandra, and Sera, what emerged were places in the transcript where Cassandra and Sera were articulating purposeful silences that were maintained, sometimes for years, because they were produced by a desire – a desire to maintain smooth and uncomplicated (or less complicated) family relationships, family dinners, long-term friendships, acceptance both inside and outside the academy, spousal conversations, and possibilities of intimate relationships. Where might the productive relationships between desire and silence be occurring? And so we set off to see if we could engage a Deleuzian mapping of desire via the silences that we were seeing/hearing/ missing. We did not wish to overlay the transcripts and trace the silences in order to fix meaning or explanations, but rather to produce a mapping of the silences as understood through the counterintuitive framing of desire. Such mapping produces the question: *How does a desiring silence function to keep/maintain/produce smooth social, familial, and professional relations?*

---

[4] Alecia Jackson first coined the term "desiring silence" in her chapter "What am I Doing when I Speak of this Present? Voice, Power and Desire in Truth-Telling," in *Voice in Qualitative Inquiry*, edited by Alecia Y. Jackson and Lisa A. Mazzei (London: Routledge, 2009). Jackson's chapter mobilizes Deleuzian desire to interpret what is happening in the context of her research: she describes how desire functions to produce certain truths. Mazzei extends this work in the article, "Desiring Silence: Gender, Race and Pedagogy in Education," *British Educational Research Journal*, 37 (2011). In this article she extends her thought to consider how desire is functioning to produce silence that serves to produce and protect white privilege.

Schematic cues

Becoming and differen... Th...   ...'s work, and they serve as his
respo...   ...ning as a transcendent, linear
proce...   ...ame, which relies on a stable
identit...   ...as in grouping. That is, traditional ...   ...oup; for example, the social
catego...   ...ble because of its distinction
from ...   ...ategories of *working-class* or
white ...   ...nd readily recognizable and
predict...

How ...   ...ordination to sameness, and
becomin...   ...ints. There is no origin, no
destinat...   ...coming is directional (away
from sa...   ...articular *within* that would
render t...   ...manent to (not outside of)
the socia...   ...ribed as an escape, it always
"takes p...   ...t do not leave the world
behind ..

To illu...

A lin...   ...on the contrary, it passes
betwe...   ...f becoming that unites the
wasp ...   ...of the wasp, in that it
becom...   ...but also of the orchid, in
that it ...   ...liberated from its own
reprod...

The *becomi...*   ...id. The becoming is the
something ...   ...ment through a unique
event that p...   ...te of being-in-between,
the "contin...

Desire – ...   ...desire, not because we
lack somethi...   ...cause of the forces and
actions that ...   ...fluence of Nietzsche:

Where N...   ...l of forces, resulting in
an infinit...   ...applied it at the ontological lev...   ..., relating, and existing

[5] Brian Massumi   ...*m Deleuze and Guattari*
(Cambridge, M...
[6] Gilles Deleuze ...   ...slated by Robert Hurley,
Mark Seem and ...   ...ss, 1983), 293 [emphasis
in original].
[7] C. Stagoll, "Bec...   ...rk: Columbia University
Press, 2005), 20...   ..."Deleuze and the Girl,"
International Jo...   ...7.

which he calls desire. Forces want to act and to be acted upon, they want to give themselves and change their nature; they look for syntheses which will be able to produce something new.[8]

Rationality and intentionality are not part of Deleuzian desire. Nor is negativity, "loss, failure, … and the ontological lack."[9] What matters for Deleuze is not what desire means; instead, he wants to know "whether it works, and how it works, and who it works for."[10] While Foucault focused much of his analysis on knowledge and power, Deleuze chose desire as that which was most worth considering in social theory.[11] For Deleuze, "Desire is a part of the perceptual infrastructure: it is constitutive of the objects desired as well as the social field in which they appear. It is, in other words, what first introduces the affective connections that make it possible to navigate through the social world."[12]

Deleuze and Guattari further explain and provide a sense in which their conception of desire differs from a psychoanalytic perspective:

> To a certain degree, the traditional logic of desire is all wrong from the very outset: from the very first step that the Platonic logic of desire forces us to take, making us choose between production and acquisition. From the moment that we place desire on the side of acquisition, we make desire an idealistic (dialectical, nihilistic) conception, which causes us to look upon it as primarily a lack: a lack of an object, a lack of the real object.[13]

Desire – Lacanian. Desire for Lacan is a condition created by the establishment of ourselves in relation to our objects of desire. Desire for Lacan is desire of the Other. We attempt to satisfy needs as governed by exchanges with others, for "Lacan argues that it demonstrably belongs to humans to desire-directly-as or through another or others."[14] Žižek maintains that "The original question of desire is not directly 'What do I want', but 'What do others want from me? What do they see in me? What am I for those others?' "[15] This is further elaborated by Schrift, who writes that "To view desire as lack assumes that desire is derivative, arising in response to the perceived lack of the object desired or as a state produced in the subject by the lack of the object."[16]

Desiring machine. Desiring machines, introduced by Deleuze and Guattari in *Anti-Oedipus*, are referred to as the assemblage in *A Thousand Plateaus*. The desiring machine is that which provides connections for a plugging-in of forces, flows, and intensities. The machine, as such, with no subjectivity or center, is a hub of connections and productions – it deterritorializes and presents the possibility for transformation, proliferation, and becoming.

---

[8] Goodchild, *Deleuze & Guattari*, op. cit., 33.

[9] Rosi Braidotti, *Metamorphoses: Towards a Materialist Theory of Becoming* (Malden, MA: Polity Press, 2002), 57.

[10] Gilles Deleuze, *Negotiations: 1972–1990*, trans. Martin Joughin (1990; repr. New York: Columbia University Press, 1995), 22.

[11] Goodchild, *Deleuze & Guattari*, op. cit., 34.

[12] Alan D. Schrift, *Nietzsche's French Legacy: A Genealogy of Poststructuralism* (New York: Routledge, 1995), 69.

[13] Gilles Deleuze and Félix Guattari, *A Thousand Plateaus: Capitalism and Schizophrenia*, translated by Brian Massumi (Minneapolis: University of Minnesota Press, 1987), 25.

[14] Matthew Sharpe, "Jacques Lacan," *Internet Encyclopedia of Philosophy*, accessed September 25, 2008, www.iep.utm.edu

[15] Slavoj Žižek, *How to Read Lacan* (London, Granta Books, 2006), 49.

[16] Schrift, *Nietzsches French Legacy*, op. cit., 69.

Alan Schrift discussed *Anti-Oedipus* as introducing "the desiring machine as a machinic, functionalist translation of Nietzschean will to power. A desiring machine is a functional assemblage of a desiring will and the object desired."[17] The desiring machine is thus an assemblage of intensities that is autonomous, self-constituting and creative, which function as an ontology of change, transformation, or "becoming." The machine is not anthropocentric, there is no "subject" that lies behind the production of desire, and this "desire" is due not to lack nor a desire for an object, but rather to a production of intensities produced in order to actualize potentials to an ever-increasing degree.

Deterritorialization. In discussing Deleuze and Guattari's use of language, Philip Goodchild writes that "Although they may use some of the same words, ideas, and concepts, these are always 'deterritorialized' – their meanings are changing, following lines of flight."[18] Deterritorialization is the process of un-coding habitual relations, experiences, and usages of language in order to separate the foundational human image-opinion construct that orients thought in a specific manner. A re-composition or reterritorialization is the production of a higher quality of deterritorialization, which is the power of taking a quality beyond its actual occurrence and granting it a general extension, the power to actualize, to become differently.

Claire Colebrook provides the following example:

> Deterritorialisation occurs when an event of becoming escapes or detaches from the original territory. Think of the way humans organise or territorialise themselves through language. Language can then become inhuman or deterritorialised in art; no longer meaningful, controllable or recognisable.[19]

Immanence. Immanence is produced from the flows of life – the now that is not governed by a system of laws and relations. Immanence constantly re-opens thinking to the outside without allowing a fixed image of that outside. Immanence does not allow any experience to be enslaved by a single image that would elevate itself above others. In positioning Deleuze as a philosopher of immanence, Colebrook writes:

> If we allow thought to accept some transcendent foundation – such as reason, God, truth or human nature – then we have stopped thinking. And if immanence is philosophy for Deleuze it is also an ethics: *not allowing experience to be enslaved by any single image that would elevate itself above others.*[20]

Intensities. Intensities are those affects that operate on us in myriad ways. The effects that are produced are then referred to by Deleuze as intensities. Affect is intensive because it is something that happens to us, across us, with us. Claire Colebrook provides the following illustration:

> If we see the world, usually, as a set of extended objects and as part of a uniform and measurable space, this is because we have synthesised intensities. Intensities are not just

---

[17] *ibid.*, 68.
[18] Goodchild, *Deleuze & Guattari*, 42.
[19] Claire Colebrook, *Gilles Deleuze* (London: Routledge, 2002), 59.
[20] *Ibid.*, 79 [emphasis ours].

qualities – such as redness – they are the becoming of qualities: say, the burning and wavering infrared light that we eventually see *as* red.[21]

Transcendence. Transcendence refers to normative or universal values, that which comes before and supercedes our notions of morality and goodness. Kant posited this as that which is before or beyond experience. We are separated from the world, in this view, as humans, as that which is above or beyond and that we consider to be universally true. For many, this transcendence is understood as God. For philosophers such as Deleuze, who put forth a philosophy of immanence, a foundation such as reason, God, truth, or human nature serves to enslave or preclude experience or thinking, as it forces us to submit to the strictures of a single truth, law, or perspective.

[21] *Ibid.*, 39.

Chapter 6

Deleuze: Thinking with desire

Desire constantly couples continuous flows and partial objects that are by nature fragmentary and fragmented.[1]

Desiring-production is pure multiplicity, that is to say, an affirmation that is irreducible to any sort of unity.[2]

A desiring silence

To think with Deleuze is to consider the forces of desire that are acting through and with our research participants, and to make sense of what results from such interaction. Consistent with the aims set out in Chapter 1, we continue in Deleuzian fashion not to seek "a 'true' interpretation," but rather we seek "to make sense, to give a direction."[3] To do so, we engage the concepts of Deleuze and Guattari to approach the question of desire. Our treatment of desire in the context of this chapter is not in keeping with desire as lack in a Lacanian sense, but as Deleuzian desire that is generative and seeking, resulting in the production of privilege, power, and voice. Both Deleuze and Guattari discuss the debt they owe to Lacan. While this debt to Lacan is properly acknowledged, it is also properly disclaimed by them as they "want to free it [desire] from the normative cage within which psychoanalysis has enclosed it."[4] If desire does not begin from lack (desiring what we do not have), then where does it begin, or put differently, what spawns desire?

In a conversation about *Anti-Oedipus*, Félix Guattari discussed the fact that while psychoanalysis has been compromised, it discovered "desire, machineries of desire:"[5]

They're constantly whirring, grinding away, churning stuff out, in any analysis. And analysts are always starting up machines, or restarting them, on a schizophrenic basis. But they may be doing or setting in motion things they're not fully aware of ... There's

---

[1] Gilles Deleuze and Félix Guattari, *Anti-Oedipus: Capitalism and Schizophrenia*. Translated by Robert Hurley, Mark Seem and Helen Lane (1977; repr. Minneapolis: University of Minnesota Press, 1983), 5.

[2] *Ibid.*, 42.

[3] Philip Goodchild, *Deleuze & Guattari: An Introduction to the Politics of Desire* (London: Sage, 1996), 29.

[4] Gilles Deleuze, *Negotiations: 1972–1990*. Translated by Martin Joughin (New York: Columbia University Press), 13–14.

[5] *Ibid.*, 15–16.

no question that psychoanalysis has ... been like a bomb smuggled inside ... it's forced people to organize things differently, it's uncovered desire.[6]

As we read the data, what emerged in the threshold was how Cassandra and Sera kept quiet. By this we mean they described episodes where they or someone else kept quiet. We began to hear these silences as desire functioning to produce an effect. As it is Deleuzian desire that we are thinking with to understand the silences, we have to ask, how does desire function to produce silence? What are the machineries of desire that are constantly "churning stuff out" to produce connections that form the becoming of Sera and Cassandra? What are the silences producing? The charge then becomes not to define desire, but to understand the interests that produce desire, and the interests that desire seeks to produce and/or protect, to ask the Deleuzian question, how does it work? Such thinking prompts the question: *How does a desiring silence function to keep/maintain/produce smooth social, familial, and professional relations?*

For example, when Sera describes finding people in university settings that "I consider my people," she is talking about those connections that do not demand a desiring silence to conceal her background growing up "sitting next to the juke box in bars while my parents were drinking and in different places because they weren't together." When she is not in the company of her people, however, a desiring silence is produced when the machinery demands otherwise; a desiring silence in the form of a masked identity, one that maintains the illusion of sameness and belonging. This naming of a *desiring silence* is not to be confused with a desire *for* silence, as in "to desire" silence; instead, silences are produced and produce an effect, emerging from a "*production* of production."[7] This production of production then is Sera becoming otherwise. The mask of a desiring silence protects Sera from her background in the production of this new effect of belonging.

Desire as persistent force

Desire, according to Deleuze and Guattari, is not a "thing" or a characteristic, but rather a force. It is a coming together of forces/drives/intensities that produce something. As we look at the data, we ask not what Cassandra and Sera are doing, but what is happening. We want to know how they are becoming. We want to look for the drives that emanate from the intersecting desires by colleagues and students and family to produce something unexpected in the form of a desiring silence.

Turning desire on its head results in an opening up of how silences work, and why they persist, because those "speaking" with silence act and are acted upon in a transformative process. Sera and Cassandra are silent with their families, and are produced by the effect of a desiring silence as being good daughters and sisters, rather than to be denied by their families when they are criticized for being too uppity, too book smart but not street smart, as described by Sera: "So I know that my mom and my dad brag on the fact that I have a PhD, but they also are very quick to say oh, you're just a PhD, you don't know about stuff." When Cassandra responds to a question about how relationships with family and friends from her hometown may have changed, she responds that "to this day when I'm around family I act the way I always have," and continues by saying, "I know that I'm being successful because – pretty much they'll say things like, they call me Jane

---

[6] *Ibid.*, 16.
[7] Simon O'Sullivan and Stephen Zepke, "Introduction: The Production of the New," in *Deleuze, Guattari and the Production of the New*, edited by Simon O'Sullivan and Stephen Zepke (London: Continuum, 2008), 1.

there, my middle name. They say, 'That Jane, she ain't changed a bit.'" This is not to suggest that Sera and Cassandra are always consciously making decisions about how to speak and act, but that they plug into a desiring machine that is continually whirring away and that "churns stuff out." The desiring machine of family plugs into Sera's and Cassandra's becoming in the academy in ways that seek to reterritorialize and freeze their becoming. Such arresting is not *finally* possible because desires still circulate and plug into one another, resulting in a becoming that produces a new desiring silence.

Desiring subjects

Assuming a "desiring subject" is also concomitant with a necessary rethinking of the intentional, rational humanist subject. It is a thinking of a "subject group," according to Deleuze and Guattari, rather than *a* subject. Mark Seem writes that once we loose ourselves from *an* ego, "where singularity and collectivity are no longer at odds with each other," there is the possibility to "de-normalize and de-individualize through a multiplicity of new, collective arrangements against power."[8] To approach Sera's and Cassandra's interview data in this way is to consider their subjectivity as emergent through the productive forces of desire. Agency, therefore, is not located solely within the individual, but rather is assembled, performed, constructed. Sera and Cassandra's subjectivity is becoming with each experience, each telling, each desiring. Deleuze and Guattari write that "There is no such thing as either man [*sic*] or nature now, only a process that produces the one within the other and couples the machines together."[9]

In discussing personal relationships, Sera talked about how, as a single woman, she was viewed as much more attractive when she was less educated. "People say oh, that's so neat. You have a PhD. You're a doctor or a professor or whatever they say when they find that out ... and then they hit the road." In this example, there is a process, a coupling of forces that produces a reaction, a retreat, a silence by men who encounter Sera's becoming academic. While she may be able to swear, and drink, and know the culture of bars due to her upbringing, her education plugs into the machine to produce a silence on the part of those who encounter her out of context. What does desire produce? It produces Sera as one who both belongs and doesn't belong. It produces Sera as both traditional and radical. It produces Sera's becoming as a "site of necessary trouble."[10]

We gesture back to Butler and forward to Barad here to further think the subject as de-centered, non-foundational, and never fully constituted. If, as Butler writes, identity categories (PhD, first-generation, woman, black, academic) are "sites of necessary trouble," then we ask, how is desire functioning to produce and protect these fragile and unstable becomings?[11] Such questioning helps us turn to a performative understanding of discursive practices that, according to Barad, if properly constructed, is "a contestation of the excessive power granted to language to determine what is real."[12] Such a move shifts

---

[8] Mark Seem, "Translator's Introduction," in Gilles Deleuze and Félix Guattari, *Anti-Oedipus*, op. cit., xxi.

[9] Deleuze and Guattari, *Anti-Oedipus*, 2.

[10] Judith Butler, "Imitation and Gender Insubordination." In *Women, Knowledge, and Reality: Explorations in Feminist Philosophy*, 2nd edn, edited by Ann Garry and Marilyn Pearsall (New York: Routledge, 1996), 371–87.

[11] *Ibid.*

[12] Karen Barad, "Posthumanist Performativity: Toward an Understanding of How Matter Comes to Matter." In *Material Feminisms*, edited by Stacy Alaimo and Susan Hekman (Bloomington: Indiana University Press, 2008), 121.

the focus of our inquiry "from questions of correspondence between descriptions and reality ... to matters of practices/doings/actions."[13] What are the practices/doings/actions that are manifest in a desiring silence that strives to protect fragile or troublesome becomings?

Rather than return to the safe space of knowing and of meaning, we think with Deleuze about what is producing the silence. We want to know (with Deleuze) how desire is functioning to produce silence, and what is being produced as a result. With these prompts to guide us, and with Deleuze looking over our shoulders, we began to see/hear what we thought might be examples of a desiring silence.

A desiring silence

One such example of a desiring silence is in Sera talking about what she can't say, or won't say, to her mother:

> She's a massively born-again Christian. She's evangelical, right wing, loves President Bush, she's always been a poor, single parent. And I was reading about this, they're called hidden messages. A rhetoric of morality, in this case, and it was talking about this one evangelical preacher whose name is Joel Osteen ... it took apart [that] these are really issues of class that are housed in issues of morality, and this is how it works. And so I said to my mom have you heard of this Joel Osteen? And she says, "I love him. I love him."
>
> Okay, but how do you feel about prosperity theology? And she says, "I just think it's right on." And I'm looking at her life thinking how can she think this? What she's saying is that God doesn't bless her. She's not living good enough because God hasn't given her material resources. And yet she believes in it. It's like poor people that believe in individualism or whatever. It's like this *so* doesn't serve you. And what I realize is that I can't then have the conversation. I can't turn around and say blah, blah, blah, academics, blah, blah, blah because she'll just dismiss it as ridiculous.

Looking at the data through the lens of Deleuzian desire, we seek to know how desire is working and who it is working for in the above example. Sera wants to have this conversation with her mother about what she has learned and how she sees her mother ascribing to a politics that further disadvantages her, and yet she also recognizes that to have the conversation is to further distance her from her mother. What is desire producing when Sera says, "I've been able to accept her more?" While her mother brags on her for having a PhD, she doesn't see Sera as "smart" where it really counts (for her mother) in terms of street smart. Sera knows that to push this conversation further with her mother is both to risk alienation and to affirm her mother's notion that she lacks common sense. Desire functions to produce a silence that maintains the illusion of sameness.

> While in the threshold, we noticed other similar places where the women were describing moments of silence in their interviews, desiring silences that produce/

---

[13] *Ibid.* We extend this notion of practices/doings/actions more fully in Chapter 7, in our thinking with Barad and intra-activity. While many of the material feminists do not cite Deleuze *per se*, we view much of the current work in this area that takes up ontology as being an enactment of what Deleuze and Guattari were writing about in both *Anti-Oedipus* and *A Thousand Plateaus*.

maintain relished outcomes and effects, or silences on the part of colleagues and family members that might be functioning in the same way. We sought to plug Deleuze's notion of desire into these texts, to plug the texts back into Deleuze, and to see what was being produced in and by the desiring machine, in order to catch a glimpse of how a desiring silence was functioning in Sera's and Cassandra's relationships. We did so as a way to return to our analytic question: *How does a desiring silence function to keep/ maintain/produce smooth social, familial, and professional relations?* In other words, to ask the Deleuzian question: how does it work, and who is it working for?

As researchers, our interest is not in pinning down what the silences mean, nor what these women and their colleagues and students desire, nor even to suggest that we can *know* that all silences are desiring silences. What we wish to do instead is ask: What are the desires that are producing the silence on the part of Sera, Cassandra, and the network of subjectivities (academic, daughter, colleague, mother) and, in turn, what are the silences producing (status, avoidance of conflict, fitting in)? Why do they persist, sometimes for years? Who benefits? Is it only those who speak the desiring silences that are both producing them and benefitting from them? In other words, how does desire function?

In the process of plugging the narratives into our past encounters with Deleuze, one of the impressions that was noticeable was that of silence, written about by Lisa in a previously published article. This research sought to examine how a desiring silence produced by white teachers functioned to maintain for them the privilege ascribed to whiteness.[14] It was these nagging, persistent silences that produced many consequences, both expected and unexpected. In our interview with Cassandra, she discussed her work on university diversity committees and that her contributions are valued. She also described the persistent and almost pathological silence that she has encountered in such work.

> I was in the position of assistant to the provost for women's concerns for a while and while I was talking to him I told him that one of these days I was gonna write a book called *Games Academicians Play* and he asked me "What did I mean?"
>
> I said, "You form a committee where somebody doesn't really want you to accomplish anything, they form a committee and so you discuss the problem for a year and you come up with the recommendation for improving the situation and then you file a report and then it sits somewhere and then when somebody brings the problem up again you form another committee to study it, and you have several meetings where you discuss it to death."
>
> [And] he just kind of went on to the next topic.

Like the white teachers in Lisa's previous research, the white male administrator who silently responds to Cassandra is maintaining privilege through the production of a desiring silence. What happens in this exchange is that "Desiring silence then re-produces an unspoken white presence."[15] Cassandra recognizes the silence surrounding diversity and the administrator's failure to respond to her critique.

---

[14] Lisa A. Mazzei, "Desiring Silence: Gender, Race, and Pedagogy in Education." *British Educational Research Journal* 37 (2011).
[15] *Ibid.*

Returning to the data, we cannot say that nothing has changed. However, before proceeding further with our analysis, we must emphasize that race as an identity category, both black and white, is not a return to an essentializing notion of race. It is recognition and reinsertion of racial markers as simultaneously culturally and biologically produced via the forces of desire. Again, calling attention to race is done not for the purposes of essentializing, but to illustrate the entangled nature of the forces of race and racial identity in the production of desire, or desire in the production of silence.

The forces of Cassandra and the administrator meet and interact, and in the process each of them changes, a process that Deleuze and Guattari will later call a "process of becoming or double deterritorialization: one force acts on another by lending it a fragment of its 'code', offering some of its conventions and habits."[16] This meeting of forces, of desires, imposes senses and values on the other force, and *vice versa*. Through what Goodchild describes as "this exchange of fragments of code, the overall memory or territory belonging to each force is expanded, possibly in a way that overrides former codes and conventions."[17]

By recognizing and naming the silence, Cassandra interacts in this process of becoming or double deterritorialization. Rather than what might seem a futile effort, her naming of the silence as "games academicians play" serves as an un-coding of habitual relations (not dealing with the issue of diversity – both racial and gender). At the same time, we might read the silence or force spoken by the white male administrator when he "goes onto the next topic" as also enmeshed in this exchange of fragments and codes, attempting to reterritorialize the Otherness that is Cassandra's blackness and womanness by preventing an escape. Deterritorialization occurs when an event of becoming exceeds or escapes its original trajectory. Because Cassandra both names the desiring silence and attempts to deterritorialize it, the effect produced is no longer controllable or recognizable. We can conclude that "each force acts upon the other in a process of transformation,"[18] in other words, it is deterritorialized. As Goodchild explains, "In terms of territories, each force deterritorializes the other."[19]

Just as subjectivity and desire are a series of entanglements, so are the silences enacted in Cassandra's interview. The "white administrator" is silenced by Cassandra, in that she is the one giving his account. He is ventriloquized by Cassandra, and is further silenced by us as researchers, since we privilege her account. Diversity is conflated with race and gender, which may permit a voicing of diversity that talks about race and gender without talking about race and gender.[20] A further opening up and disruption requires a questioning of our own desires as researchers and how we plug into the desiring machines to produce new desires and silences.

In an examination of how desire functions to produce silent discourses that serve to perpetuate a continuation of privilege with white teachers and researchers, the challenge is not

---

[16] Goodchild, *Deleuze & Guattari*, op. ci., 38.

[17] *Ibid.*

[18] *Ibid.*, 33, 38.

[19] *Ibid.*

[20] If "diversity" is substituted as a catch-all for difference (gender, race, ethnicity, etc.) then it can be substituted to gesture toward the fact that issues of race and racial inequities are being addressed, when in fact they are being avoided. Diversity becomes a euphemism for speaking about the unsavory topic of racial discrimination, not unlike the many euphemisms that are used to mask death. People don't talk about death and dying; they talk about passing, leaving, etc.

to define desire, but to understand the confluence of interests that both produce desire, and that desire seeks to produce and/or protect. In the case of white teachers in Lisa's previous research, she observed that

> the visibleness of white as a marker of their bodies has previously been deemed invisible because of its normative presence. The same can be said of the failure for males to notice their privilege for the same reason. This failure to have previously named white-ness [and maleness] thereby produces a desire to protect the invisibleness and hence a maintenance of whiteness as an unchallenged norm.[21]

Similarly, the visibleness of privilege may not be noticeable to this white male administrator except in the presence of Cassandra's deterritorializing gaze. She brings to the attention of the provost that the reports produced by diversity committees are met with silence, and is further responded to with silence. If the report is shelved, if the conversation is cut short, then the invisibleness of whiteness, maleness, and its attendant privilege that pretends inclusiveness through tokenism is strengthened. Desiring silence maintains its place in the desiring machine. In the above example, the multiple forces of desire emanate from becomings, of a white male and his becomings [in the center] and a black female and her becomings [from the outside/inside, in the Spivakian sense]. The becomings are manifested in the conversations, both virtual and actual, and desire persists to deterritorialize and reterritorialize. The vital element "of such relations of becoming is that differing modes should mutually act upon each other and transform each other."[22]

Practices/doings/actions

In the case of these first-generation women, the mark of first-generation is invisible because there are no outward symbols. The desire then produces a silence that maintains this invi-sibleness, for in the presence of a desiring silence is the production and protection of an unchallenged norm. Sera and Cassandra "fit" into social and familial contexts by not calling attention to their education, status, and privilege. They further "fit" into academic contexts by not calling attention to their first-generation status, their otherness that can remain hidden if they are silent in ways that reproduce an image of the academic that is, at times, illusory. Silence functions both to protect and to limit – it works both for and against Sera and Cassandra, often at the same time.

In our interview with Sera, she talked about the intimidation and insecurity that she experienced as a PhD student working as a graduate teaching assistant.

> I didn't really chalk it up to being first-generation. I just chalked it up to being not smart. It was like oh, I don't know if I can do this. I'm acting a lot of the time. I feel like that you hear people say fake it until you make it. And I feel like I did a lot of that. Especially when I was teaching classes [as a graduate teaching assistant], and I had no idea what I was talking about. But I would write it on the board, and students would ask a question. And I would say well, these are the four things. But I couldn't explain them at all at first for a while.

---

[21] Mazzei, "Desiring Silence," op. cit.
[22] Goodchild, *Deleuze & Guattari*, 38.

She continues in the conversation to talk about her first position at Prairie College immediately after graduate school, and how intimidation and insecurity persisted.

> Once I had my PhD, I expected myself to be this person I thought I was supposed to be. And I was in the very, very wrong place for me [at Prairie College]. Not only did I feel like I didn't know enough to be a professor, even though I just went through seven years of all this deep learning and deep thinking. I knew that if a student asked me a question, I still might not know the answer.

Sera produces a silence that masks the identity of first-generation and (in)experience. Desire is functioning as a force to become and produce images.[23] That she doesn't belong/fit with these students at Prairie College that she is teaching, perceived by her as being better educated and more savvy, is on display when she described them in her interview as "different from my public school experience and different from my state school experience."[24] This lack of belonging and of fitting in, and trying to pass, produces a silence that maintains (or seeks to maintain) an image of seeming authority. A powerful image is an unnamed and silent identity that continues to be masked through a silence that protects a necessary image. Desiring silence then re-produces an unspoken acceptance. By writing the points on the board, Sera can avoid a further exposition of what she knows, or fears she does not know. Her desire further produces a silence on the part of the students, because the board in this instance coalesces with Sera to produce this authoritative stance – knowledge is carved in stone, metaphorically, silently communicating truth.

We return momentarily to Lacan to illustrate how a Deleuzian reading of desire produces something very different. Desire, for Lacan, is desire of the Other. In other words, Cassandra and Sera desire what the other desires of them. They attempt to satisfy needs as governed by the expectations held of them by others. Lacan argues "that it demonstrably belongs to humans to desire-directly-as or through another or others."[25] So, for instance, if Cassandra is asking, "What do my white male colleagues want from me?" or if Sera asks "What am I for those others [students]?" then this is a Lacanian demonstration of desire. For Lacan, then, "The original question of desire is not directly 'What do I want', but 'What do others want from me? What do they see in me? What am I for those others?'"[26] If we are to assume a psychoanalytic stance toward desire that is motivated by the unattainable lack, then we can find instances in both Sera's and Cassandra's narratives that indicate actions (and perhaps silences), both on the part of them as individuals and also on the part of colleagues, that attempt to achieve the fulfillment to be gained through attainment. The following account given by Cassandra is offered to further illustrate our point.

---

[23] Claire Colebrook, *Gilles Deleuze* (London: Routledge, 2002), 94.

[24] In a US context, Sera is speaking about the large inner-city public high school that she attended, in which she described students being "shuttled" to different places. She also refers to attending a large state or public university. This contrasts with the exclusive high-school education that many of her students at Prairie College may have received, and with their being enrolled in a small, private liberal arts college.

[25] Matthew Sharpe, "Jacques Lacan," *Internet Encyclopedia of Philosophy*, accessed September 25, 2008, www.iep.utm.edu

[26] Slavoj Žižek, *How to Read Lacan* (London: Granta Books, 2006), 49.

I had been brought here to be a mentor to the African American students and to create courses and programs and so forth to talk about diversity, and so some of the white students felt that I was paying too much attention to the black students and so they wrote these long, very critical letters of me that accused me of reverse discrimination and that I was showing favoritism to the black students because they would come in to my office ... They would be sitting all on the floor and everything and we just hung out together. I was a mother figure, that was pretty much the same thing that I did at Southern State University so I knew how to work with those students and I knew that [they] need a lot of personal attention. Now there was never a time when I didn't give the same amount of attention to any white student who wanted it. But it became so huge that it went all the way up through the provost's office and I found myself spending a lot of time writing letters of rebuttal and that kind of thing.

We know from the conversation above with Cassandra that one of the reasons she was hired was to be a mentor to the African-American students and to create courses and programs that addressed issues of diversity. And she recounts how she filled this role. We can read the above through a psychoanalytic lens that suggests that Cassandra is brought in to fill the unattainable lack – the desire on the part of the Other to find affirmation in the fact that they are doing something commendable – hiring an African-American woman who provides visible evidence (unavoidable due to the presence of her blackness and womanness) of their commitment to diversity, and also creating a welcoming space for minority students in the department. We situate Sera and Cassandra and those with whom they are enmeshed as subjects acting as a result of their position ("I desire what the Other desires of me"), rather than acting as a result of the forces of desire as conceptualized by Deleuze.

However, this same excerpt from Cassandra's interview, viewed through a Deleuzian mapping of desire, produces a very different reading. In contrast to Lacan, Deleuze and Guattari provide an immanent and immediate account of desire, one that rejects a constraining, transcendent desire that posits how one "ought to be" or "needs to be" according to normative expectations of what is good and just. Cassandra was hired to be a mentor and develop programs for the African-American students. She also came to understand that she was hired, in part, because she made others look good; she said, "They needed someone to fill that position in that grant and they wanted it to look like they were making an effort." In other words, she could be touted as an example of the university becoming more diverse in the hiring of a black woman. If we are to consider the silences on the part of colleagues and administrators who are not forthright about some of their motivations to hire Cassandra, we begin to consider the functioning of desire very differently. We look for that which is being produced by the silences that prevent an open acknowledgment of the motivations and desires on the part of university administrators. We also *hear* the silences that disallowed a supportive and collegial stance when Cassandra was challenged by white students who felt they were being slighted, discriminated against, or silenced.

We could read the silence on the part of colleagues and administrators as a desiring silence, one designed to perpetuate authority, privilege, and control that is maintained in a hegemonic and normative silence, one that produces complicity in continuing a system that is anything but good and just. Perhaps those who hired her believed her not to be competent because she was hired as a "token," a gesture, a symbol. Their desire therefore to regulate themselves and to resist being wrenched from their comfort zone produces a silence that attempts to re-inscribe privilege, authority, and identity. Their silent voice in this case also coalesces with power to maintain whiteness. They are thus free from a dismantling of their own subjectivity that may occur because they engage in the form of a desiring silence. Their desire produces certain ways for them "to 'become' ... to voice certain truths"[27] that escape the scrutiny and gaze of racist/sexist motivations. If white academics are not attentive to these silent voices, then white privilege is maintained.

Neither the Lacanian nor the Deleuzian reading is *right or wrong*, but thinking with Deleuze opens up the possibility of thought that "does not respect the artificial division between the three domains of representation, subject, concept, and being; it replaces restrictive analogy with a conductivity that knows no bounds."[28] It demands a more rigorous reading that does not attempt to fill the void, but rather engages desire as producing a becoming. It is a reading central to thinking desire as productive in the entanglement of forces and becomings. Deleuze and Guattari thus prompt a thinking not of what desire is, but how it functions and who it benefits.

Productions of desire

In our continuing practice of plugging one text into another, it seems that desire is functioning to produce silent discourses. These silent discourses in some cases serve to maintain a status quo that is, in part, a gendered response, but they also seek to perpetuate a continuation of status that is experienced on the part of Sera and Cassandra as tenuous and false, in that they feel as if they do not belong, and/or others continue to remind them that they need to stay in their place. The desire with these women, then, springs not from what they lack, but from a desire to preserve and produce *more* of what they have; in other words, a sense of belonging. For example, Sera fitting in with those she identifies as "my people," and Cassandra being told by friends and family that "she ain't changed a bit." It is this notsaid, this silent and desirous voice, that is produced by a longing for maintaining a normative and unchallenged (even unrecognized) belonging (status) that is important here. Working within "a problematic of silence,"[29] coupled with this view toward the silences as "producing" something, may lead us to turn on its head not only desire, but also silence as well, in a way that forces us to bring "production into desire on the one hand and desire into production on the other."[30]

If we think of silence as an enactment of a desire to be recognized as governed by social norms, then we acknowledge that the desire on the part of these women is a desire to be recognized "within the constraints of normativity."[31] If they are recognized within such constraints, then their mark *both* as someone esteemed by their families without alienation, *and* as "forgetting where they're from" (according to Cassandra), remains intact. Privilege remains unchallenged and is thus exercised as a desiring silence that lets them both fit in and masquerade as someone else, or as a part of their becoming. Instead of asking, "What is

[27] Alecia Y. Jackson, "'What am I Doing When I Speak of This Present?': Voice, Power, and Desire in Truth-Telling." In *Voice in Qualitative Inquiry*, edited by Alecia Y. Jackson and Lisa A. Mazzei (London: Routledge, 2009), 172.

[28] Brian Massumi, *A User's Guide to Capitalism and Schizophrenia* (Cambridge, MA: MIT Press, 1992), 5.

[29] Lisa A. Mazzei, *Inhabited Silence in Qualitative Research: Putting Poststructural Theory to Work* (New York: Peter Lang, 2007).

[30] Deleuze, *Negotiations*, op. cit., 17–18.

[31] Jackson, "What am I Doing When I Speak of This Present?" 171.

desire?" the impetus is to ask instead, "How is desire functioning to protect something?" In the case of Sera and Cassandra, it might be protecting their identity, their insecurity, their passings; their risks of becoming. Sera and Cassandra both speak of "fitting in" of "being silent," and of trying to anticipate (rather than ask) how they should be, what they are supposed to know, and what is expected of them in the new arena of academia. Sera elaborated more in her description of her "horrible dissertation" and her fraught relationship with committee members.

> I took on ideology and I took on rhetoric, and I feel like I can see how those things work, and I put it all together in my dissertation. And I said well, it makes a lot of sense to me. And everyone on my committee had areas that they liked … And I know why I put it in. I had this whacky doodle idea that I was entertaining them because they were bored. So I thought to myself, well, they don't have time to read this book. I'm going to paraphrase this book because it's really interesting, and I know that this person is going to really like reading it. And so I thought well, I'll add some stuff to the conclusion because it will be interesting to them. Why did they let me do that? They should have [told me] this has to go, it makes no sense. So I feel like I was doing a lot of audience adjusting, and I really feel like a lot of times I would go into my professor's office, and we would have a nice social relationship. And what I really should have been saying was I don't understand this. Help me do this. And we weren't doing any of the work. We were doing, I have to spend an hour with you. Let's touch base and see how things are going. And I really should have just been much more assertive, but I was passing a lot. I was just trying to get through and not to be noticed.

In her quest to be recognized within the constraints of normativity, in other words, to pass as belonging to this academic "club," to know the rules of the game, to attain the approval of her committee, Sera's passing was produced by a desiring silence that protects her identity as an impostor. Perhaps her committee members assume that she knows the rules of the game because her silence has convinced them that she does. Perhaps the committee members are silent because they do not want to blow her cover. Perhaps the committee members are silent because they wish to be recognized within the constraints of normativity. Perhaps none of these is the reason that the silences are produced. Deleuze would not have us look for reasons or causes, but to be once again confronted with the question of how desire works and who it works for.

How does it work?

Desire, for Deleuze and Guattari, does not seek something that is absent, but instead produces an effect. Deleuze "swerves" around the "despotic nature of signification"; in other words, around the tiresomeness of an insistence on meaning, for as he insists with Guattari, " 'Interpretation is our modern way of believing and being pious.' "[32] What matters for Deleuze and Guattari is not what desire means; instead, they want to know, what does desire do?

A movement *away* from meaning and interpretation does not lead to a shunning of attempts to know or understand what is being communicated by Sera and Cassandra. Instead,

---

[32] Jeffrey T. Nealon, "Beyond Hermeneutics: Deleuze, Derrida and Contemporary Theory." In *Between Deleuze & Derrida*, edited by Paul Patton and John Protevi (London: Continuum, 2003), 160.

through an engagement with Deleuzian desire, we are challenged to focus on what is producing the silence (desire) and/or what the silence produces (power, privilege, status), what we have named above, as we think with Deleuze and Guattari, a *desiring silence*. A movement away from meaning is an ethical response that attempts to disturb thought so as not to reproduce what we already think, know, and experience. It seems to us that, in our approaching this desiring silence, desire and silence are producing each other, much in the same way that power/knowledge operates for Foucault – they express each other, rely on each other, and produce something that is not singular to one or the other.[33] As researchers in this process of thinking with a Deleuzian theory of desire, the question is not what is lacking, but what desires are producing the silences, and what do these silences in turn produce?

Regulation and resistance

In her ethnographic study with those learning to teach, Deborah Britzman asserts "Much about the experience of learning to teach is negative: learning what to avoid, what not to do, and what not to become even as one finds oneself performing these disclaimed actions."[34] Similarly, much of the structure in the academy for those on a tenure track is modeled after the experience of learning to teach; what to avoid, what not to do, and what not to become as one is forging an academic identity that is "unique" and that is always already tied to the criteria in the Faculty Handbook that, in US universities, serves as the "bible" for what faculty need to do and be in order to become tenured and promoted. Both Sera and Cassandra have learned that regulation and conformity are necessary for their survival in the academy. In order to fit in and meet the criteria for becoming tenured, they are told, both implicitly and explicitly, to produce a desiring silence, and in turn they enforce the silence to produce a response that avoids scrutiny, singling out, and disciplining, as evidenced in the example below.

In the case of Sera, there are several desires that are forced into the social field: the desire to be a good mother, good academic, good colleague, and to do all of these things as an as-yet-untenured faculty member. Sera said,

> I've been told okay, if you're going to say that you need time off, don't say it's because of your kids … And so in my work relationships, I've been told that while on the surface people will say oh lovely that you have kids. Oh that's just wonderful. Even for married people, it's say that you need time off because you need to do research, you need time off because you're going to a conference, *not* you need time off because of spring break for your kids. Okay. Got it.

In order to "fit in" or fly under the radar in order to be viewed favorably by colleagues who ultimately will be deciding whether Sera is a "good" faculty member, a desiring silence produces multiple responses. The good mother knows that it is important, even necessary, to spend time with her children, particularly at times when school is not in session, but desire functions to produce a silence that masks her intentions with an acceptable (silent) response so the image of "good" faculty member is preserved. Sera is silent in order to

---

[33] See Chapter 4 for a lengthy discussion on power/knowledge and how we are thinking with Foucault.

[34] Deborah Britzman, *Practice Makes Practice: A Critical Study of Learning to Teach* (Albany: SUNY Press, 2003), 4.

produce that which is needed to maintain status. A seeming irony, of course, is that the advice that produces this desiring silence is given by those who assess her worthiness to become tenured, thereby also maintaining the privilege that they enjoy as tenured faculty themselves.

Maintaining privilege

A look at the following excerpt from Cassandra's transcript requires us to rethink desiring silence as an investment in whiteness and its attendant privileges. It is a recognition of these collective desires on the part of white students and administrators (and, in some cases, ourselves) as producing a desiring silence that maintains and sustains whiteness through a connection of desires, flows, and intensities. In our interview with Cassandra, she talked about a situation that occurred early in her career at Regional State University, in which letters were written to her department chair by white students accusing her of reverse discrimination. She then went on to describe a more recent experience.

> A couple of years ago, I had a similar situation when two graduate students ... said I was incompetent and they wrote these long letters, which ended up in the Dean's office and I had to write a rebuttal to that and fortunately it was resolved in my favor so that those letters no longer exist in my work folder, but the thing that has been a constant obstacle for me is that if one or two students are upset with you that they could do something like that and if you don't respond to it, it could actually end up in your permanent folder without any recourse ... They [the white administrators], of course, later found that the charges that the students had raised were totally unfounded and if they had asked me about that before they put the letter in my folder, then they would have known that.
>
> I know that that happens to people, probably several other people even within the College because students do things like that but the interesting thing for me is I never know whether it's because I'm black, or whether it's because I'm a woman, or whether it's because it's both, because there is this phenomenon that has been written about in some of the feminist literature, and it's specifically black feminist about the "double whammy" and so in my case, ... I find myself questioning as to whether they would do it to some of my colleagues. They do do it to some of my female colleagues from time to time, but I don't know that they've ever done it to any of my male colleagues [who are all white].

In the above example, desiring silence produces a response on the part of Cassandra's white colleagues. Desire functions to produce a silence that results in an avoidance of loss of power and control that is maintained in a hegemonic and normative silence.[35] Desiring silence therefore functions to sustain the system of white privilege within which these white colleagues and students function. Their participation in a process to regulate and resist produces a desiring silence that attempts to re-inscribe privilege, power, and identity. Their silent voice coalesces with power to maintain whiteness as privilege.

Why do Cassandra's colleagues, and in this particular instance her white male colleagues, remain silent and accept accusations by white students that she is not doing her job, when

[35] Lisa Mazzei,"Desiring Silence."

her record and the fact that she has been tenured and promoted would indicate otherwise? Why does Cassandra have to insist that the voice of one or two disgruntled students is not evidence that she is failing in her work as a good academic, citizen, scholar, and colleague? She must deterritorialize this desiring silence by rebutting accusations that her white colleagues accept as truth, coming as they are from white graduate students. Perhaps it is a challenge to the privilege enjoyed by her department chair and dean, as both white and male, that is producing this desiring silence (or what this desiring silence might be producing). The following is an example of how this works, based on Lisa's research with white teachers:

> If we think of silence as an enactment of a desire to be recognized as governed by social norms, then we acknowledge that the desire on the part of these white pre-service teachers is a desire to be recognized "within the constraints of normativity" (Jackson, 2009, p. 171). If they are recognized within such constraints, then their mark as white teacher remains intact. Privilege remains unchallenged and is thus exercised as a desiring silence that maintains an invisible mask of whiteness. In other words, these white pre-service teachers do not speak of whiteness, or more specifically their own race, therefore whiteness is reinscribed as that which need not be named.[36]

To say that these disgruntled students may be responding to Cassandra based on her race and/or gender is to acknowledge that she is not recognized within the constraints of normativity. Cassandra is aware of how her presence as an African-American woman, both in her college and also on strategic university committees, is welcome because the presence of her blackness and womanness makes the others look good – they are inclusive and diverse. She also is candid in discussing the delicate dance that risks exposing the motivations and practices of students, administrators, and colleagues. We don't know enough from the transcript, but perhaps she has challenged their own silence by her presence in the classroom, which makes visible their whiteness in contrast to the otherness that is her blackness. For the administrators, not to "go along" with the assertions made by the white students might mean to risk their own normative identity and its attendant privilege.

In discussing whiteness, Elizabeth Ellsworth writes about how whites *do* notice their positioning, their privilege, their status, and *keep silent* to fit in and maintain acceptable (normative) "white" behavior and attitudes.[37] Because there is no evidence that Cassandra's white male colleagues have faced similar charges from students, this desiring silence may serve to prevent an open dialogue regarding race that further reinscribes racial stereotypes, thus protecting white privilege. If they don't talk about whiteness and white privilege, then they can go about the business of their work without interruption. Those students and faculty who are white are therefore not made to feel uncomfortable by noticing and/or talking about something that they wish to avoid – white privilege – hence desire continues to produce a desiring silence.

[36] *Ibid.*
[37] Elizabeth Ellsworth, "Double Binds of Whiteness." In *Off White: Readings on Race, Power, and Society*, edited by Michelle Fine, Lois Weis, Linda C. Powell, and L. Mun Wong (New York: Routledge, 1997).

Keeping them in their place

We know from the description of their upbringing and high school experiences that the likelihood that either Sera or Cassandra would go to college was low. They have worked very hard to obtain their degrees, to fit into the academy, and to be successful in their fields. They work equally hard to fit in with friends and families, because they are the first in their families who have attended college. Many times, this fitting in is possible only through a desiring silence. As stated earlier, we desire, according to Deleuze, not because we lack something that we do not have. Desire is a force that acts on us and that coalesces with other desires producing, among other things, silence. These silences do not just appear or happen out of ether. They are produced in response to the dominant reality of the multiple communities to which Sera and Cassandra belong, and attempts to maintain that which they wish to preserve: belonging. Sera and Cassandra are produced as silent, desiring subjects with their families and friends. They do so to avoid being criticized for being too uppity or too book smart, even though they and their families are very proud of their accomplishments. Cassandra explained how this has shaped her interactions with family and friends from her hometown:

> I would do this flip-flop kind of thing all the time, but not only with my friends, but with my family as well and even to this day when I'm around my family I act the way that I always have and I know, and not just my family, but the friends, the people in the community, and I know that I'm being successful because – pretty much they'll say things like, they call me Jane there, my middle name.
>
> They say, 'That Jane, she ain't changed a bit.' And that lets me know that I'm being successful in terms of my relating, but what I have to do is I have to try as much as possible to fit in and to be, – I will speak the local dialect when I'm around them and just that's the role, – that's what I have to do in order to keep my social relations at home, for example.

There is also a sense from Sera that she is kept in her place by being reminded by others that her background is very different from those of many of her academic colleagues. She uses the phrase "my people" on several occasions to describe those friends and colleagues with whom she can be herself, who share "the same roots," and with whom she at times can just "be the girl." Friends who, like her, have "made it" in the form of college education and/or teaching, but who, like her, have "a very working class way of approaching things" and yet have learned how to negotiate both worlds. She also goes to great pains to keep her personal life out of the academy because of the way she feels it may be used against her, particularly in the entangled desiring machine of a religiously affiliated university.

> It's very strategic on my part. At work, I don't talk about a personal life. Like if I have a boyfriend or whatever, and I don't, but sometimes I do. But it's very important that I'm a single parent because I can't really hide that, but I know that that kind of stuff counts against me, so I'm not going to be the single parent that *also* has a boyfriend.

Desire functions in the above examples to normalize and sustain privilege. To consider how desire works is not to locate *a* desire and attach it to *a* subject – for example, the desire on the part of Cassandra's family to keep her as she has always been, or desire on the part of

Sera to avoid scrutiny as a single mother with a boyfriend. Desire works in the machine because it is the desires that many bring to the enterprise: Sera, Cassandra, family, friends, colleagues, the church, the academy. These desires plug into the machine in a transformative process that produces many outcomes, prompting the Deleuzian question, who does it work for?

Who does it work for?

Desire is assembled and shaped over time by our experiences. We learn what we want, how to get it, how to maintain it, and what it means through the act of connection. Sera and Cassandra have learned how to maintain their status in the academy, often through the production of a desiring silence. They have survived/thrived because they have connected their desires with those of others in the production of new becomings. Claire Colebrook further elaborates:

> Desire begins from connection; life strives to preserve and enhance itself and does so by connecting with other desires. These connections and productions eventually form social wholes; when bodies connect with other bodies to enhance their power they eventually form communities or societies.[38]

Deleuze's method does not begin from assumed terms, "such as 'man' or 'human interests': it shows the historical composition of those terms from intensities. This means, contra ideology, that desire is not repressed by politics so much as it is coded."[39] The intensities that coalesce to produce what is understood as good daughter, sister, friend, colleague, academic also coalesce to produce desires that interact with other forces and intensities. While the codes that govern Sera and Cassandra are strong, so too are the interests that produce an emergent desire.

These coded images of what it means to be a good academic are particularly laden with gendered compositions based on the historical nature of who has been in the academy, thus the connections that produce a coded image of the academic. Both Sera and Cassandra speak of the differential treatment and deference given to their male colleagues that is not afforded to them. It is the unspoken nature of this maleness, this space of otherness that they inhabit by virtue of being both female and also first-generation, that attempts a new coding: a becoming and deterritorialization. As in the previous example with Cassandra and the white male administrator, each force acts upon the other in a process of transformation: it is deterritorialized.

Sera presented the following description of how she is perceived in relation to a male colleague, which we can use to think about how the connections are enmeshed to produce new connections.

> I think that students perceive or are going to perceive males with more power and be less quick to devalue them. Here's an example. A male colleague and I, we're probably pretty similar. A little bit rambly, his students are going to accept that in him as a

[38] Colebrook, *Gilles Deleuze*, op. cit., 91.
[39] *Ibid.*, 93.

positive stereotype … he's a little spacey and that's okay. Whereas with me, it's going to be a quicker dismissal.

I think it's both [age and gender] and, what he looks like, a caricature of an Italian cartoon. And I hear students say oh, he's so cute. I have seen very clearly that as a woman, you're going to have a harder time in these few areas. That's just how it is. And the hard part is trying to get the male professors to see because that's always been a struggle. It's so frustrating. But it doesn't mean it's going away. Is there a strategy for dealing with it? Probably not. Because you say something about it, and then they're just like oh, you're a bitch.

The coded intensities in the example above are on the plane of immanent desire that is shaped by the relations (between Sera and her colleague; Sera and her students; students and Sera's colleague), connections (between those present in the above example and beyond), and the meanings that exist in society. Desire, for Deleuze and Guattari, "is the social unconscious."[40] Understanding how desire is functioning and what is being produced is not to focus on the individual desires of Sera, but on the desires as produced and functioning within the social unconscious, in this case, the university. It is looking for definitions of what is normal (transcendence) and how desire, and desiring silence, are functioning to both maintain and resist normalcy (immanence). What the students say, how Sera's male colleague is perceived, and her recognition that push-back will land her the label of "bitch" are all coded within a Catholic institution that still maintains a strong coding of a patriarchal structure where the percentage among full-time faculty is 62 percent male. However, we go back to Deleuze to be reminded that "when forces meet and interact, the relation that they construct affects their own nature and changes them in the process."[41] The codes may be strong, but they are still susceptible to deterritorialization.

While forces function to preserve and maintain this sense of "normal," they are enacted within a social whole. Social wholes, as described by Claire Colebrook, take "*desires* – or those connections which enhance life – in order to produce interests – 'coded', regular, collective and organised forms of desire."[42] It is this investment in not calling attention to oneself, in these collective desires producing a desiring silence, that maintains and sustains ordinariness and reveals itself for what it is in Deleuzian terms: a connection of desires, a conjunction of flows, and a continuum of intensities. It is the social whole of the academy that continues to produce a desiring silence that allows entry and acceptance for Sera and Cassandra as first-generation women academics. While there are many forces that operate in society to foreclose desire, multiplicity, and creation from coming into existence, "these operate less as a blockage against the realization of a potential, than by interposing themselves so that other relations come into play."[43]

Thinking with desire

Thinking with Deleuze and Guattari's desire offers an immanent and immediate account of desire, one that complicates our reading and listening as we account for the productive presence of silence in the narrations of our research participants. Deleuze, with Guattari,

[40] Goodchild, *Deleuze & Guattari*, 5.
[41] *Ibid.*, 18.
[42] *Ibid.*, 91.
[43] *Ibid.*, 5.

extends our thinking by complicating the production of silence in our interviews with Sera and Cassandra to prompt a question of what is produced and what is producing silence: a productive silence that we named a *desiring silence*. For Deleuze and Guattari, desire is about production. Desire's production is active, becoming, transformative. It produces out of a multiplicity of forces, which form the assemblage. Sera and Cassandra (and their family, friends, and colleagues) desire, not because they lack something that they do not have, but because of the productive force of intensities and connections of desires. We used this productive notion of forces in our analysis to turn desire on its head as a way to open up how silences were functioning in the research narratives, why they persisted, and who benefitted.

While our focus has been, for the most part, on Sera and Cassandra, their experiences are but one aspect of the social whole, the desiring machine producing becomings that are taking the institutions of the university, the white male administrators, colleagues, and family into different states of intensity and transformation. Because Deleuze is interested in what is to be learned about living, we return not to the question of what it means, but how it works. Goodchild writes that one "accomplishes little by talking about 'desire' in the abstract; much more is to gained by developing strategies for the liberation and creation of desire,"[44] an aim which we have sought to demonstrate in this chapter. Deleuze uses the word *thought* to refer to philosophy that takes itself seriously. Goodchild concludes that Deleuze offers a radically different approach as long as "we turn to his work not to settle old questions [what does it mean] or old scores [why] but instead to become unsettled. In short, as long as we are willing to do philosophy"[45] in our thinking with desire.

More on desire

The following texts are offered, not as *the* texts to consult, but as providing an entry point for those who are new to the writings of Deleuze and would like to learn more about desire. We list the secondary texts first as a continuation of the "schematic cues" presented in the interludes, which readers can use as a brace as they enter this new theoretical terrain. Following the secondary texts are suggested entry points for approaching the writing of Deleuze, and finally, research exemplars that illustrate additional examples of thinking with Deleuzian concepts.

Secondary texts

Colebrook, Claire. *Gilles Deleuze*. London: Routledge, 2002.

Goodchild, Philip. *Deleuze & Guattari: An Introduction to the Politics of Desire*. London: Sage, 1996.

Hardt, Michael. *Gilles Deleuze: An Apprenticeship in Philosophy*. Minneapolis: University of Minnesota Press, 1993.

May, Todd. *Gilles Deleuze: An Introduction*. Cambridge: Cambridge University Press, 2005.

Primary texts

Deleuze, Gilles and Félix Guattari. *Anti-Oedipus: Capitalism and Schizophrenia*. Translated by Robert Hurley, Mark Seem and Helen R. Lane. 1972; repr. Minneapolis: University of Minnesota Press, 1983.

---

[44] *Ibid.*, 42.
[45] Todd May, *Gilles Deleuze* (Cambridge: Cambridge University Press, 2005), 25.

——A *Thousand Plateaus: Capitalism and Schizophrenia*. Translated by Brian Massumi. 1980; repr. Minneapolis: University of Minnesota Press, 1987.

Research exemplars

Mazzei, Lisa A. "Desiring Silence: Gender, Race and Pedagogy in Education," *British Educational Research Journal* 37 (2011).

International Journal of Qualitative Studies in Education 23, no. 5 (2010). Special Issue: "Thinking with Deleuze in Qualitative Research." Contributors include: Karin Hultman and Hillevi Lenz Taguchi; Alecia Y. Jackson; Maggie MacLure, Rachel Holmes, Christina MacRae, and Liz Jones; Lisa A. Mazzei; Kate McCoy; Marg Sellers; Warren Sellers and Noel Gough; Eve Tuck.

Why Barad?

Beginning with our placement of Derrida at the beginning of this book, our movement to the other theorists with whom we have been thinking is done in our efforts to expand/stretch/distort previous ways of knowing. This ordering of chapters is not to suggest a teleological progression, but rather to illustrate the relationships between the theorists we have chosen, and how they have stretched the work of other theorists who have come before. It also reflects a move from an emphasis on the discursive, with Derrida and Spivak; to the discursive ↔ material, with Foucault and Butler; to the material ↔ discursive,[1] with Deleuze and Barad. It is in the work of Foucault, and by extension Barad, that we come to be reminded that "theories, discourses, have material consequences."[2]

Karen Barad draws heavily on the work of Foucault's theory of discourse and Butler's theory of performativity (in addition to Niels Bohr's theory of complementarity) in a project that is at some level to be likened to Cixous' "shaking up of the order"[3] as she moves to reinstall the material as "equal" in the material ↔ discursive binary. This reinstallment of the material is being taken up by critical and poststructural feminists alike, along with a conviction that "materialism is once more on the move after several decades in abeyance."[4] It is not that the material hasn't been present, it is that it hasn't been accorded its due in the discursive, laden writings of poststructural theorists and methodologists. "Theorists such as Gilles Deleuze and Michel Foucault do, in fact, accommodate the material in their work,"[5] and yet we find in the work of material feminists[6] and, for purposes of this chapter,

---

[1] We are using the double arrow to indicate the intra-action, or that which is simultaneously materially and discursively produced, reflective of a key shift in material feminist thought. We do so as a gesture toward a removal of the hyphen or slash used to indicate the relationship between the material and the discursive without privileging one over the other. In a conversation with Hillevi Lenz Taguchi about this chapter, she stated that she would like to get rid of the hyphen (but she hasn't dared to yet). This is a nod to Hillevi and a move in that direction. We would also like to acknowledge the insights and guidance provided by Hillevi in the development of this chapter.

[2] Susan Hekman, *The Material of Knowledge: Feminist Disclosures* (Bloomington: Indiana University Press, 2010), 90.

[3] Hillevi Lenz Taguchi, "Becoming-With-the-Barkboat in the Event: A Relational Materialist and Deleuzian Approach to Analysis of Interview Data," unpublished manuscript, 5.

[4] Diana Coole and Samantha Frost, "Introducing the New Materialisms." In *New Materialisms: Ontology, Agency, & Politics*, edited by Diana Coole and Samantha Frost (Durham: Duke University Press, 2010), 2.

[5] *Ibid.*, 3.

[6] Barad's work is situated in a body of work by feminists named new materialists or material feminists, who enact Deleuzian becoming and a material ↔ discursive rewriting of subjectivity, informed by, or at least engaging, a Deleuzian philosophy of immanence. See for example: Olkowski, Hekman, Grosz, Mol.

specifically the work of Karen Barad, a fruitful theorizing of the relationship between discursive practices and the material world. Further, we see the work of Karen Barad as an enactment of what has been encountered in the work of Deleuze as theoretical abstractions. Deleuze and Guattari theorize this ontological shift in a philosophy of immanence. In *Anti-Oedipus*, they write: "There is no such thing as either man or nature now, only a process that produces the one within the other and couples the machines together."[7] Here they seem to be writing about the entangled nature of the material and discursive. To make this shift, we will demonstrate in Chapter 7 how the material is always already discursively produced, and the discursive is always already materially produced. For example, during her interview with us, Cassandra talks about an episode in which a colleague tells a student, "I don't agree with that," speaking against Cassandra's expertise. To make the shift from discursive to material ↔ discursive is to read these words not merely as a construction based on gender and racial stereotypes, but as material, not just as an assault on her intellect, but as a negation of her as a black female. These words, this material assault, would not have the same import if, for instance, they were spoken by a colleague directly to her. But the fact that they are "ventriloquized" by a student who mediates is a way to begin reading the data differently. How do these words, this assault, strike differently when spoken by a student, one who speaks from a position of privilege as white? This brings us to a place as researchers of considering how these constructions and interactions, then, are not just about bodies, nor just about words, but about the mutual production of both subjectivities and performative enactments.

It is the work of Karen Barad, and others named as "new materialists" or "material feminists," to ask how our intra-action with other bodies (both human and nonhuman) produce subjectivities and performative enactments. While much of what has been written under the guise of material feminism comes from the philosophy of science, it is the work of feminist scholars and the new materialists to posit posthumanist performativity in the social world. In writing of "new materialisms,"[8] Diana Coole and Samantha Frost emphasize that much of how we think of matter is contingent on assumptions based in the thinking of Descartes, from whom we developed an understanding of matter as "extended, uniform, and inert."[9] The writings of Descartes provided a foundation for modern assumptions about nature as fixed and measurable, laying the groundwork for Newtonian physics, which adheres to material objects as discrete, as acting only when acted upon by an external agent, and as doing so in a cause-and-effect relationship. What they continue, in a laying out of the new materialisms, is its "antipathy toward oppositional ways of thinking."[10]

> Such thinking is accordingly post- rather than anti-Cartesian. It avoids dualism or dialectical reconciliation ... Perhaps most significant here is the way new materialist

---

[7] Gilles Deleuze and Félix Guattari. *Anti-Oedipus: Capitalism and Schizophrenia.* Translated by Robert Hurley, Mark Seem and Helen R. Lane (1972; repr. Minneapolis: University of Minnesota Press, 1983), 2.

[8] According to Susan Hekman, "At this point in the discussion the new approach does not have an agreed-upon label. Many have been proposed: several feminist critics of science favor 'the new materialism'; Nancy Tuana proposes 'interactionism' and 'viscous porosity'; Karen Barad favors 'intra-action' and 'agential realism.' The lack of consensus on a label, however, is indicative of little more than the newness of the approach. What is important is that there is a building consensus among feminists and critical theorists that a new approach is needed and that feminism is and should be on the forefront of that effort." Hekman, *The Material of Knowledge*, op. cit., 68.

[9] Coole and Frost, "Introducing the New Materialisms," op. cit., 7.

[10] *Ibid.*, 8.

ontologies are abandoning the terminology of matter as an inert substance subject to predictable causal forces ... One could conclude, accordingly, that "matter becomes" rather than that "matter is."[11]

Susan Hekman traces the early development of accounting for the material, after the linguistic turn, back to two key articles by Donna Haraway and Bruno Latour. Haraway's article, "Manifesto for Cyborgs: Science, Technology, and Socialist Feminism in the 1980s," was a critique of the failure of socialism and "the cyborg" as a deconstruction of the discourse/reality dichotomy. Hekman continues her tracing by describing Latour's article, "Why Has Critique Run Out of Steam? From Matters of Fact to Matters of Concern" as an assault on the linguistic turn and privileging of the discursive at the expense of the material, that was beginning at the time Haraway published her article.[12] The point then, and what has been extended in the work of "new materialists" such as Rosi Braidotti, Elizabeth Grosz, Susan Hekman, Nancy Tuana, Stacy Alaimo, and Karen Barad, to name a few, is an ontological re-orientation that, in many cases, is influenced by the work of Gilles Deleuze and his vitalist proclivities. In introducing what they are calling new materialisms, Diana Coole and Samantha Frost present three themes in new materialist scholarship.

> First among them is an ontological reorientation that is resonant with, and to some extent informed by, developments in natural science: an orientation that is post-humanist in the sense that it conceives of matter itself as lively or as exhibiting agency. The second theme entails consideration of a raft of biopolitical and bioethical issues concerning the status of life and of the human. Third, new materialist scholarship testifies to a critical and nondogmatic reengagement with political economy, where the nature of, and relationship between, the material details of everyday life and broader geopolitical and socioeconomic structures is being explored afresh.[13]

It is important to note that a characteristic shared by all three themes is an emphasis on the inseparable nature of the resiliency of matter and its productivity in concert with the human.

What is consistent with the above-mentioned theorists and themes is a challenge to our basic humanist assumptions, including, and perhaps foremost, "its normative sense of the human and its beliefs about human agency."[14] From a humanist perspective, humans possess the ability to act on the world, making choices that are centered within the human and that imply a unidirectional relationship with the real or the material. It is a discontent, primarily fueled by feminist scholars, with the failures of social constructionism and

---

[11] *Ibid.*, 8–10.

[12] Cited by Susan Hekman, "Constructing the Ballast." In *Material Feminisms*, edited by Stacy Alaimo and Susan Hekman (Bloomington: Indiana University Press, 2008), 85–89. The reader is encouraged to consult this essay for a fuller discussion of how the early work of Haraway and later work of Latour have contributed to a current re-examination of the material. The Haraway article that Hekman refers to is the now well noted "Manifesto for Cyborgs: Science, Technology, and Socialist Feminism in the 1980s," first published in 1985. The article by Bruno Latour is "Why Has Critique Run Out of Steam? From Matters of Fact to Matters of Concern," *Critical Inquiry* 30, no. 2 (2004): 225–248.

[13] Coole and Frost, "Introducing the New Materialisms," 6–7.

[14] *Ibid.*, 4.

postmodernism, that concerns itself with a definition of the "real" in a Cartesian sense – in other words, something "out there" to be conquered and known. Hekman writes:

> Like Latour, many feminists came to the conclusion that we should be able to account for the real [i.e. the material] beyond discourse, but exactly how this accounting should be expressed remains elusive ... There appears to be a consensus that something is amiss, but there is as yet no consensus on how the problem can be fixed.[15]

Barad would certainly concur that something is amiss. It is the work of Chapter 7 to begin to account for this real, this material, beyond merely the confines of the discursive constructions to be found in interview data when viewed only as text that conveys descriptions of things.

We go to Barad because she, and the other material feminists engaging questions of ontology, lead us to think not just how discourses function, but how they materialize. Or, to invoke a Deleuzian question, not what do they mean, but how do they work? Such questioning shifts our thinking from not only how discursive performative speech acts or repetitive bodily actions produce subjectivity, but also how subjectivity can be understood as a set of linkages and connections with other things and other bodies. Barad offers an examination of these linkages, and she does so spurred by an interest not merely in a re-insertion of the material, nor a privileging of the material, but in a shaking up of the privileging of the discursive in postmodern thought without a re-centering of the material that preceded the linguistic turn. This fundamental break presented by Barad helps us "fashion an approach that brings the material back in without rejecting the legitimate insights of the linguistic turn."[16] Such fashioning prompts the question: *How do Cassandra and Sera intra-act with the materiality of their world in ways that produce different becomings?*

Schematic cues

Agency. Agency takes on different meanings and is ascribed various levels of importance as accorded by the paradigmatic perspective from which one is located – for example, humanism, poststructuralism, or posthumanism.[17] From a humanist perspective, agency is something possessed by humans, and is seen as the ability to act on or act in the world. To ascribe "agency" to someone is to imply that one is a voluntary actor, making choices that are willed rather than determined. The agency of the subject in a poststructural paradigm "seems to lie in the subject's ability to decode and recode its identity within discursive formations and cultural practices."[18] From a posthumanist perspective, agency is distributed. In other words, intentionality is not attributable to humans, but, according to Karen

---

[15] Hekman, "Constructing the Ballast," op. cit., 90–91.

[16] Hekman, *The Material of Knowledge*, 7.

[17] In her essay "Feminism, Materialism, and Freedom," which appears in the book *New Materialisms* (edited by Diana Coole and Samantha Frost, op. cit., 139), Elizabeth Grosz proposes an opening of the terms commonly used to define subjectivity or identity that she maintains have functioned as a "kind of mantra of liberation" for feminists: "Concepts of autonomy, agency, and freedom – the central terms by which agency has been understood."

[18] Elizabeth Adams St Pierre, "Poststructural Feminism in Education: An Overview," *International Journal of Qualitative Studies in Education* 13, no. 5 (2000): 504.

Barad, is "understood as attributable to a complex network of human and nonhuman agents, including historically specific sets of material conditions that exceed the traditional notion of the individual."[19] Agency, then, is an enactment, not something that an individual possesses.

Agential realism. This is what Barad names as her proposed ontoepistemological framework. Agential realism would have us ascribe agency not only to humans, but to matter as well. A key understanding that we can apply to our research settings from Barad's agential realism is that it "provides an understanding of the role of human and nonhuman, material and discursive, and natural and cultural factors in scientific and other social-material practices."[20] In an early article, Barad identified four principal advantages of agential realism that have significant implications for research and data analysis:

> First, it grounds and situates knowledge claims in local experience. Thus objectivity is literally embodied. Second, agential realism privileges neither the material nor the cultural; rather, production is material/cultural. Third, agential realism entails the interrogation of boundaries and cultural reflexivity. Drawing different boundaries has different ontological implications. Fourth, agential realism underlines the necessity of an ethic of knowing; our constructed knowledge has real, material consequences.[21]

Nancy Tuana writes of this relationship and its consequences with the conceptual metaphor "viscous porosity," in a move that shifts "debates from 'realism' vs. 'social constructivism' to *emergent interplay*, which precludes a sharp divide between the biological and the cultural,"[22] or the material and the discursive. Tuana asserts that problems arise from what she deems questionable ontological divisions that we use artificially to separate the "natural from the humanly constructed, the biological from the cultural, genes from their environments, the material from the semiotic."[23] She illustrates her analysis with the events that have come to be known simply as "Katrina" in reference to the 2005 hurricane that struck the city of New Orleans and its aftermath. Continuing, Tuana writes, "As the phenomenon of Katrina's devastation has taught us all too well, the knowledge that is too often missing and is often desperately needed is at the intersection between things and people, between feats of engineering and social structures, between experiences and bodies."[24] An agential realist account, then, would have us look to the intersection of the "real" and the "socially constructed" for more complex and nuanced understandings.

Diffraction. Karen Barad makes a distinction between diffraction and reflection, a practice viewed as sound methodology for many qualitative researchers. She takes the metaphor from the notion of diffraction as a physical phenomenon, for instance, when ocean waves pass through an opening or obstruction and are spread differently than they would be otherwise. To think of diffraction as a methodological practice, according to Barad, is to read "insights

---

[19] Karen Barad, *Meeting the Universe Halfway: Quantum Physics and the Entanglement of Matter and Meaning* (Durham: Duke University Press, 2007), 23.

[20] *Ibid.*, 26.

[21] Hekman, *The Material of Knowledge*, 73.

[22] Nancy Tuana, "Viscous Porosity: Witnessing Katrina." In *Material Feminisms*, edited by Stacy Alaimo and Susan Hekman, op. cit., 189.

[23] *Ibid.*

[24] *Ibid.*

through one another," whereas reflection is a practice of critical self-positioning. She continues, "Both are optical phenomena, but whereas the metaphor of reflection reflects the themes of mirroring and sameness, diffraction is marked by patterns of difference."[25] Diffraction moves us away from habitual normative readings and accounts grounded in discursive readings that often fail to account for material intra-actions.

Discursive. Poststructuralist theories are those that are said to have developed as a result of the linguistic turn, which explicitly adheres to an understanding of reality as constituted through our language practices, or discursive constructions. The epistemology of the post-structuralists is therefore an acknowledgement of the centrality of language for our constitution of reality. In other words, we know the world and our place in it, and we are constructed and constrained by the language which we enter at our birth. Discourse is not literally what is said. Discourse is what enables and constrains what can be said. It is through discursive practices that we define what counts as meaningful statements. Only those statements deemed meaningful circulate in fields of discourse to produce constitutions of reality. The project of new materialists or material feminists is to re-establish the material in the discursive/material binary. Further, in the philosophies and enactments of new materialism, there is not a rejection of the discursive, but a conceiving of the discursive as always-already material, and the material as always-already a discursive construction. The two, then, are mutually constitutive of one another.

Intra-activity. Intra-activity refers to the ways in which "discourse and matter are understood to be mutually constituted in the production of knowing."[26] For Barad, intra-activity is to be differentiated from inter-activity, which describes a relationship between distinctly separate bodies, often focusing on the realm of inter-personal relationships. Key to Barad's analysis is the agential realist understanding of "matter as a dynamic and shifting entanglement of relations, rather than a property of things."[27] For Barad, this understanding of agential realism "takes into account the fact that the forces at work in the materialization of bodies are not only social and the bodies produced are not all human."[28] In Chapter 7, we present examples of how Sera and Cassandra are produced differently through positionings with office space, other bodies, clothing, and furniture. Similarly, how their entanglement with these material fixtures is also mutually shifting. Barad writes,

> The dichotomized positions of realism and social constructivism—which presume a subject/object dichotomy—can acknowledge the situated/constructed character of only one of the poles of the dualism at a time. Realists do not deny that subjects are materially situated; constructivists insist upon the socially or discursively constructed character of objects. Neither recognizes their mutually constitutive "intra-action."[29]

Material. While poststructural and/or postmodern theories have privileged the discursive, modernism and modern philosophies (e.g. Marxism; critical theory) have privileged the material. The material is that which we experience in the world. In the broadest terms, materialism maintains that whatever exists is, or depends solely upon, matter. For those who ascribe to materialist philosophies, the material precedes knowing. It is the project of

25 Barad, *Meeting the Universe Halfway*, op. cit., 71–72.
26 Lenz Taguchi, "Barkboat," 5.
27 Barad, *Meeting the Universe Halfway*, op. cit., 224.
28 *Ibid.*, 224–25.
29 Karen Barad, "Agential Realism: Feminist Interventions in Understanding Scientific Practices." In *The Science Studies Reader*, edited by Mario Biagioli (New York: Routledge, 1999), 2.

material feminists to reclaim the material and to explore how we are constituted by both the material and the discursive without privileging one over the other.

Myra Hird, in the article, "Feminist Engagements with Matter,"[30] makes an important distinction between the emerging field of material feminism (in which the analysis in Chapter 7 is situated) and what she describes as the more familiar "material feminism" that accounts for significant feminist analysis:

> This latter field is concerned with women's material living conditions – labor, repro-duction, political access, health, education, and intimacy – structured through class, race, ethnicity, age, nation, ableism, heteronormativity, and so on. These analyses, in broad brushstroke, draw attention to the often mundane, repetitive, and tedious activities of daily life – hauling water, chopping firewood – that occupy women's lives. Although certainly paying attention to the often overlooked minutiae of 'living woman,' these analyses tend not to engage with affective physicality or human–nonhuman encounters and relations. What distinguishes emerging analyses of material feminism – alternatively called "new materialism," "neo-materialism," and "new sciences" – is a keen interest in *engagements* with matter.[31]

Meaning. We stated in our discussion in the Preface how we are working against inter-pretivism and against humanism. While this is the case, and we have tried to eliminate many words from our vocabulary in writing this text, we are still burdened with much of the lan-guage that comes from our humanist history: meaning, encounter, experience. In an exten-sion from our thinking with Deleuze, these signifiers cannot hold the same places that they did in humanism. For example, an encounter in a humanist paradigm might be meant to evoke an experience. An encounter in posthumanism might be meant to signal a change, an intra-action, a collective subjectivity as named by Deleuze. We still attempt to limit our use of these referents, but in doing so, we take them on, as gestured to by Barad, and also in an ongoing effort to produce new concepts and ways of knowing in being. Barad uses the word "meaning" to denote that which we know as produced by the discursive, and the word "matter" to denote that which we know and encounter as the material. She presents meaning not as an attempt at truth, but to indicate *how we know as produced in the entanglements between the material and the discursive*.

Ontoepistemology. Critical to an understanding of Barad's project is the concept of ontoepistemology, sometimes written as onto-epistem-ology. To think of ontoepiste-mology is to think of knowing in being. To engage this from the standpoint of how it informs research methodology, it is more accurate to think about the study of practices of knowing in being as the understandings that are needed to come to terms with how specific intra-actions matter. Barad's critique, and that of other material feminists, is that the separation of epistemology from ontology is a carry-over from metaphysics, that assumes "an inherent difference between human and nonhuman, subject and object, mind and body, matter and discourse."[32] An ontoepistemological stance asserts that practices of knowing *and* being cannot be isolated from one another, but rather are mutually implicated. In the words of Barad, "We don't obtain knowledge by standing outside the world; we

---

[30] Myra J. Hird, "Feminist Engagements with Matter." In *Feminist Studies* 35, no. 2 (2009): 329–30.
[31] *Ibid.*
[32] Barad, *Meeting the Universe Halfway*, 185.

know because we are of the world."[33] We therefore know as a result of our being in the world.

Phenomena. Our use of "phenomena" in Chapter 7 is not to be confused with "phenomenon," as in a fact or an occurrence. In the context of Barad's work as a scientific philosopher and physicist, phenomena are conceptualized as *"differential patterns of mattering"*[34] that are produced through the intra-actions of matter (e.g. waves) and apparatus (e.g. equipment, instruments). Barad goes onto explain that these differential patterns of mattering or "diffraction patterns" are produced in the agential intra-actions between different types of matter that need not necessarily involve humans. The primary ontological units, then, for Barad "are not 'things' but phenomena."[35]

Posthumanist performativity To begin a further exploration of the entanglement of matter (the material) and meaning (discursive) is to remind ourselves of the humanist perspective that has burdened the concept of agency, and relationships of humans to the material, for centuries. Humanism asserts the centrality of thought, reason, and outcome as solely centered in and determined by humans, a position that grew out of the Renaissance in contradistinction to the authority of the church. Andrew Pickering, describing traditional sociology of science, classifies it as "humanist in that it identifies human scientists as the central seat of agency ... traditional sociology of science refuses to ascribe agency to the material worlds."[36]

Conversely, posthumanism does not ascribe agency as something to be possessed by the human actor, a seemingly difficult shift to comprehend. In the posthuman, "Material and human agencies are mutually and emergently productive of one another."[37] Karen Barad writes:

> From a humanist perspective, the question of nonhuman agency may seem a bit queer, since agency is generally associated with issues of subjectivity and intentionality. However, if agency is understood as an enactment and not something someone has, then it seems not only appropriate but important to consider agency as distributed over nonhuman as well as human forms.[38]

If agency is distributed in the sense that Karen Barad describes, a corresponding approach to our research settings and data is required to better account for these mutually constitutive sites of agency.

Subjectivity. Poststructural theories of subjectivity posit a notion of the "self" as a site of disunity and conflict that is always in process, and produced within power relations. Chris Weedon defines subjectivity as "the conscious and unconscious thoughts and emotions of the individual, her sense of herself, and her ways of understanding her relation to the world."[39] Subjectivity is not stable, but is constructed in relationships with others and in everyday practices. A woman's subjectivity is not stabilized or essentialized by identity categories (race, class, gender) because her ways of existing in the world can shift depending on social relations, historical experiences, and material conditions.

---

[33] *Ibid.*

[34] *Ibid.*, 140.

[35] *Ibid*, 141.

[36] Andrew Pickering, "The Mangle of Practice." In *The Science Studies Reader*, edited by Mario Biagioli (New York: Routledge, 1999), 373.

[37] *Ibid.*, 375.

[38] Barad, *Meeting the Universe Halfway*, 214.

[39] Chris Weedon, *Feminist Practice & Poststructuralist Theory*, 2nd edn (Malden: Wiley-Blackwell, 1997), 32.

Chapter 7

Barad: Thinking with intra-action

Nature is agentic—it acts, and those actions have consequences for both the human and nonhuman world. We need ways of understanding the agency, significance, and ongoing transformative power of the world—ways that account for myriad "intra-actions" (in Karen Barad's terms) between phenomena that are material, discursive, human, more-than-human, corporeal, and technological.[1]

Making room for the material

In writing of what she terms a "(post)critical feminist methodology" Patti Lather urges an interrogation of the enabling limits of research practices in order "to grasp what is on the horizon in terms of new analytics and practices of inquiry."[2] We take up Lather's call in this chapter by demonstrating how material feminist readings can produce meanings that take into account the ways in which the discursive and material intra-act to enable an encounter with the previously unthought – to consider how "discourse and matter are understood to be mutually constituted in the production of knowing."[3] Our aim is to propose not merely how these readings of our data *with* and *through* a materialist lens open up new ways of seeing and thinking, but how they in fact produce a different encounter with our data as we interrogate our own positioning and intra-actions as researchers. Such thinking requires that we *not* center on our research subjects (or ourselves as researchers) as the site of agency and therefore the focus of our inquiry, but rather, that we consider the enactment of agency and the co-production of these enactments. Nancy Tuana admonishes that the "knowledge that is too often missing and is often desperately needed is at the intersection between things and people, between...experiences and bodies."[4] We approach the moments of becoming to understand how matter functions in the "intra-actions" (as re-told and remembered) of Sera and Cassandra. We do so in order to produce an understanding of subjectivity constituted in

---

[1] Stacy Alaimo and Susan Hekman, "Introduction: Emerging Models of Materiality in Feminist Theory." In *Material Feminisms*, edited by Stacy Alaimo and Susan Hekman (Bloomington: Indiana University Press, 2008), 5.

[2] Patti Lather, *Getting Lost: Feminist Efforts Toward a Double(d) Science* (Albany, SUNY Press, 2007), 1.

[3] Hillevi Lenz Taguchi, "Becoming-With-the-Barkboat in the Event: A Relational Materialist and Deleuzian Approach to Analysis of Interview Data," unpublished manuscript, 5.

[4] Nancy Tuana, "Viscous Porosity: Witnessing Katrina." In *Material Feminisms*, edited by Stacy Alaimo and Susan Hekman, *op. cit*. In this haunting and illustrative account, Tuana describes how the forces, human and nonhuman, coalesced to produce the events both leading up to and following "Katrina" that could not have happened otherwise.

the inseparable connections between the linguistic, social, political, and biological; what we will discuss later in the chapter as the mangle and the entangled production of subjectivity. Such treatment of subjectivity, as constituted in these multiple realms, prompts the question: *How do Cassandra and Sera intra-act with the materiality of their world in ways that produce different becomings?*

Introducing what they name "new materialisms," Diana Coole and Samantha Frost ask: How is it that we can ignore the "power of matter and the ways it materializes in our ordinary experiences or fail to acknowledge the primacy of matter in our theories"?[5] How does our intra-action with other bodies (both human and nonhuman) produce subjectivities and performative enactments not previously thought? It is the work of "new materialists," and of this chapter, to reinstall the material "without rejecting the legitimate insights of the linguistic turn."[6]

In framing this development, Susan Hekman discussed the critique leveled at the linguistic turn in previous work by Donna Haraway and Bruno Latour: "For both Haraway and Latour the point of critique is not to abandon reality but to redefine it in discursive terms. The point is not to privilege the discursive over the material but to understand the material in discursive terms."[7] Hekman continues her discussion in agreement with Haraway and Latour, asserting that we have shunned what the material may still have to offer feminists. And, while feminists have indeed benefitted from discursive understandings of subjectivity, Hillevi Lenz Taguchi reminds us of its continuing limitations.

> Turning to the discursive has been immensely productive for feminist researchers, and has opened up totally new possibilities of understanding gender, sexuality and the body, without getting trapped in genital or essentialising categorisations. So, what is the problem? The most obvious problem put forward by material feminist researchers is that mainstream discursive approaches don't consider the agency of the material in the production of knowledge.[8]

For Karen Barad, the new material is grounded in an ontoepistemology, or *knowing in being*, that presents a shaking up of the privileging of the discursive in postmodern thought without a re-centering of the material that preceded the linguistic turn. For Barad, this ontoepistemology asserts that "the primary ontological units are not 'things' but phenomena."[9] If, as qualitative researchers, we are to realign our thinking from an emphasis on epistemology to ontology, or ontoepistemology, then data and meaning-making become not merely a re-insertion of the material into our analyses. Thinking of knowing in being does not mean that we privilege the material, but we adhere to a fundamental break in a privileging of the discursive and a thinking of knowledge as the sole domain of epistemology, what Barad refers to as an "onto-epistem-ology."

[5] Diana Coole and Samantha Frost, "Introducing the New Materialisms." In *New Materialisms: Ontology, Agency, and Politics*, edited by Diana Coole and Samantha Frost (Durham: Duke University Press, 2010), 1.

[6] Susan Hekman, *The Material of Knowledge: Feminist Disclosures* (Bloomington: Indiana University Press, 2010), 7.

[7] Susan Hekman, "Constructing the Ballast." In *Material Feminisms*, edited by Stacy Alaimo and Susan Hekman, op. cit., 88.

[8] Lenz Taguchi, "Barkboat," op. cit., 3.

[9] Karen Barad, *Meeting the Universe Halfway: Quantum Physics and the Entanglement of Matter and Meaning* (Durham: Duke University Press, 2007), 141.

There is an important sense in which practices of knowing cannot fully be claimed as human practices, not simply because we use nonhuman elements in our practices but because knowing is a matter of part of the world making itself intelligible to another part. *Practices of knowing and being are not isolable; they are mutually implicated.* We don't obtain knowledge by standing outside the world; we know because we are of the world. We are part of the world in its differential becoming. The separation of epistemology from ontology is a reverberation of a metaphysics that assumes an inherent difference between human and nonhuman, subject and object, mind and body, matter and discourse. *Onto-epistem-ology*—the study of practices of knowing in being— is probably a better way to think about the kind of understanding that we need to come to terms with how specific intractions matter.[10]

Approaching knowledge as understood ontoepistemologically requires a different approach to thinking theory with data. Susan Hekman writes that, while it is far easier to criticize the excesses produced by the linguistic turn, what is far more difficult is expressing a theoretical position that moves to an articulation of a new theoretical approach. Judith Butler, often critiqued by new materialists for her privileging of the linguistic, is interested in how subjectivity is constructed through discursive practices that produce performative enactments. While Barad critiques Butler for a privileging of the discursive to the exclusion of the material, particularly in *Gender Trouble* and *Bodies that Matter*, Butler's later work seems to be gesturing toward making room for the material.[11] In *Undoing Gender*, Butler says about the body that it "has its invariably public dimension; constituted as a phenomenon in the public sphere, my body is and is not mine."[12] If our bodies both belong and don't belong to us, if they are indeed, as Butler says, constituted in the public sphere, how might we account for the body, the material elements of the public sphere, and the intra-actions that are always already occurring in our research sites?

Orienting our researcher selves ontoepistemologically, we understand Sera's and Cassandra's performative enactments as "emergent in a relational field."[13] This relational field is one in which matter and meaning (the material and discursive constructions) are "understood to be mutually constituted in the production of knowing."[14] Given our location ontoepistemologically in this field, our task as researchers is to "put to work [our] bodymind faculties to extend [our] knowing into other potential realities."[15]

We seek, in our thinking with theory and data, that which is simultaneously materially and discursively produced. This mutual production of the material as discursive and the discursive as material further pushes us as researchers to consider how such an orientation might function to produce knowledge differently from a material ↔ discursive stance. In an intra-active reading of the following account given in her interview, we look not for

---

[10] *Ibid.*, 185 [emphasis ours].

[11] We reference Susan Hekman's discussion of Judith Butler in *The Material of Knowledge*, op. cit.; Hekman in this analysis specifically refers to Butler's discussion in *Giving an Account of Oneself* (New York: Fordham University Press, 2005) and *Undoing Gender* (New York: Routledge, 2004).

[12] Butler, *Undoing Gender*, op. cit., 21.

[13] Karin Hultman and Hillevi Lenz Taguchi, "Challenging Anthropocentric Analysis of Visual Data: A Relational Materialist Methodological Approach to Educational Research." *International Journal of Qualitative Studies in Education* 23, no. 5 (2010): 527.

[14] Lenz Taguchi, "Barkboat," 5.

[15] *Ibid.*

evidence of Cassandra's actions; rather, we look for the mutual constitution of agency that is simultaneously materially and discursively produced: between black and white bodies, black bodies and white institutions, and the constraining and judgmental. Race as an identity category in this intra-active reading is not a return to an essentializing notion of race. It is a re-insertion of racial markers as simultaneously culturally and biologically produced. The entanglement of blackness and what it both says and evokes is an effect of evolution, sun exposure from working in fields, culture as tied to regional practices of segregation, and historical constructions of enslavement and freedom. Again, calling attention to race is not done for the purposes of essentializing, but for the purpose of accounting for the way in which the material of race (the body in this case) and the discursive constructions of race (what our ideas are regarding race that come to us through language) are entangled to produce something other than would be produced singularly. In fact, it is to say that one cannot be produced without the other.

We attempt to understand how the discursive constructions of Cassandra and those around her intra-act with their material conditions. We recognize such intra-actions as entangled with her subjectivity (albeit unstable) as a black woman in a mostly white university. How others respond to her is an entanglement of the discursive constructions of race and the material construction of skin, hair, and dress. The body "says" something, and those who encounter Cassandra "say" something about the body that they encounter. We attempt to recognize the production of phenomena that depend on her constituted self *and* the discursive field of this predominantly white university in which she finds herself, one that is located in a rural community:

> One of the things I've learned as I was coming up in grade school and high school was you have to be twice as good to be considered as good [as whites] and that still registers a little bit with me because I feel like if I get ninety-nine things right and one wrong, then they're going to focus in on the one thing that I didn't get right. That kind of fits in in some way with your impostor thing because you're not focused on the things that you do well nearly as much as you are the one area that you think that you might have been able to do better. I don't know if that's a natural kind of thing for people to feel or not, but it kind of keeps you on edge. I think that I'm much better at it, much more at ease with who I am now, but I'm not afraid, I'm on guard. I'm ready for it. I'm waiting for it. I'm pleasantly surprised when I don't get it but I'm waiting to see, now who in this audience or in this class – what are they going to come up with?

To encounter what is simultaneously materially and discursively produced requires not just a reading with/through a materialist lens, but it is a reading that relies on a re-insertion of ontology into the task of knowing. Cassandra's statement that "if I get ninety-nine things right and one wrong, then they're going to focus in on the one thing that I didn't get right" is an assumption that she lives with every day. This assumption is a result of her discursive construction as a black woman, but it is further produced and reinforced in the history of slavery that inhabits the area of the country in which she lives, and in having grown up farming "from daylight to twilight" working for "other people who had larger farms." She cannot escape her body, nor can she escape the constructions that make her body different from the white students and colleagues. A return to the data prompts a reading that seeks the discursive construction of Cassandra as a black woman in the south as never quite good enough, possible in an intra-action between her discursive self and her material self – between the discursive construction of the institution, and the material constitution of a regional university that has difficulty attracting a large number of minority faculty and students due to its rural location.

Barad writes that "neither discursive practices nor material phenomena are ontologically or epistemologically prior."[16] In the case of Cassandra, it is not that her sense of self as it has been discursively produced ("they're going to focus on the one thing I didn't get right") precedes her ontologically. It is that, as Barad continues, "Neither can be explained in terms of the other. Neither is reducible to the other."[17] They exist simultaneously and continuously intra-act in an ongoing production of who Cassandra is and what she is becoming in a way that is different at Regional State University than it would have been when she was teaching at Southern State University, a historically black institution. It is not possible to point to her physical presence or what others see/think based on discursive constructions as one being prior to the other. What is important is not what produces the effect (Cassandra believing that she can never be good enough), nor whether the material or discursive is privileged, but what it produces, similar to Deleuze's question: how does it work?

Encountering the material and discursive simultaneously shifts our thinking from one of not only how discursive performative speech acts or repetitive bodily actions form subjectivity, but how subjectivity can be understood as "a set of operational linkages and connections with other things, other bodies."[18] We approach the data bringing our bodymind construction as researchers to Cassandra's *knowing in being* as a black woman, as a black woman who is often "the only black person" in a region of the country where black women were routinely at the bottom of the heap.[19] As researchers, we understand her subjectivity as produced in the push-back (from not being good enough) that occurs from these constructions, not in response to what she says or does, but in response to her blackness that is constituted in the public sphere – in this case, a public sphere that is mostly white. Cassandra's reality is a result of language, but these constructions are more complex than to be explained only by the discursive. What is needed is a way to account for these intra-actions in our analyses that "incorporates language, materiality, and technology into the equation."[20]

We go to the essay "Cassie's Hair"[21] by Susan Bordo to develop further the entangled nature of the intra-actions in the example with Cassandra. In this essay, Bordo presents a discussion of how "living inside" race becomes far more complicated, and does so in a way that incorporates language, materiality, and technology. As a white woman with an adopted multi-racial child, she begins the piece with a story about her daughter Cassie coming home from day care "with a dozen tiny braids marking a complex and delicate pattern on her tiny head."[22] Bordo describes her response first of being mystified that someone could have the skill and patience to produce this work of art, but further that Cassie "seemed, for the first time, undeniably black." She also goes on to describe her friend Annice's outrage at what had happened.

[16] Barad, *Meeting the Universe Halfway*, op. cit., 152.

[17] *Ibid.*

[18] Elizabeth Grosz, cited by Karin Hultman, "Pedagogical Photo-Documentation of Children and Other Agential Forces," paper presented at the AERA Annual Meeting, April, 2010, Denver, CO, USA.

[19] See Gail Collins, *When Everything Changed: The Amazing Journey of American Women from 1960 to the Present* (New York: Little, Brown, 2009), ch. 6.

[20] Hekman, "Constructing the Ballast," op. cit., 92.

[21] Susan Bordo, "Cassie's Hair." In *Material Feminisms*, edited by Stacy Alaimo and Susan Hekman, op. cit., 400–424.

[22] *Ibid.*, 400.

I understood why she, as a black woman whose own hair had been braided by her grandmother and aunts, might have had that reaction. Why she, as a person whose ancestors had their parental rights ignored, would be horrified at the idea of another woman appropriating, without permission, such an intimate ritual of mother–child bonding.[23]

The essay continues with a discussion of the constitution of Cassie as being materially constituted within the discourses of anglo images of beauty, of the technology of hair straightening, and the complicated entanglement of these intra-actions. Returning to Cassandra, it is impossible to think about skin and the constructions of race and beauty without accounting for the porosity of boundaries which have previously been thought of as discreet.

Re-thinking agency in the mangle

A move to the mangle helps us in a continuing analysis to account for bodies as materially constituted and agency as mutually produced. We do this not just to explain further how bodies intra-act *with* the material, but are in fact differently constituted. Extending the work of Andy Pickering and his discussion of the mangle, Susan Hekman presents the "mangle" as a way to explain "how the agency of matter is intertwined with human agency."[24] She intentionally engages the mangle as both noun and verb in writing that

> The elements of the mangle are mangled; they are mixed up with each other into a combination in which the various elements lose their clear boundaries. The mangle teaches us that rather than being shocked by this mix we should accept it and seek to understand it.[25]

Hekman goes on to discuss bodies as materially constituted or, as Butler writes, "The body has its invariable public dimension; constituted as a social phenomenon in the public sphere, my body is and is not mine."[26] Cassandra can be in her body, but how others are with Cassandra is also a result of this body that is becoming constructed in this material encounter. This is particularly relevant given the presentation of Cassandra's narrative. She is being responded to not just as a woman, or as a black woman, but as a body that produces and evokes a different, intra-active response, one that causes her to always question whether students and colleagues are waiting for her to get something wrong, which keeps her always "on edge." How the bodies of women are located in the mangle is further used by Hekman as a useful figuration for examining the situation of women in the modern world. Especially in the context of research with these first-generation women, for as women, "they have not been allowed to become the disembodied knowers"[27] that their male counterparts in the academy have. They are always already viewed differently by students and colleagues (both male and female) by virtue of their femaleness, and in Cassandra's case, her blackness as well.

---

[23] *Ibid.*
[24] Hekman, *The Material of Knowledge*, 24.
[25] *Ibid.*, 24–25.
[26] Butler, *Undoing Gender*, 21.
[27] Hekman, *The Material of Knowledge*, 25.

Hekman continues: "Women are their bodies, and this association has had a profound effect on the status of women in modernity."[28]

Continuing, then, to read Cassandra as both noun and verb form of the mangle, she is intra-actively constituted in the following account in an association that will not let her be separated from her body:

> I've had students actually challenge me and I knew that they thought I didn't even know what was in the textbook, because they would ask me a question that was right there, sometimes within the first few pages of the chapter that we were studying and it was if they felt that I hadn't even read the book, that I wouldn't know the answer to that question that they were asking, which I thought was rather stupid, but I would answer the question ... Some of the students from time to time have actually gone to my colleagues and told them what I said and asked them what they thought about it. Sometimes my colleagues come back and tell me that it had happened and then other times the students themselves would come back and tell me, "Well, yes I was talking to Dr. So and so and they said"... Most of the time [my colleagues] would support me, but there would actually be times that my colleagues would disagree with what I said, even though it was on a topic where I was considered the expert and they were not. I would never challenge their expertise in their area, but they would say, "I don't agree with that," and the students would then feel that I obviously didn't know what I was talking about because Dr. So and so didn't agree with me.

We look to the above to consider how this failure to challenge her colleagues' responses, and an acceptance of this perceived ritual of "testing" on the part of students, become intra-actively produced in the language of bodies. In the context of our study on first-generation academics, many of the women talk about instances of feeling insecure, of playing the game, of fitting in. Sera captures this in the oftentimes repeated phrase, "Fake it until you make it." And while this may be a strategy that many new academics employ, how do we understand this differently, or rather, what different knowledge is produced, if we are to re-think Cassandra's subjectivity as always already and continuously re-produced in this milieu that is the mangle? If her "I" is both produced by forceful discursive codes but not wholly created by them, we see this as evidence of the linguistic, social, political, and biological as inseparable from her constitution.[29]

To explain the entanglement in the above data excerpt from Cassandra, a return to the concept of Hekman's mangle as composed of multiple elements is useful: bodies that are sexed and raced, bodies that are located in a particular place in the social hierarchy, and bodies that have had a range of experience.[30] Cassandra is a subject constituted in the "I" of the mangle and cannot extricate herself from this entanglement. She is a black woman, working among mostly white colleagues, teaching mostly white students in a state where slavery was once legal. When students go to other professors in order to "challenge" her expertise, they are doing so from a position of privilege. She may be more educated than they are, but in this mangle, she is not constituted as such. When the words "I don't agree"

[28] *Ibid.*
[29] *Ibid.*
[30] Ibid, 100–101.

are spoken by a colleague, they are a forceful negation of her race and gender. Words become material, writes Barad. In this moment, the words become a performative agent, writing and acting on her body, further putting her "on edge," as she described in the previous data excerpt. In this mangle, there is strong intensity and force in the phrase, "I don't agree," or "Dr. So and so said."

It is not Cassandra's "blackness" that produces her differently, it is the intra-action of bodies, discourses, and institutions that do so. Hekman concludes:

> The result may be a subject that fits neatly into the definition of subject the social scripts circumscribe. Or the result may be an "I" who cannot find a script that fits, that resists the scripts available to her/him. In all cases, however, there is no single causal factor determining the subject; the elements of subjectivity intra-act in a complex web.[31]

How this subject negotiates this complex web is what we explore in the next section, in what Barad names as an "entangled state of agencies."[32]

An entangled state of agencies

Karen Barad discusses the "entangled state of agencies"[33] that exceed the traditional notions of how we conceive of agency, subjectivity, and the individual. For Barad, "agency is an enactment, not something that someone or something *has*."[34] Such entanglements require an "analysis that enables us to theorize the social and the natural together";[35] that is, in theorizing the social and natural together, Sera and Cassandra intra-act with the matter of their worlds in ways in which they are transformed by matter and *vice versa*. For Barad, matter is a "dynamic and shifting entanglement of relations."[36] How, then, might we take into account, in our reading of Sera's and Cassandra's narratives through a materialist becoming, "the fact that the forces at work in the materialization of bodies are not only social and the bodies produced are not all human"?[37] The following account by Cassandra is relevant here:

> I had been brought here to be a mentor to the African-American students and to create courses and programs and so forth to talk about diversity, and so some of the white students felt that I was paying too much attention to the black students and so they wrote these long, very critical letters of me that accused me of reverse discrimination and that I was showing favoritism to the black students because they [the black students] would come in to my office.
>
> My office is small now, but it was even smaller then and they would be sitting all on the floor and everything and we just hung out together. I was a mother figure, that was

---

[31] *Ibid.*
[32] Barad, *Meeting the Universe Halfway*, 22–23.
[33] *Ibid.*
[34] *Ibid.*, 235 [emphasis ours].
[35] *Ibid.*, 25.
[36] *Ibid.*, 224.
[37] *Ibid.*, 225.

pretty much the same thing that I did at Southern State so I knew how to work with those students and I knew that [they] need a lot of personal attention.

Now there was never a time when I didn't give the same amount of attention to any white student who wanted it. But it became so huge that it went all the way up through the provost's office and I found myself spending a lot of time writing letters of rebuttal and that kind of thing.

Thinking this data with Barad, we shift our focus away from Cassandra and the students as making choices or acting on and being acted on. We look for how the forces of offices and bodies work together, in a way that moves us away from what is *told* by Cassandra toward what is *produced* in this intra-action. Cassandra described her office as "small now, but... even smaller then." This office, as a force producing a materialization of bodies, creates an intimate (cramped) space that welcomes (deters) students and that invites a closeness (repulsion) of bodies "sitting on the floor" and hanging out together. This material of the office produces a social environment of refuge and intimacy for the black students, who are in the minority at Regional State University. It creates a belonging space where, for a brief moment, they are on the inside looking out, rather than *vice versa*. These black students, "sitting on the floor," are able to refuse constraining norms about power and prestige and in turn produce Cassandra differently as a mentor. This office, this material force, also produces Cassandra in a way that shifts her identity from one who students "thought I didn't even know what was in the textbook," as in the previous data excerpt, to one who provides "a lot of personal attention."

This office, this material force, is not the only force producing intra-actions. The fact that the white students experience this space as exclusionary and accuse Cassandra of "reverse discrimination" is an example of how the forces, both human and not human, material and otherwise, intra-act to produce different becomings. We become aware of the constraints produced in the confines of an office that is seen/experienced as safe space for the black students, but exclusionary space for the white students. In this entangled state of agencies, we see that what is produced by the intra-actions renders Cassandra as welcoming for the black students and as a conundrum for the white students, who accuse her of reverse discrimination.

We undertake the above analysis with Barad for the purpose of reassessing how we understand social phenomena and how we un-naturally divide the world into categories that include the "social" and the "natural." The office is both social and natural, material and discursive. The question is not why does this happen, but how does this happen? The implication for how we think data differently, given this entangled state, is to move away from thinking the interview and what is "told" discursively, toward a thinking of the interview and what is "told" as discursive, as material, as discursive *and* material, as material ↔ discursive, and as constituted *between* the discursive and the material in a posthumanist becoming.

Posthumanist performativity

In the above example with Cassandra and the office, we confront agency as distributed. If agency is distributed in the sense that Karen Barad describes, a corresponding approach to how we know and what we know is required in an accounting of sources of meaning and agency. In other words, if as qualitative researchers we make meaning only based on what we hear in the narrative accounts given by our participants, then we fail to also consider how what we and our participants know might be based on what is produced in our intra-actions with data. Put differently, we focus only on the scripted, spoken words produced by our "subjects" in our strategies to capture data and make meaning, thereby limiting our understandings of what our research participants are saying, or trying to say. We gather and produce "evidence" of these voiced encounters in the form of transcripts that re-produce and classify *direct* speech-acts. In a move to unloose such strictured notions of data, and meaning, and agency, we can turn to a performative understanding of discursive practices, which, according to Barad, if properly constructed "is not an invitation to turn everything ... into words" but is instead "a contestation of the excessive power granted to language to determine what is real."[38] Such a move shifts the focus methodologically "from questions of correspondence between descriptions and reality...to matters of practices/doings/ actions."[39] Intra-actions are absent classical ontological conditions of exteriority between observer and observed, thereby removing the possibility of objectivity and representation in the humanist sense.[40]

Consideration of the narration of Cassandra and Sera as presenting a performative practice requires a re-interpretation of the material, or a re-thinking of the relationship between the material and the discursive. Such re-positioning demands that we re-think voice, and data, and the subject, not as a separation of the theoretical from the material, but as an enactment, as a performative practice, one that asks "how matter and embodiment come to matter in the process of research itself,"[41] and in the process of how participants account for what they tell us and how we view their tellings as enactments rather than descriptions. In the previous example, the office produces a different embodiment on the part of Cassandra and the students. To focus merely on the words spoken is to fail to think *with* the concept of intra-activity. In other words, such an orientation means that we are to embark on a re-thinking of meaning as constituted between the discursive and the material – as constituted without a beginning, or without being constrained by the reductive binary of the discursive and the material. Such a re-thinking might be in keeping with Barad's "agential realism" that "rejects the notion of a correspondence relation between words and things and offers in its stead a causal explanation of how discursive practices are related to material phenomena."[42]

Returning to the previous example, in which one of Cassandra's colleagues tells a student, "I don't agree with that," there is not a one-to-one correspondence relation between words and things. Yes, the word disagree is easy to define, and most people would probably *agree* on a fairly stable definition. But taking the words at face value fails to account for how the discursive constructions of Cassandra and those around her intra-act with their material conditions. They fail to account for the importance of how these words would materialize differently in her previous role at Southern State University, a historically black college, than they do at Regional State University. In this example, we cannot separate the discursive

---

38 Karen Barad, "Posthumanist Performativity: Toward an Understanding of How Matter Comes to Matter." In *Material Feminisms*, edited by Stacy Alaimo and Susan Hekman, op. cit., 121.
39 *Ibid.*
40 *Ibid.*, 133.
41 Hillevi Lenz Taguchi, "The Researcher Becoming Otherwise; The Materiality of Collaborative Deconstructive Research," paper presented at the 1st International Conference in Feminist Pedagogy, Uppsala University, Sweden, 2008.
42 Barad, *Meeting the Universe Halfway*, 44–45.

practice from its production in the material. Nor can we fail to take into account its material effects.

While much of what has been written under the guise of new materialisms comes from the philosophy of science, Susan Hekman's work and that of some qualitative researchers is building on the scientific to posit posthumanist performativity in the social world.[43] A key understanding that we can apply to our research settings from Barad's agential realism is that it "provides an understanding of the role of human and nonhuman, material and discursive, and natural and cultural factors in scientific and other social–material practices,"[44] as we tried to show in the example of the office above. This reading of the office takes seriously that "agential realism privileges neither the material nor the cultural…production is material/cultural."[45] Similarly to the way that Barad describes how scientists who observe are interacting with apparatus in ways that effect knowing due to an intra-action with the apparatus, we can translate this performative understanding of scientific practices that she describes as similarly relevant in the context of social science research. What opens up then is "the fact that knowing does not come from standing at a distance and representing but rather from *a direct material engagement with the world*."[46] We take this notion of knowing from engagement with the world to our reading of the texts to see how knowing in being is present in the narratives of Sera and Cassandra. A further entanglement of the material and discursive occurs by attributing agency not to individuals, but to a dynamism (or *becoming*, to use Deleuzian language) that is the "ongoing reconfigurings of the world."[47] This ongoing reconfiguring results methodologically in a blurring and destabilizing of the boundaries between the spoken and the visual, discursive and material, toward a "speech-act" that is both discursive and material.

Nancy Tuana names this blurring as a "viscous porosity" to describe the interaction of phenomena between humans and the environment and social practices and natural phenomena.

> There is a viscous porosity of flesh—my flesh and the flesh of the world. This porosity is a hinge through which we are of and in the world. I refer to it as viscous for there are membranes that effect the interactions. These membranes are of various types—skin and flesh, prejudgements and symbolic imaginaries, habits and embodiments. They serve as one of the mediators of interaction.[48]

In reading the excerpt below from Sera's interview, we read differently if we blur the boundary of agency between the material and the discursive as mutually shared and produced by Sera and the suit, as knowing in being in her engagement with the material, and as a viscous porosity that acts as a hinge between Sera and the suit.

[43] See, for example, Hillevi Lenz Taguchi, *Going Beyond the Theory/Practice Divide in Early Childhood Education: Introducing an Intra-Active Pedagogy* (London: Routledge, 2010); Hultman and Lenz Taguchi, "Challenging Anthropocentric Analysis of Visual Data," op. cit.

[44] Barad, *Meeting the Universe Halfway*, 26.

[45] Hekman, *The Material of Knowledge*, 73.

[46] Barad, *Meeting the Universe Halfway*, 49 [emphasis in original].

[47] *Ibid.*, 141.

[48] Tuana, "Viscous Porosity," op. cit., 199–200.

I was in one of these classes where you have undergraduates and graduates take the classes together. So I had a sense of this one person who everybody just thought was this total nerd. You know, every time she had to teach, people were like whatever. But I thought she was like the coolest thing. She was really funny if you listened to her. And she was really nerdy, but in a great way. And so she and I were always pleasant to each other.

And then she said, oh, hey, I'm doing the Regional Communication Association. I'm the vice president and I need somebody to man this registration table. Would you do that? And I said well, sure … And I bought a suit, and I manned this registration table. And I remember putting on the suit feeling like I am so powerful. I couldn't get over how different I felt in the suit about answering questions and talking with people at the registration table. She didn't say wear a suit, but I figured I should. And so I bought one. And then I experienced that.

The above is a performative dimension of Sera's subjectivity, and a process of taking up certain subject positions in response to discursive constraints. These constructions ask of her to dress, speak, and act according to professional norms that dictate what is acceptable and unacceptable in a business environment. And certainly, normative constraints offer a range of subject positions – "suit-wearing" being one of many. Yet what is of interest from a posthumanist performative perspective is to consider how the suit and Sera intra-act in a mutual production of agency. Suits are constructed to render an image on the part of the wearer as conferring status, conformity, and confidence. In Sera's wearing of the suit, she not only wears a suit because it is what she "figured she should do," but also the suit produces this in/with her. "An agential realist elaboration of performativity allows matter its due (in this case the suit) as an active participant in…ongoing intra-activity".[49] In this case it also helps provide an understanding of *how* discursive practices matter in our notions of what the suit should produce.[50]

In the above data excerpt, the suit seems to have a life of its own, and certainly intra-acts with Sera's body to produce a subject who is confident. It is not just that Sera appears to know what she is doing and that she belongs as viewed/experienced by conference participants, it is that she intra-acts with the suit in a way that exudes confidence, and those who are helped by Sera at the registration table intra-act with the suit as well. While the suit conveys a particular image, the wearer of the suit (in this case Sera) is produced in a mutual becoming with the suit. The suit molds Sera's body, producing a different carriage and a sense, on the part of her and the others, that she is in her place, she belongs, and is no longer an impostor. Similarly, we can talk about Sera's intra-action and positioning in relation to the registration table. She is positioned behind the table as this is how the table is intended to function and to position her. This placement of Sera behind a registration table is also an element of this intra-action that distances her from the participants in a way that places her in a position of authority. The table produces a response, not just in Sera, but in how those who approach Sera do so differently, again, because of this placement. The forces, then, of Sera, the suit, and the table produce Sera as a material ↔ discursive production.

What is interesting about the above passage is that Sera remembers this event as an important threshold when prompted by the interviewer to recall her consideration of graduate school as a possible choice. The intra-action with the suit, and with the "nerdy"

[49] Barad, *Meeting the Universe Halfway*, 136.
[50] *Ibid.*, 126.

graduate teaching assistant she looked up to, produces other instances in her "talk" that describe her material enactments as producing a structural relation that might have been otherwise. Sera has become the academic, the intellectual, and part of that becoming is intra-acted many mornings after her children are out of the house and off to school.

> I guess what I'm seeing now is that I like the academic life more than I [thought] … I see myself doing this work for a long time. I know people struggle with, well, I could make a bunch of money in industry or I could be a consultant. And maybe it's because I feel comfortable here and because I feel like I'm really learning a lot right now. Every morning, what I like to do is drink a cup of coffee and read an article or read a chapter or something. And I love that.

Sera describes herself as an intellectual, and part of that description is enacted in the body. She is comfortable in her department, in her university, and with colleagues. This comfort is exhibited in her being able to be what she refers to as "who I am," and in her practice of sitting with articles while drinking coffee. This comfort extends to her differentiating herself from being an academic (whom she describes as being "very mechanical") in contrast to the intellectual who, according to Sera, is "always thinking about things deeply." Rosi Braidotti wants to "think through the body, not in a flight away from it,"[51] and so it is with Sera when she describes her practices of reading; she too is thinking through the body. Braidotti presents an "enfleshed materialism"[52] as a site of difference and becoming, a becoming that Karen Barad names as diffraction.

Reading/thinking/seeing diffractively

> Nothing will unfold for us unless we move toward what looks to us like nothing.[53]

Much space has been given in this book to reading texts through one another in the methodological process that we described in Chapter 1 as plugging one text in to another. While Derrida and Spivak privilege the discursive, a move to account for the material is found in the work of Foucault and, some would argue, in the more recent work of Butler. Foucault, for instance, was interested in how the discursive is made visible through practices. While these practices, for Foucault, are both social and material, he does not conceptualize an intra-activity between the two, something that is introduced in the work of Barad and other material feminists. What is urged by the material feminists, then, is not a deconstruction of the discourse/reality dichotomy and the constructing of a new paradigm,[54] but a movement to reading diffractively that requires an emphasis not on how discourses function, but on how they materialize. A diffractive reading is not about what is told, or experienced – it is about the ways in which what is experienced is formed in the intra-action between the material and discursive.

An emphasis on the discursive has proven very profitable, as discussed at length in the previous chapters in this book. As Heckman wrote, "We have learned much from the

---

[51] Rosi Braidotti, *Metamorphosis: Towards a Materialist Theory of Becoming* (Malden: Polity Press, 2002), 5.
[52] *Ibid.*, 15.
[53] Barad (quoting Alice Fulton) in *Meeting the Universe Halfway*, 39.
[54] Hekman, *The Material of Knowledge*, 6.

linguistic turn. Language *does* construct our reality."[55] And yet, while qualitative researchers under the influence of poststructuralism have eschewed the material due to its modernist proclivities, "we are discovering now, however,…that this is not the end of the story."[56] Maggie MacLure gestured toward the presence of the material in qualitative research when she said,

> In the case of qualitative research, the suppression of materiality happens even though the *spoken* voice is central to the research endeavour. In interviews, case studies, "participant observation" and so on, people are speaking to one another. Yet much of what constitutes voice evades capture, or prompts its own erasure from the official texts of research, which prefer to forget that speech issues from our insides.[57]

Perhaps the material has been present in qualitative research all along, as we have tried to demonstrate in our thinking with Barad in this chapter. What we have accounted for up to this point is the intra-action with our participants and the material of their contexts. As qualitative researchers, a further extension is to begin to read/think/see diffractively. Such reading/thinking/seeing diffractively requires us to insert ourselves into the material production of the texts, both "official" and unofficial, by installing "ourselves in the event that emerges in our reading" so that we might "ask ourselves how we are affected in our encounter with it."[58] Such a practice of reading diffractively adheres to Barad's admonishment that "To 'see' one must actively intervene."[59] A diffractive reading of data, then, is not an insertion into the context in an autoethnographic sense, nor is it a reflection that takes our own researcher subjectivity into account, but it is an installing of ourselves that attempts to make sense of the blurring and viscous interactions that Nancy Tuana names as a viscous porosity. We have written in the examples with Sera and the suit, and Cassandra and the office, how they are installed and how boundaries are blurred. What we hope to enact in this final section is how, as researchers, we insert and install ourselves in a diffractive reading. Because we are not "interpreting" the experiences of Sera and Cassandra, we install ourselves into a situation in a blurring of what "happens" and how we make sense of what happens.

In order to put to work a diffractive reading, we go back to examples presented earlier in this chapter in the process of spreading meanings differently than they would be otherwise. One of the ways this happens is based on the assumption that "diffraction does not fix the object and subject in advance."[60] To read diffractively, then, is to try to reposition ourselves as researchers otherwise than merely always-already subject, and our participants and their material conditions as otherwise than always-already object. Reading diffractively means that we try to fold these texts into one another in a move that "flattens out"[61] our relationship to the material. In so doing, "We install ourselves in the event that emerges in our reading, and we ask ourselves how we are affected in our encounter with it."[62] We will illustrate in the

---

[55] Hekman, "Constructing the Ballast," 92.
[56] *Ibid.*
[57] Maggie MacLure, "Qualitative Inquiry: Where are the Ruins?" Keynote Presentation to the New Zealand Association for Research in Education, University of Auckland, December 2010.
[58] Lenz Taguchi, "Barkboat," 16.
[59] Barad, *Meeting the Universe Halfway*, 51.
[60] *Ibid.*, 30.
[61] Hultman, "Pedagogical Photo-Documentation," op. cit.
[62] Lenz Taguchi, "Barkboat," 16.

following discussion how this installation of our researcher selves into the events as narrated by Sera and Cassandra produces a different account, not only of the mutual production of agency between Cassandra and her students, but also of Cassandra and the office, and of Sera and the suit. We will further examine how such positioning changes not only the questions we ask of the data, but the questions we ask of ourselves as researchers.

Barad enacts for us her example of a diffractive reading in "an agential realist under-standing of material-discursive relations of power through each other"[63] with a case study of shop-floor dynamics in the Indian jute industry as presented by Leela Fernandes. What is interesting in the context of the present discussion is to engage the questions that Barad presents as guiding an examination not only of how power structures are productive, but how they are themselves produced in this process of intra-action. The questions below are adapted from those presented by Barad, and through/with them we wish to re-engage a diffractive reading of material-discursive relations of power and agential realism through each other in the narratives of Sera and Cassandra.

- In what sense are social relations produced and what does this production entail?
- What is the nature of the processes that "shape" these relations?
- What is the relationship between the material and discursive dimensions of power relations?
- How are we to make sense of the nature of power dynamics? Of materiality?[64]

Reading Sera's description of what we name as her intra-action with the suit in a process of becoming is not just about what she says, what she experiences, and how we describe the phenomena of her relationship to/with/in the material. It is also very much about our own material $\leftrightarrow$ discursive reconfiguring that is occurring as we re-insert ourselves into the event. In other words, how we are becoming as researchers as we read and engage with Sera's account diffractively. How we seek what is produced in our own intra-action with Sera, and with the intra-action of our own material engagements toward an understanding of the relationship between the material and discursive dimensions of power relations.

> The point is not simply to put the observer or knower back in the world (as if the world were a container and we needed merely to acknowledge our situatedness in it) but to understand and take account of the fact that we too are part of the world's differential becoming. And furthermore, the point is not merely that knowledge practices have material consequences but that *practices of knowing are specific material engagements that participate in (re)configuring the world*.[65]

Returning to the data, it is not just about what Sera says, but how we imagine ourselves as intra-actively produced in tandem with Sera and how we re-imagine her. When first reading the data, we encounter Sera's narrative in part as a product of a discursive construction left over from the 1980s that indicated how one must dress to be successful. We return to the constraints that such discursive constructions produced in our own resistance to and intra-action with clothing that "said" something about who we were. Suits with big

---

[63] Barad, *Meeting the Universe Halfway*, 326.
[64] *Ibid.*, 229. See also Chapter 6 for Barad's presentation and discussion of her diffractive reading.
[65] *Ibid.*, 91.

shoulder pads, wide lapels, and "ties" that said the more you can look like a man while still presenting a feminine image, the greater chance you will have for advancement. We could feel the affect, what it produced in us as women trying to assert ourselves and to be taken seriously and our compliance with norms and resistance in ways that brought the material back into our reading and knowledge making – both intellectually and physically. The suit intra-acted with our discursive constructions to produce a different subjectivity. We therefore at some level can continue to read this intra-action as a result of a discursive construction that prescribes a specific list of do's and don'ts in order for women (and men) to be taken seriously in the work place.[66]

In becoming-with-Sera in this event[67] we re-insert ourselves in ways not already coded with our discursive readings and materialist intra-actions, but try to take part in the phenomena that produce this as such an important example of difference. For Sera, who grew up "raised by wolves," "sitting next to the juke box in bars" while her parents were drinking, and without material things (necessities) that we take for granted, like having a television in the house while growing up, this event is not about success, but about *becoming*. We are brought back to our own need to conform and fit in, not by choosing clothes, but by adopting them, and yet, for Sera, perhaps this is not about conforming at all, but about "changing topologies of power."[68] Sera transforms the suit into a site of power. Our reading in becoming-with-Sera challenges us to resist our own "interpretation and experience" of intra-actions with suits as marking belonging and gravitas, rather than as an intra-action that displaces and reinscribes power.

Sera, perhaps for the first time in her life, is encountered by others as "in the know," a result of a production of power relations that we can understand as a material discursive construction. The structural relations that produce this different topology are to be found not only in the suit, but in the subject position of Sera: she is positioned on the side of the registration table that indicates to others that she is in charge, knows the answers, and is someone whom others need to treat with respect in order to get what they need. The material conditions intra-act to both introduce and produce a topology of power relations and a subject position not previously experienced. It is also a result of this relationship between the material and discursive dimensions of power and Sera's becoming that presents a consideration of the possibility of graduate study to her for the first time. If, however, Sera were to be positioned in front of the table, or to be casually seated on the edge of the table, not only would she be differently constituted, but the table would be as well.

Barad's questions are also a productive site for a diffractive reading of the account presented from Cassandra. Returning to the site of her first office, one described as "small now, but ... even smaller then," we can think about how offices exhibit the relationship between the material and discursive dimensions of power relations. We have come to understand, at least in Western contexts, that offices are used as material symbols of structural hierarchy and status. Those who are seen as powerful (or see themselves as powerful) are rewarded with, among other things, offices that are larger, more central, and often with a view. In other

---

[66] We refer here to John T. Malloy's *Dress for Success*, first published in 1975 and updated to include a *New Women's Dress for Success*, described by some in the 1980s as required reading for those in the business professions.

[67] For a lovely discussion of this, see, Lenz Taguchi, "Barkboat."

[68] Barad, *Meeting the Universe Halfway*, 223.

words, the discursive constructions of organizational power are presented materially in offices in ways that may function to intra-actively shape relations.

A diffractive reading of the above example from Cassandra produces a questioning of how the material of the office space both produces, and is produced by, relations of power. It prompts us to consider the nature of power dynamics and how they are intra-actively produced. If we are to flatten the data, then we insert ourselves not just *in* the data, but *in* the office, in an attempt to change our *"perceptual style* and *habits of seeing."*[69] We can think of this process of changing our perceptual style as an act of diffraction that spreads knowledge differently, as in the example of ocean waves passing through an obstruction. As explained by Barad, "theorizing and experimenting are not about *intervening* (from outside) but about *intra-acting* from within, and as part of, the phenomena produced."[70]

Moving into the building that houses the department where Cassandra is located, we may see/experience a variety of offices. Characteristics that we may notice include: the absence or presence of a window; the absence or presence of nice, perhaps matching furniture rather than cast-offs from the last office vacated; location in a noisy corridor or next to the elevator; and location in a corridor with other departmental colleagues. We may also notice adornments either on the door of the offices or on the walls that communicate important information about the occupant. For instance, is the occupant male or female; gay or straight; white or a person of color; feminist; activist; Professor or Assistant Professor; PhD or EdD; from a top-tier institution, and so forth. The point of the above is not to classify, nor to reinscribe binaries, but to illustrate the ways in which the material and discursive intra-act to produce a subject, in this case Cassandra, who is a product and is positioned in the relations of power as an intersection between the material and discursive that is her office. In this example, students approach her office with a sense of her perceived position in the department and university – untenured, black, female, assistant professor. What we begin to "see" is how the office as both a material and discursive construction is reproducing power relations.

As students pass by or enter Cassandra's small office, they quickly ascertain that the office possesses none of the markers of status, nor does she, as black female assistant professor. For the black students, this office, this assistant professor, produces an intra-action that produces Cassandra as nonthreatening, as a "mother figure" who is there to provide encouragement and who serves as a role model for the potential that higher education has to offer. Despite the fact that the material ↔ discursive constructions in the space of the office do not say status, the presence of this woman in this space does, to these black students. For the white students, this office excludes them from a majority space as they pass by, perhaps to speak with Cassandra, and continue their walk as they peer in and see the office filled with black students "sitting on the floor." The office is therefore constituted differently, as both place of refuge and place of banishment simultaneously. Further, their sitting on the floor constitutes the office space as a less formal gathering place, in contrast to an office that is usually used for more formal meetings and discussions. The office as transformed invites friendly "interactions" with its occupants. It is not difficult to imagine laughter, teasing, joking, and play. Because many of these white students had perhaps not experienced being in the minority before, this safe space for the black students becomes a threatening space for the white students, producing an intra-action and a discourse of "reverse discrimination." This black

---

[69] Hultman and Lenz Taguchi. "Challenging Anthropocentric Analysis of Visual Data," op. cit., 525.
[70] Barad, *Meeting the Universe Halfway*, 56.

assistant professor, who shows "favoritism to the black students," who is also seen as excluding the white students, is clearly not someone in power, therefore an attempt to put her in her place is manifest in "critical letters" written to the occupants of the offices that possess the markers of power. Cassandra is thus produced in multiple ways as one who welcomes and excludes, as one who is valorized by the black students and chastised by the white students. She must also produce a discursive response to this entangled becoming, in the form of letters of rebuttal that she writes to the administration.

A final diffraction is to think about how the office space itself creates a diffraction. The office door, the opening, the threshold, can be viewed as the place through which waves pass, creating a diffraction. This diffraction passes both ways: in inviting those who enter and those who fail to enter. This opening further serves to reconstitute the office door as a threshold to be crossed, or as a threshold that welcomes. One invites, the other excludes.

A further summative quote provided by Barad is helpful in an articulation of the constitutive nature of practices that we are trying to illustrate in the above example.

> Indeed, as Butler and Bohr emphasize, that which is excluded in the enactment of knowledge-discourse-power practices plays a *constitutive* role in the production of phenomena—exclusions matter both to bodies that come to matter and those excluded from mattering....Turning the mirror back on oneself is not the issue, and reflexivity cannot serve as a corrective here. Rather, the point is that these *entangled practices* are productive, and who and what are excluded through these entangled practices matter: different intra-actions produce different phenomena.[71]

It is in and through an understanding of these entangled practices presented by Barad that we can begin to understand how diffractive readings can help us in our work as qualitative researchers to produce knowledge differently.

Thinking intra-actively

Thinking with Barad's intra-action helps us fashion an approach that re-inserts the material into the process of analysis. It is a reclaiming of the material absent in its modernist limitations. It is the work of Karen Barad and others named as "new materialists" or "material feminists" to ask how our intra-action with other bodies (both human and nonhuman) produce subjectivities and performative enactments. In our thinking with Barad, we were able to consider not just how discourses were functioning to produce Cassandra and Sera, but how they materialize. Such questioning shifts our thinking away from how performative speech acts or repetitive bodily actions produce subjectivity, but also how subjectivity can be understood as a set of linkages and connections with other things and other bodies, both human and nonhuman. We presented examples of how Sera and Cassandra were produced differently through intra-actions with office space, other bodies, clothing, and furniture, and similarly how their entanglement with these material fixtures resulted in a mutual constitution of the material and discursive. It is through an enactment of a diffractive analysis and a re-thinking of our relationship to/with data, and to/with the material in our research sites, that we see much productive potential for research methodologists.

[71] *Ibid.*, 57–58.

More on intra-activity (and posthumanist performativity)

The following texts are offered, not as *the* texts to consult, but as providing an entry point for those who are new to the writings of Barad and other new materialists and would like to learn more about intra-action and posthumanist performativity. We list the secondary texts first as a continuation of the "schematic cues" presented in the interludes, which readers can use as a brace as they enter this new theoretical terrain. Following the secondary texts are suggested entry points for approaching the writing of Barad, and finally, research exemplars that illustrate additional examples of thinking with these new materialist concepts.

Secondary texts

Alaimo, Stacy and Susan Hekman (eds). *Material Feminisms*. Bloomington: Indiana University Press, 2008.

Coole, Diana and Samantha Frost (eds). *New Materialisms: Ontology, Agency, and Politics*. Durham: Duke University Press, 2010.

Hekman, Susan. *The Material of Knowledge: Feminist Discourses*. Bloomington: Indiana University Press, 2010.

Primary texts

Barad, Karen. *Meeting the Universe Halfway: Quantum Physics and the Entanglement of Matter and Meaning*. Durham: Duke University Press, 2007.

——"Posthumanist Performativity: Toward an Understanding of How Matter Comes to Matter." In *Material Feminisms*, edited by Stacy Alaimo and Susan Hekman, 120–54. Bloomington: Indiana University Press, 2008.

Research exemplars

Hultman, Karin and Hillevi Lenz Taguchi. "Challenging Anthropocentric Analysis of Visual Aata: A Relational Materialist Methodological Approach to Educational Research." *International Journal of Qualitative Studies in Education* 23, no. 5 (2010): 511–42.

Taguchi, Hillevi Lenz. *Going Beyond the Theory/Practice Divide in Early Childhood Education: Introducing an Intra-Active Pedagogy*. London: Routledge, 2010.

Chapter 8

Diffractions

> Thinking is not something "we" do; thinking happens to us, from without. There is a necessity to thinking, for the event of thought lies beyond the autonomy of choice. Thinking happens.[1]

Our title for this last chapter is picked up from the notion of diffraction, as developed by Karen Barad, to explore the ways in which our plugging of theory into data into theory not only produces new analytical questions, but also produces different researcher selves. Through a discussion of how we were constituted as researchers in the mangle, and our desires for future work, we will briefly present some of our learnings as a result. While we could write another book about what we have learned, much of which was presented in Chapter 1 as a way to foreground our process, we wish to focus on how we have been constituted as researchers in the threshold, and what happens in the difficulty of staying there. In this last chapter, we would like to focus on: How does the threshold both make and unmake us?

We introduced the figuration of the threshold in Chapter 1 as a way to situate our "plugging in," or how we put the data and theory to work in the threshold to create new analytical questions. In the space of the threshold, we became aware of how theory and data constitute or make one another – and how, in the threshold, the divisions among, and definitions of, theory and data collapse. Rosi Braidotti carefully explains that "figurations are not figurative ways of thinking, but rather more materialistic mappings of situated, or embedded and embodied positions."[2] What we weren't anticipating was the extent to which this embedded/embodiedness would occur in the way that theory and data constituted us, and how, in the threshold, the divisions among writing, thinking, data, participants, and researcher selves collapsed.

We used and worked the concept of the threshold with each other to excess. By this, we mean that whenever one of us was straying too far from the data, we would remind ourselves to return to the threshold. We began in the threshold, as this is how our analytic questions emerged. The place of the threshold for us then became our *code word* for using the data to illustrate the theory and *vice versa*, rather than falling into the traps of our received methodology: large data "dumps" with thin analysis; use of theory to situate our researcher selves without using the data to illustrate; lapsing into interpretive comments

---

[1] Claire Colebrook, *Gilles Deleuze* (London: Routledge, 2002), 38.

[2] Rosi Braidotti, *Metamorphoses: Towards a Materialist Theory of Becoming* (Malden: Polity Press, 2002), 2.

rather than working our analytic questions to exhaustion; ascribing humanist agency in the context of what we had deemed posthumanist work. Naming the above does not mean we were able to avoid *all* of these traps *all* of the time, as we are always already in the process of deconstruction. Such naming, however, induced a vigilance that kept us constantly aware of our attempts to flee this difficult space of excess. Further, naming them with each other meant that we were not only plugging the theory into the data into the theory, we were also plugging in each other's insights, questions, and critiques at the same time.

We not only read the data with Derrida, Spivak, Foucault, Butler, Deleuze, and Barad looking over our shoulder, but also we read with each of us looking over the other's shoulder. What happened to us in the threshold is what Colebrook describes in the opening quote for this chapter as, simply, thinking. Again, while what we set out to accomplish was to *think* with theory, how we were constituted in this process of thinking was not fully predicted or expected. What emerged as a result of thinking with multiple theorists and their concepts across the data was not merely exhausting in the sense of fatiguing, it was exhausting in that we were constantly pulled back into the threshold, into the data, into new thinking. We began to think and enact data analysis differently because, once in the threshold, there was no way out.

The threshold, then, for us became the site of diffraction – an opening that spread our thoughts and questions in unpredictable patterns of waves and intensities. We wrote in Chapter 1 that the excess of a threshold is the space in which something else occurs: a response, an effect. Once you exceed the threshold, something new happens. Being in the threshold, in this intensive mode, was not something easily achieved. Much of how doctoral students are taught to write dissertations, and much of what we are asked to "produce" for scholarly journals, still demands a separation of theory and analysis: present your theoretical framework up front and then tell what you "found" in your data. Being in the threshold, and our continuous reminders with post-it notes and texts and emails and comments on drafts, was about not straying too far from the theory *or* from the data.

While qualitative researchers have written about the complicated nature of the writing-up aspects of research, we go again to Braidotti and her discussion of the writing style for *Metamorphoses* that she describes as being "post-personal."[3] One of the ways she characterizes this style is that it is working against the writer/reader binary. Being in the threshold, thinking with the theory, forced us to write in such a way as to not talk to the reader about what sense we made of the data, but to try to bring the reader into the threshold with us. We could never stray far from the theory, or from how we were trying to bring the theory and data together in a way that the reader could think alongside us in the threshold. Braidotti continues: "The question of style is crucial to this project. As readers in an intensive mode, we are transformers of intellectual energy, processors of the 'insights' that we are exchanging."[4]

In the intensive mode of the threshold, we found ourselves both transformed and transforming of/by this intellectual energy of which Braidotti writes. Perhaps we were acutely aware of Barad and intra-activity as this was the last chapter in the book. Perhaps we were open to the prospect of our place in the desiring machine having spent time in the production of Deleuzian desire. Perhaps, in keeping with a Deleuzian methodology, trying to explain a reason is a waste of time. But in the last days of intensive writing and revising

---

[3] *Ibid.*, 9–10.
[4] *Ibid.*

together across a continent, there was a tangible sense of presence and buzz of energy as texts were flying, words were coming in and out of focus, and intensities were produced and being produced. We were in the mangle and our work as methodologists will be forever different.

Braidotti writes about a nomadic style of writing that is against linearity. A nomadic style risks obliqueness, and this is where we struggled very intensely. We wanted this text to be useful, to be accessible, and to serve as the teaching resource that we wish we had *as* graduate students and *with* our own past and present graduate students. And yet, for it to be these things, we had to resist the nomadic temptation and write linearly. While the concepts that we engage are not simplistic, we hoped that the structure of interlude, schematic cues, and an exhaustive use of example and explanation might help us achieve our aims. But this linearity and structure was also confining, or at least it seemed so. The hardest task in thinking with theory was *writing linearly about something that is happening simultaneously*. While we were writing and thinking and plugging in and dipping in and out of the threshold, we found it very difficult to write about what was happening in a way that was coherent to others than ourselves. These concepts that we were working with are not necessarily more complex than others that we might have chosen, but they occur all at one time. The writing is limiting in that it is difficult to capture this simultaneity. It is a Deleuzian flow, producing something that is not expected.

We also had to attempt to contain the Deleuzian flow. We were very cognizant of the need to "show" rather than explain by opening up and distorting the data repeatedly. In order to illustrate what we were attempting, we had to focus intently on specific data "chunks" that could be repeated and re-viewed across the various theorists and concepts. And while we have explained throughout the text how the theorists rhizomatically emerged and how the concepts bubbled up, we had to resist the lines of flight that were tempting to take us to other concepts, other theorists, other data. While there is a productivity to be found in the dissonance and unexpectedness of, say, working *between Deleuze and Derrida*, we were careful not to blend theorists or concepts in our analysis. This is not to say that we always succeeded, but we tried nonetheless. Our desire (in a Deleuzian sense) was to work against the stance of the *bricoleur* and to push the concepts with the data to exhaustion.

What we offer, not by way of conclusion, but by way of opening up new ways of thinking with theory, is a bit of wisdom from Derrida, who, as you know from the beginning of this book, is someone we cannot think without. In speaking of the collection of essays and interviews titled *Negotiations*, Derrida states that he did not choose the title *Negotiations*, but that the word imposed itself on him. And in speaking of the etymology of the word negotiations in the context of his writing, he refers to negotiation as meaning "no leisure" or "unleisure." Unleisure is, according to Derrida, "the impossibility of stopping, or settling in a position."[5] And so it is with a lack of leisure that we continue to think with theory in qualitative research.

---

[5] Jacques Derrida, *Negotiations: Interventions and Interviews 1971–2001*. Translated by Elizabeth Rottenberg (Stanford: Stanford University Press, 2002), 12.

Bibliography

Alcoff, Linda. "The Problem of Speaking for Others." *Cultural Critique* 20 (1991): 5–33.

Alaimo, Stacy and Susan Hekman. "Introduction: Emerging Models of Materiality in Feminist Theory." In *Material Feminisms*, edited by Stacy Alaimo and Susan Hekman, 1–19. Bloomington: Indiana University Press, 2008a.

——*Material Feminisms*. Edited by Stacy Alaimo and Susan Hekman. Bloomington: Indiana University Press, 2008b.

Audi, Robert (ed.). *The Cambridge Dictionary of Philosophy*. Cambridge: Cambridge University Press, 1999.

Baker, Peter Nicholas. *Deconstruction and the Ethical Turn*. Gainesville: University Press of Florida, 1995.

Barad, Karen. *Meeting the Universe Halfway: Quantum Physics and the Entanglement of Matter and Meaning*. Durham: Duke University Press, 2007.

——"Posthumanist Performativity: Toward an Understanding of How Matter Comes to Matter." In *Material Feminisms*, edited by Stacy Alaimo and Susan Hekman, 120–56. Bloomington: Indiana University Press, 2008.

Bordo, Susan. "Cassie's Hair." In *Material Feminisms*, edited by Stacy Alaimo and Susan Hekman, 400–24. Indianapolis: Indiana University Press, 2008.

Boucher, Geoff. "The Politics of Performativity: A Critique of Judith Butler." *Parrhesia* 1 (2006): 112–41.

Bové, Paul A. "Discourse." In *Critical Terms for Literary Study*, edited by F. Lentricchia, 50–65. Chicago: University of Chicago Press, 1990.

Braidotti, Rosi. *Metamorphoses: Towards a Materialist Theory of Becoming*. Malden: Polity Press, 2002.

Briggs, Charles L. *Learning to Ask: A Sociolinguistic Appraisal of the Role of the Interview in Social Science Research*. Cambridge: Cambridge University Press, 1986.

Britzman, Deborah P. *Lost Subjects, Contested Objects: Toward a Psychoanalytic Inquiry of Learning*. Albany: SUNY Press, 1998.

——*Practice Makes Practice: A Critical Study of Learning to Teach* (revised edn). Albany: SUNY Press, 2003.

Butler, Judith. *Gender Trouble: Feminism and the Subversion of Identity*. New York: Routledge, 1990.

——"Contingent Foundations: Feminism and the Question of 'Postmodernism'." In *Feminists Theorize the Political*, edited by Judith Butler and Joan W. Scott, 3–21. New York: Routledge, 1992.

——*Bodies that Matter: On the Discursive Limits of "Sex."* New York: Routledge, 1993.

——"For a Careful Reading." In *Feminist Contentions: A Philosophical Exchange*, edited by Seyla Benhabib, Judith Butler, Drucilla Cornell, and Nancy Fraser, 127–44. New York: Routledge, 1995.

——"Imitation and Gender Insubordination." In *Women, Knowledge, and Reality: Explorations in Feminist Philosophy*, 2nd edn, edited by Ann Garry and Marilyn Pearsall, 371–87. New York: Routledge, 1996.

——*Excitable Speech: A Politics of the Performative*. New York: Routledge, 1997a.

——*The Psychic Life of Power: Theories in Subjection*. Stanford: Stanford University Press, 1997b.

——*Undoing Gender*. New York: Routledge, 2004.

——*Giving an Account of Oneself*. New York: Fordham University Press, 2005.

——*Judith Butler in Conversation: Analyzing the Texts and Talk of Everyday Life*. Edited by Bronwyn Davies. New York: Routledge, 2008.

Chakraborty, Mridula Nath. "Everybody's Afraid of Gayatri Chakravorty Spivak: Reading Interviews with the Public Intellectual and Postcolonial Critic." *Signs: Journal of Women in Culture & Society* 35, no. 3 (2010): 621–45.

Childs, Peter and Patrick Williams. *An Introduction to Post-Colonial Theory*. New York: Prentice Hall, 1997.

Cixous, Hélène. "Savoir." In *Veils*, edited by Hélène Cixous and Jacques Derrida, translated by Geoffrey Bennington, 1–16. Stanford: Stanford University Press, 2001.

——*Stigmata: Escaping Texts*, 2nd edn. London: Routledge, 2005.

Cixous, Hélène and Mireille Calle-Gruber. *Rootprints: Memory and Life Writing*, translated by Eric Prenowitz. London: Routledge, 1997.

Clarke, Simon. *The Foundations of Structuralism*. Sussex: Harvester Press, 1981.

Colebrook, Claire. *Gilles Deleuze*. London: Routledge, 2002.

Collins, Gail. "The Crying Game." *The New York Times*, December 16, 2010.

Coole, Diana and Samantha Frost. "Introducing the New Materialisms." In *New Materialisms: Ontology, Agency and Politics*, edited by Diana Coole and Samantha Frost, 1–43. Durham: Duke University Press, 2010a.

——*New Materialisms: Ontology, Agency and Politics*. Edited by Diana Coole and Samantha Frost. Durham: Duke University Press, 2010b.

Davies, Tony. *Humanism*. London: Routledge, 1997.

Deleuze, Gilles. *Cinema II*. Translated by Hugh Tomlinson and Robert Galeta. Minneapolis: University of Minnesota Press, 1985/89.

——*Foucault*. Translated by Sean Hand. Minneapolis: University of Minnesota Press, 1986/88.

——*Negotiations: 1972–1990*. Translated by Martin Joughin. New York: Columbia University Press, 1990. Originally published in Pourparlers (Paris: Les Editions de Minuit, 1990).

Deleuze, Gilles and Félix Guattari. *Anti-Oedipus: Capitalism and Schizophrenia*. Translated by Robert Hurley, Mark Seem, and Helen Lane. Minneapolis: University of Minnesota Press, 1983. Originally published as *L'Anti-Oedipe* (London: Viking Penguin, 1972).

——*A Thousand Plateaus: Capitalism and Schizophrenia*. Translated by Brian Massumi. Minneapolis: University of Minnesota Press, 1987. Originally published as *Mille Plateaux*, Vol. 2 of *Capitalisme et Schitzophrénie* (Paris: Les Editions de Minuit, 1980).

Deleuze, Gilles and Claire Parnet. *Dialogues II*. Translated by Hugh Tomlinson and Barbara Habberjam. New York: Columbia University Press, 1987/2002.

Derrida, Jacques. *Positions*. Translated by Alan Bass. Chicago: University of Chicago Press, 1972/1981.

——*Margins of Philosophy*. Translated by Alan Bass. Chicago: University of Chicago Press, 1972/1982.

——*Of Grammatology*. Translated by Gayatri Spivak. Baltimore: Johns Hopkins University Press, 1976.

——*Writing and Difference*. Translated by Alan Bass. Chicago: University of Chicago Press, 1978.

——*Dissemination*. Translated by Barbara Johnson. Chicago: University of Chicago Press, 1981.

——"Différance." In *Margins of Philosophy*, translated by Alan Bass, 1–27. Chicago: University of Chicago Press, 1982.

——"Passions: 'An Oblique Offering'." Translated by David Wood. In *Derrida: A Critical Reader*, edited by David Wood, 5–35. Oxford: Blackwell, 1992.

——*Specters of Marx: The State of Debt, the Work of Mourning, and the New International*. Translated by Peggy Kamuf. New York: Routledge, 1994.

——*Deconstruction in a Nutshell: A Conversation with Jacques Derrida*. Edited and with commentary by John D. Caputo. New York: Fordham University Press, 1997.

——*Negotiations: Interventions and Interviews 1971–2001*. Translated by Elizabeth Rottenberg. Stanford: Stanford University Press, 2002.

——*Rogues*. Translated by Pascale-Anne Brault and Michael Naas. Stanford: Stanford University Press, 2003.

Derrida, Jacques and Anne Durourmantelle. *Of Hospitality: Cultural Memory in the Present*. Translated by Rachel Bowlby. Stanford: Stanford University Press, 2000.

Descartes, René. *Discourse on Method and Meditations on First Philosophy*. Translated by Donald A. Cress. Indianapolis: Hackett, 1998.

Dreyfus, Hubert L. and Paul Rabinow. *Michel Foucault: Beyond Structuralism and Hermeneutics*. Chicago: University of Chicago Press, 1983.

Eagleton, Terry. *Figures of Dissent*. London: Verso, 2003.

——*Literary Theory: An Introduction*. Minneapolis: University of Minnesota Press, 1982.

Ellsworth, Elizabeth. "Double Binds of Whiteness." In *Off White: Readings on Race, Power, and Society*, edited by Michelle Fine, Lois Weis, Linda C. Powell, and L. Mun Wong, 259–69. New York: Routledge, 1997.

Foucault, Michel. *The Archeology of Knowledge and the Discourse on Language*. Translated by A. M. Sheridan Smith. New York: Pantheon Books, 1972.

——*Language, Counter-Memory, Practice: Selected Essays and Interviews*. Translated by D. F. Bouchard and S. Simon. Ithaca, NY: Cornell University Press, 1977.

——*Discipline and Punish: The Birth of a Prison*. Translated by Alan Sheridan. New York: Vintage Books, 1979.

——*The History of Sexuality. Volume 1: An Introduction*. Translated by Robert Hurley. New York: Vintage Books, 1980a.

——*Power/Knowledge: Selected Interviews and Other Writings: 1972–1977*. Translated by Leo Marshall, Colin Gordon, John Mepham, and Kate Soper, edited by Colin Gordon. New York: Pantheon Books, 1980b.

——"The Subject and Power." In *Michel Foucault: Beyond Structuralism and Hermeneutics*, edited by Hubert L. Dreyfus and Paul Rabinow. Chicago: University of Chicago Press, 1982.

——"What Is Enlightenment?" In *The Foucault Reader*, edited by Paul Rabinow, 32–50. New York: Pantheon Books, 1984.

——*Politics, Philosophy, Culture: Interviews and Other Writings of Michel Foucault, 1977–1984*. New York: Routledge, 1990.

——*Ethics: Subjectivity and Truth*. New York: The New Press, 1994.

——*Power*. Translated by Robert Hurley *et al.*, edited by Paul Rabinow. *Essential Works of Foucault 1954–1984, Vol. III*. New York: The New Press, 2000.

Glesne, Corrinne. *Becoming Qualitative Researchers: An Introduction*, 2nd edn. White Plains, NY: Longman, 1992.

Goodchild, Philip. *Deleuze & Guattari: An Introduction to the Politics of Desire*. London: Sage, 1996.

Grosz, Elizabeth. "Darwin and Feminism: Preliminary Investigations for a Possible Alliance." In *Material Feminisms*, edited by Stacy Alaimo and Susan Hekman, 23–51. Bloomington: Indiana University Press, 2008a.

——*Chaos, Territory, Art: Deleuze and the Framing of the Earth*. New York: Columbia University Press, 2008b.

——"Feminism, Materialism, and Freedom." In *New Materialisms: Ontology, Agency and Politics*, edited by Diana Coole and Samantha Frost, 139–57. Durham: Duke University Press, 2010.

Hekman, Susan. "Constructing the Ballast: An Ontology for Feminism." In *Material Feminisms*, edited by Stacy Alaimo and Susan Hekman, 85–119. Bloomington: Indiana University Press, 2008.

——*The Material of Knowledge: Feminist Disclosures*. Bloomington: Indiana University Press, 2010.

Hird, Myra J. "Feminist Engagements with Matter." *Feminist Studies* 35, no. 2 (2009): 329–46.

Hultman, Karin and Hillevi Lenz Taguchi. "Challenging Anthropocentric Analysis of Visual Data: A Relational Materialist Methodological Approach to Educational Research." *International Journal of Qualitative Studies in Education* 23 (2010): 525–42.

Jackson, Alecia Y. "Rhizovocality." *International Journal of Qualitative Studies in Education* 16, no. 5 (2003): 693–710.

——"Performativity Identified." *Qualitative Inquiry* 10, no. 5 (2004): 673–90.

——"Desiring Silence." Paper presented at the 3rd Annual International Congress for Qualitative Inquiry, Champaign-Urbana, IL, May 4, 2007.

——" 'What am I Doing When I Speak of this Present?' Voice, Power, and Desire in Truth-telling." In *Voice in Qualitative Inquiry: Challenging Conventional, Interpretive, and Critical Conceptions in Qualitative Research*, edited by Alecia Y. Jackson and Lisa A. Mazzei, 165–74. London: Routledge, 2009.

——"Deleuze and the Girl." *International Journal of Qualitative Studies in Education* 23, no. 5 (2010): 579–87.

Jackson, Alecia Y. and Lisa A. Mazzei, "Experience and 'I' in Autoethnography: A Deconstruction." *International Review of Qualitative Research* 1, no. 3 (2008): 299–318

——(eds) *Voice in Qualitative Inquiry: Challenging Conventional, Interpretive, and Critical Conceptions in Qualitative Research*. London: Routledge, 2009.

Jones, Sandra J. "Complex Subjectivities: Class, Ethnicity, and Race in Women's Narratives of Upward Mobility." *Journal of Social Issues* 59, no. 4 (2003): 803–20.

——"A Place Where I Belong: Working-Class Women's Pursuit of Higher Education." *Race, Gender & Class* 11, no. 3 (2004): 74–87.

Kearney, Richard. *States of Mind, Dialogues with Contemporary Thinkers*. New York: NYU Press, 1995.

de Kock, Leon. "Interview with Gayatri Chakravorty Spivak: New Nation Writers Conference in South Africa." *Ariel: A Review of International English Literature* 23, no. 3 (1992): 39–40.

Kondo, Dorinne K. *Crafting Selves: Power, Gender, and Discourses of Identity in a Japanese Workplace*. Chicago: University of Chicago Press, 1990.

Kramnick, Isaac (ed.) *The Portable Enlightenment Reader*. New York: Penguin Books, 1995.

Lather, Patti. *Getting Lost: Feminist Efforts Toward a Double(d) Science*. Albany: SUNY Press, 2007.

MacLure, Maggie. *Discourse in Educational and Social Research*. Philadelphia: Open University Press, 2003.

——"Broken Voices, Dirty Words: On the Productive Insufficiency of Voice." In *Voice in Qualitative Inquiry: Challenging Conventional, Interpretive, and Critical Conceptions in Qualitative Research*, edited by Alecia Y. Jackson and Lisa A. Mazzei, 97–113. London: Routledge, 2009.

——"Qualitative Inquiry: Where are the Ruins?" Keynote speech presented at the New Zealand Association for Research in Education Conference, Auckland, New Zealand, December 6–9, 2010.

Malabou, Catherine and Jacques Derrida. *Counterpath: Traveling with Jacques Derrida*. Translated by David Wills. Stanford: Stanford University Press, 2004.

Massumi, Brian. *A User's Guide to Capitalism and Schizophrenia: Deviations from Deleuze and Guattari*. Cambridge: MIT Press, 1992.

May, Todd. *Gilles Deleuze: An Introduction*. Cambridge: Cambridge University Press, 2005.

Mazzei, Lisa A. "Silent Listenings: Deconstructive Practices in Discourse-Based Research." *Educational Researcher* 33, no. 2 (2004): 26–34.

——*Inhabited Silence in Qualitative Research: Putting Poststructural Theory to Work*. New York: Peter Lang, 2007.

——"Silence Speaks: Whiteness Revealed in the Absence of Voice." *Teaching and Teacher Education* 24, no. 5 (2008): 1125–36.

——"An Impossibly Full Voice." In *Voice in Qualitative Inquiry: Challenging Conventional, Interpretive, and Critical Conceptions in Qualitative Research*, edited by Alecia Y. Jackson and Lisa A. Mazzei, 45–62. London: Routledge, 2009.

Mazzei, Lisa A. and Alecia Y. Jackson. "Introduction: The Limit of Voice." In *Voice in Qualitative Inquiry*, edited by Alecia Y. Jackson and Lisa A. Mazzei, 1–13. London: Routledge, 2009.

Mazzei, Lisa A. and Kate McCoy. "Thinking with Deleuze in Qualitative Research." *International Journal of Qualitative Studies in Education* 23, no. 5. (2010): 503–9.

Mol, Annemarie. *The Body Multiple: Ontology in Medical Practice*. Durham: Duke University Press, 2002.

Morton, Stephen. *Gayatri Chakravorty Spivak*. New York: Routledge, 2003.

Nealon, Jeffery T. "Beyond Hermeneutics." In *Between Deleuze and Derrida*, edited by Paul Patton and John Protevi, 160–68. London: Continuum, 2003.

Olkowski, Dorothea. *The Universal (In the Realm of the Sensible): Beyond Continental Philosophy*. New York: Columbia University Press, 2007.

O'Sullivan, Simon and Stephen Zepke. "Introduction: The Production of the New." In *Deleuze, Guattari and the Production of the New*, edited by Simon O'Sullivan and Stephen Zepke, 1–10. London: Continuum, 2008.

Pickering, Andrew. "The Mangle of Practice: Agency and Emergence in the Sociology of Science" (1993). In *The Science Studies Reader*, edited by Mario Biagioli, 372–93. New York: Routledge, 1999.

St Pierre, Elizabeth A. "Methodology in the Fold and the Irruption of Transgressive Data." *International Journal of Qualitative Studies in Education* 10, no. 2 (1997): 175–89.

——"Poststructural Feminism in Education: An Overview." *International Journal of Qualitative Studies in Education* 13, no. 5 (2000): 477–515.

——"Afterword: Decentering Voice in Qualitative Inquiry." In *Voice in Qualitative Inquiry: Challenging Conventional, Interpretive, and Critical Conceptions in Qualitative Research*, edited by Alecia Y. Jackson and Lisa A. Mazzei, 221–36. London: Routledge, 2009.

——"Qualitative Data Analysis after Coding." Paper presented at the AERA Annual Meeting. April 2011. New Orleans, LA, USA.

de Saussure, Ferdinand. *Course in General Linguistics*. Translated by Robert Harris. La Salle: Open Court, 1986.

Schrift, Alan D. *Nietzsche's French Legacy: A Genealogy of Poststructuralism*. New York: Routledge, 1995.

Secomb, Linnell. "Words That Matter: Reading the Performativity of Humanity through Butler and Blanchot." In *Judith Butler in Conversation: Analyzing the Texts and Talk of Everyday Life*, edited by Bronwyn Davies. New York: Routledge, 2008.

Seem, Mark. Translator's Preface to *Anti-Oedipus: Capitalism and Schizophrenia*, by Gilles Deleuze and Félix Guattari, xi–xxiv. Minneapolis: University of Minnesota Press, 1983.

Sharpe, Matthew. "Jacques Lacan." In *Internet Encyclopedia of Philosophy*. www.iep.utm.edu

Shetty, Sandhya and Elizabeth Jane Bellamy. "Postcolonialism's Archive Fever." *Diacritics* 30, no. 1 (2000): 25–48.

Smith, Daniel W. "Deleuze and the Theory of Desire." Paper presented at the Deleuze Summer Camp, Wales UK, August 20–24, 2007.

Spivak, Gayatri C. Translator's preface to *Of Grammatology*, by Jacques Derrida, ix–lxxxvii. Baltimore: Johns Hopkins University Press, 1976.

——*In Other Worlds: Essays in Cultural Politics*. New York: Routledge, 1988.

——*Outside in the Teaching Machine*. New York: Routledge, 1993.

——"Teaching for the Times." In *Dangerous Liaisons: Gender, Nation, and Postcolonial Perspectives*, edited by Anne McClintock, Asmit Mufti, and Ella Shohat, 468–90. Minneapolis: University of Minnesota Press, 1997.

——*A Critique of Postcolonial Reason: Toward a History of the Vanishing Present*. Cambridge: Harvard University Press, 1999.

Stagoll, Cliff. "Becoming." In *The Deleuze Dictionary*, edited by Adrian Parr, 21–22. New York: Columbia University Press, 2005.

Taguchi, Hillevi Lenz. "The Researcher Becoming Otherwise: The Materiality of Collaborative Deconstructive Research." Paper presented at the annual meeting of the American Educational Research Association, New York, April 23–28, 2008.

——*Going Beyond the Theory/Practice Divide in Early Childhood Education: Introducing an Intra-Active Pedagogy*. London: Routledge, 2010.

——"Becoming-with-the-Barkboat in the Event: A Relational Materialist and Deleuzian Approach to Analysis of Interview Data," unpublished manuscript.

Tarc, Aparna Mishra. "In a Dimension of Height: Ethics in the Education of Others." *Educational Theory* 56, no. 3 (2006): 287–304.

Tuana, Nancy. "Viscous Porosity: Witnessing Katrina." In *Material Feminisms*, edited by Stacy Alaimo and Susan Hekman, 188–213. Bloomington: Indiana University Press, 2008.

Tuck, Eve. "Breaking up With Deleuze: Desire and Valuing the Irreconcilable." *International Journal of Qualitative Studies in Education* 23, no. 5 (2010): 634–50.

Varadharajan, Asha. *Exotic Parodies: Subjectivity in Adorno, Said, and Spivak*. Minneapolis: University of Minnesota Press, 1995.

Weedon, Chris. *Feminist Practice & Poststructuralist Theory*, 2nd edn. Malden: Wiley-Blackwell, 1997.

Žižek, Slavoj. *How to Read Lacan*. London: Granta Books, 2006.

Subject index